Elegant Silvers

ELEGANT SILVERS

Striking Plants for Every Garden

Text by
JO ANN GARDNER
and
KAREN BUSSOLINI

Photos by
Karen Bussolini

TIMBER PRESS
Portland ~ Cambridge

Frontispiece: *Artemisia schmidtiana* 'Silver Mound' with *Opuntia humifusa*.

Published in 2005 by

Timber Press, Inc.
The Haseltine Building
133 S.W. Second Avenue, Suite 450
Portland, Oregon 97204-3527, U.S.A.

Timber Press
2 Station Road
Swavesey
Cambridge CB4 5QJ, U.K.

www.timberpress.com

Printed in China

Library of Congress Cataloging-in-Publication Data

Gardner, Jo Ann, 1935-
  Elegant silvers : striking plants for every garden / text by Jo Ann
Gardner and Karen Bussolini ; photos by Karen Bussolini.
      p. cm.
  Includes bibliographical references and index.
  ISBN 0-88192-703-1 (hardcover)
  1. Landscape plants. 2. Landscape gardening. I. Bussolini, Karen.
II. Title.
  SB407.G344 2005
  635.9'68--dc22
                                        2004012683

A catalog record for this book is also available from the British Library.

To Madalene Hill,
friend and inspiration

CONTENTS

ACKNOWLEDGMENTS

WE ARE VERY GRATEFUL TO THE MANY PEOPLE who have been generous with their time, opening their gardens, patiently answering questions, and sending special information as well as plants and seeds for us to observe. Without their help, we would not have been able to complete this guide to the large and complex world of silvers. We are especially indebted to Panayoti Kelaidis and Lauren Springer, who so cheerfully shared their gardens, their knowledge, and their enthusiasm for our project.

The following individuals and institutions were very helpful: garden designer Nancy Webber, Austin, Texas; Elizabeth Sullivan, Karl Gercens, and Dr. Thomasz Anisko, Longwood Gardens; Mark Weathington, Norfolk Botanical Garden; David Price, Bok Tower Gardens; Nancy Edmonson, Marie Selby Gardens; Robert E. Bowden, Harry P. Leu Gardens; Madalene Hill, McAshan Gardens; Denver Botanic Gardens; Sean Hogan, Cistus Design Nursery; Wave Hill; The New York Botanical Garden; Julie McCaffrey and Sue Markgraf, Chicago Botanic Garden; Dorte Hviid, Berkshire Botanical Garden; Minnesota Landscape Arboretum; Matt Parks, Stillinger Herbarium at the University of Idaho; John Fairey, Peckerwood Garden; Carl Schoenfeld, Yucca Do Nursery; Colleen Belk, Barton Springs Nursery; Selena Souders, Big Red Sun; Bill Bauer, Gardens; V. J. Billings, Mountain Valley Growers; Caroline Burgess, Keri Larsen, and Barbara Scoma, Stonecrop Gardens; Lindsay McGarrity, Venzano; Martha and Charles Oliver, Primrose Path Nursery; Myrna Ougland and Eric Hammond, and Heronswood Nursery; Theresa Miesler, Shady Acres Herb Farm; Tom Bodnar, Twombly Nursery; Ellen Hornig, Seneca Hill Perennials; Libby Bruch and staff, Quailcrest Farm; Karen Langan, Mulberry Creek Herb Farm; Bert Wilson, Las Pilitas Nursery; Nona Koivula, All-America Selections; Pierrre Bennerup, Sunny Border Nurseries; Tony Avent, Plant Delights; Jan Boonstra Pazlinak, Bluestone Perennials; Kathleen Nelson, Kathleen Nelson Perennials; Marty, Sunnybrook Farms Nursery; Harlan Hamernick, Bluebird Nursery; Susan Jellinek and Andrew Tokely, Thompson and Morgan Seeds; Rebecca Day-Skowron, Rocky Mountain Rare Plants; Nancy DuBrule, Natureworks; Mark Gross, Pan American Seed; Michele Meyers, Herb Society of America; Kathleen Powis,

Horticultural Society of New York; David Small, The Heather Society; and Monika Burwell, earthly pursuits.

We are grateful to those who provided silver plants for trial: Dan Heims, Terra Nova Nurseries; Renee Beaulieu, White Flower Farm; Kerry Strope, Proven Winners; Donna Greenbush, Flower Fields/Ecke; and Christine Kelleher, Blooms of Bressingham/Yoder. Thanks to Benary Seeds of North America and All-America Selections for seeds.

Thanks to Lynden Miller, the late Joanna Reed, Bill Harris, Jessica Chevalier, and Michael Peden; also Nora Holmes, Steven Ruce, Lily Shohan, Russell Studebaker, Geraldine Laufer, Tom Cooper, Tom Fischer, Joseph Hudak, Bernard S. Jackson, Jo Ann Darling, Lois Rose, Judith Siegel, Dave and Jo Ann Gardner (no relation), Betty Rahman, John Ignacio, Jefferey Stuhr, Peter Kallen, Thyrza Whittemore, Jan Axel, Judith Chatfield, Tiziana Grifoni, Tom Peace, Elizabeth A. Gillick, Margery Daughtrey, Megan at Sycamore Farms, Patricia Taylor, Mark Bussolini, Jim Hoyle, Molly Asher, and Westport librarian Anne de la Chapelle. For help above and beyond the call of duty we thank Bobbe Katzman and Darla Breckenridge and our technical staff, Mac McDevitt, Simon Moore, and Owen Merrick.

A special thanks to Professor Avinoam Danin at the Hebrew University of Jerusalem for his help and permission to use his slide of silvers in the Negev Desert and to Nell Gardner for her help and permission to use her photograph of the Piper's Silver Garden, to Tom Christopher for permission to use material from his book *The 20-Minute Gardener* with Marty Asher, to Carl Shoenfeld for permission to use Yucca Do's directions for constructing a dry bed garden, and to Stonecrop Gardens for its alpine soil formula. We are honored by Nigel Nicolson's loan of an archival photograph of the White Garden at Sissinghurst Castle. We are indebted to John W. Hazard Jr., friend of garden writers, and to Neal Maillet at Timber and editor Lisa Theobald for their patience and support.

Thanks are insufficient to John and Jackson Scofield and to Jigs Gardner (who did double duty in the editorial line) for their forbearance as we became ever more absorbed in researching and writing about silvers.

PREFACE

ELEGANT SILVERS GREW OUT OF A SHARED PASSION for silver plants and the need for a comprehensive guide to growing and using them throughout the entire landscape. This book is about silvers in their entirety, distinctive plants designed by nature to withstand extremes of heat, cold, drought, wind, or, in the case of variegated silvers, to grow in deep, moist shade. Silvers are assets to gardeners across the land wherever they live, in cool or hot growing zones from Canada to Texas and beyond. As gardeners everywhere, not just in the arid U.S. West, become more aware of water restrictions during drought periods, they want to know about beautiful plants that can grow with little or even no extra water once they are established. Silvers are available to use in the garden whether the need is for drought-tolerant plants, windbreaks, something to light up a woodland, or a dash of quicksilver to enliven a color scheme. By learning about their defining characteristics and adaptability, what site and soil problems they address, and their design possibilities, gardeners will be able to make full use of this wonderful and unusual group of plants.

Selecting silvers to feature in this book has proved far more difficult than we imagined when we began our exploration of the genre. We started by focusing on the beauty of the plant and its silver presence in the garden. From many silvery types we selected those with compelling foliage, silhouette, or ensemble of complementary flowers (perhaps attractive to hummingbirds). Fragrance and texture were considerations, too. We not only admire silvers for the way they look, but for their soothing or energizing perfumes and for the feel of their leaves. Many of these are ancient herbs, whose culinary and other uses we still appreciate.

We were so excited by our discoveries that we wanted to share every one with our readers. Constraints of time and space forced us to be more selective. Geographic range proved to be less important than we first thought, because many regional silvers, like agaves, yuccas, and echeverias, can be grown outdoors in containers where they're frost tender and then wintered over indoors, or, like *Dichondra argentea*, they are purchased every growing season in the same way as annuals. An increasing number of desirable tropical and subtropicals are of great interest to gardeners in cooler climates, and as our own experiences show, they are

Fragrant silver-leaved *Salvia* 'Vicki Romo' and *Pelargonium tomentosum* 'Peppermint' planted where they can be touched and smelled, at Wave Hill.

not difficult to winter over. Recent introductions from Australia—an increasing source of garden-worthy silvers such as *Plectranthus argentatus* and *Leucophyta brownii*— deserve more attention. Native silver trees and shrubs adapted to the toughest sites are underused, so we felt it imperative to include as many as possible.

The numbers mounted as we selected the best species, varieties, subspecies, and cultivars in important genera such as the artemisias and salvias. These encompass a range of growing and design possibilities. *Artemisia ludoviciana* 'Purshiana', for instance, can take damp conditions that would be intolerable to other cultivars of the same species. Among pulmonarias and heucheras, too— their numbers swell as we write—some are better adapted to heat and humidity. Finally, we ran out of space. We regret having to omit the many regional and speciality silvers for which there was no room—native agastaches, oenotheras, conradina, and bog rosemary (*Andromeda polifolia*).

Mrs. Desmond Underwood's *Grey and Silver Plants* (1971) was confined to downy silvers, plants that produce tiny hairs on their green surfaces as a protection against harsh conditions. In Roger Spencer's *Growing Silver, Grey and Blue Foliage Plants* (1987), the author expanded the downy repertoire to include some variegated plants as well as glaucous blue-greens lightly covered with a protective waxy layer, such as *Centranthus ruber*. We have explored all types of plants within the silver spectrum from nearly white to gleaming blues. The blues we include are coated with a heavier layer of wax than the glaucous blue-greens to produce plants with silver-blue, gray-blue, metallic blue, and powder-blue coloration. Think of the frosted boughs of Colorado spruce (*Picea pungens* var. *glauca*) in contrast to the unmistakably blue-green foliage of baptisias or aquilegias. The blue-greens are fine companions for silver-blue silvers, though, because they often share the same habitat, and in a garden setting they can bridge the gap between silvers and greens.

We have stressed a plant's provenance throughout, because plants succeed best where they are grown in conditions similar to those in their native habitat. Trying to force them to grow in unnatural places is difficult and often disappointing. Imaginative gardeners can simulate the right conditions with extraordinary success, as Madalene Hill has done in growing lavenders in the hot and humid southern United States. We have devoted as much space as possible to describing each silver's special needs, because as gardeners ourselves, we know how frustrating it is to find out about a wonderful plant but not know the particulars of how to grow it. The same is true of designing with silvers, a subject that has not been addressed in such detail in previous works. It is just as vital to understand a silver plant's design possibilities as it is to know how to grow it well.

The issue of nomenclature has been troublesome because of the absence of an ultimate authority. Our primary sources were the *Index of Garden Plants: The New Royal Horticulture Society Dictionary* (1994) and the *Royal Horticulture Society Plant Finder 2003–2004* (2003). We also consulted Liberty Hyde Bailey's *Hortus Third* and the International Plant Names Index on the World Wide Web at *http://www.us.ipni.org* (a collaboration among the Royal Botanical Gardens, Kew; the Harvard University Herbaria; and the Australian National Herbarium to standardize nomenclature). When all of these sources failed us, we turned to specialty plant organizations, plant experts, trusted plant nurseries, and common usage in the horticultural marketplace. Because botanical nomenclature is ever evolving as the understanding of plants advances, we have indicated former names and synonyms in the text by using a slash to separate the current name as we know it from the synonym or former name after the slash.

We think that nature's practical gift of silver plants brings a magical dimension to our gardens. In *The Years in My Herb Garden* (1953), herb pioneer Helen Fox observed, "The gray foliage of artemisias brings a soft cloudy or misty look which intensifies the depth of greens in mints and savories, the pink in carnations, and the violet in lavenders. The effect is similar to a rainy day when colors appear brighter than when the sun shines." As silver plants gather in and reflect the last light of day, the garden also takes on a luminosity. Perhaps silver plants' greatest virtue is to broaden the gardener's sensibility by extending the range of aesthetic possibilities. We think growing and designing with silvers will change your gardening life, as they have changed our own.

Silver-gray *Artemisia ludoviciana* 'Silver King' intensifies the depth of greens and lavenders.

CHAPTER ONE

A History of Silvers

THE SILVERS WE ADMIRE TODAY for their beauty were once regarded solely as useful plants, praised for their ability to cure or alleviate a wide variety of human complaints, from toothache to the pangs of childbirth. Classic silvers— artemisia, lavender, rue, and sage—once were no more than familiar drugs in the ancient pharmacopoeia or drugstore. The fact that their leaves were downy or

Swirling parterres of *Santolina chamaecyparissus* and *Muscari* in Central Park's Conservatory Garden, New York.

White wormwood (*Artemisia sieberi*) and sun rose (*Helianthemum vesicarium*) in Israel's Negev Desert. Photo courtesy of Avinoam Danin.

glaucous, a departure from normal green, did not create an aura of suspicion around them, as was the case with other plant oddities such as mandrake, whose bizarre-shaped roots earned it a reputation as a dangerous magical force to be approached with caution. On the contrary, no fear was attached to using the ruffled, gray-green horehound to soothe a cough or silvery gray wormwood as a cure for all stomach complaints. These were common plants—despite their unusual appearance—and a familiar part of everyday life. True, lavender was an ancient symbol of mistrust, but this association was based on the plant's sharp scent rather than its silvery leaves.

In what may be the earliest known reference, the Hebrew Bible records wormwood as a symbol of bitterness, chosen for that role because it was a bitter-tasting plant known to all, in common use as a medicinal. The Hebrew word *la'anah*, mentioned eight times in the Bible, refers to white wormwood, *Artemisia sieberi*; its former name, *A. herba-alba*, means literally white plant. With densely hairy, whitish leaves, it is a heavily branched shrub covering vast stretches of wasteland in Israel's Negev Desert. When touched by spring rain, the landscape is transformed by the interplay of white wormwood with sun rose (*Helianthemum vesicarium*)—a shrubby, silver-leaved plant with roselike flowers in shades of light and dark pink and white—in spreading drifts as if in a spectacular garden.

In printed herbals from the 1st to the 16th centuries, from Dioscorides to John Gerard, silvers were noted for their healing properties, but their looks were not ignored. In poetry celebrating his walled garden (*Hortulus*), Walahfrid Strabo, 9th-century literary monk and gardener, characterized common sage as "glowing," glaucous rue as "a shadowed grove," and southernwood as carrying a "bloom of down." In his 16th-century *Herball*, Gerard reported with typical hyperbole that "Cottonweed" (*Antennaria margaritacea*) was "covered with a most soft and fine wooll, and in such plentifull manner, that a man may with his hands take it from the stalke in great quantitie."

By 1629, with the publication of John Parkinson's *Paradisi in Sole Paradisus Terrestris*, santolina, or lavender cotton (*Santolina chamaecyparissus*), had become the

Common sage
(*Salvia officinalis*).

Victorian bedding schemes in Elizabeth Park, Hartford, Connecticut. *Tanacetum ptarmiciflorum* 'Silver Feather' outlines a bed of red-flowering *Salvia splendens*.

most popular plant for knot hedging. A small shrub (to 2 ft./0.6 m) with crimped, brilliant gray foliage on white woolly stems, it not only provided dramatically strong contrast to green hedging, it was amenable to trimming. Although santolina was and is still the premier silver for knot hedges, lavenders, germanders (*Teucrium*), and artemisias (*Artemisia abrotanum* and *A. pontica*) have venerable histories, too.

In the Victorian era, known for its excesses and predilection for novelty plantings, newly discovered frost-tender perennials such as dusty miller (*Senecio cineraria*) became important elements in carpet and ribbon designs. These, like knot hedges, were intricate plantings based on oriental carpet patterns. Massed silvers were planted in wide borders or ribbons to create astonishing effects with bright, contrasting colors. The remnants of this type of design are glaringly evident in civic bedding schemes of red hot salvia (*Salvia splendens*) with dusty miller (*Senecio* sp.). In both knot and carpet plantings, plants were regarded as rigid instruments of color. They had to conform to a strict growth pattern. Knot hedging required stiff plants amenable to trimming, and massed plantings in carpets and ribbons demanded uniformity and compact growth. As the nursery industry flourished, temporary bedding plants become more widely available to ordinary gardeners.

Although early attempts were made at single-color gardens in the early 20th century, none were as successful as those of Gertrude Jekyll. Her finely tuned aesthetic sensibilities launched the glory days of silvers as plants of individual beauty freed from the constraints of knot and carpet styles. In her grand herbaceous borders, she created painterly visions of harmony, where each plant was respected for its color and form as well as for its effect in the overall design. Her

American flag carpet bedding with silver ×*Sedeveria* "stars" shining in a background of succulent blue chalksticks (*Senecio serpens*). White "stripes" are *Santolina chamaecyparissus*. Elizabeth Park, Hartford, Connecticut.

plant palette was small by today's standards, but she was preeminently an artist whose medium was plants. She was primarily interested in using them to create painterly effects in her own marvellous gardens and in those she created in brilliant association with the young architect Edwin Lutyens.

Jekyll's silver or gray credo was reinforced in the gray borders at Munstead Wood, Surrey, England, where almost all the plants had gray foliage and all the carpeting and border plants were gray or whitish. Flowers to complement silvers and grays were white, lilac, purple, and pink. In *Colour Schemes for the Flower Garden* (1911), she advised readers that the approach to the gray gardens was best seen by first passing through the orange borders, for "here the eye becomes filled and saturated with strong red and yellow colouring . . . making the eye eagerly desirous for the complementary colour." The effect, she observed, is "astonishingly luminous and refreshing."

In the gray borders are the plants she loved and used to perfection: dusty miller (*Senecio cineraria*), lamb's ears (*Stachys byzantina*), lavender cotton (*Santolina chamaecyparissus*), and the taller blue-gray yuccas, *Yucca gloriosa*, *Y. recurva*, and *Y. filamentosa*—all plants that produce purple, pink, and white flowers. Other blues included a wild seaside plant called lyme grass (*Leymus arenarius*) and rue (*Ruta*). White flowers, indispensable for their luminous effect among grays, included the white lily (*Lilium candidum*); yarrow (*Achillea ptarmica* 'The Pearl'), which must have required vigilance to keep it from running free; everlasting pea (*Lathyrus latifolius*); and baby's breath (*Gypsophila paniculata*), a plant she adored for its long-flowering clouds of bloom (an effect that was an important component of her romantic schemes). Pinks included *Godetia* 'Double Rose', a clear pink hollyhock called *Alcea rosea* 'Pink Beauty', and pale pink double soapwort (*Saponaria officinalis*,

Senecio cineraria, loved by Gertrude Jekyll.

another spreader that needs vigilant checking). For creating a mass of purple or blue, she included ageratum (the dwarf and tall sort) and dwarf catmint (*Nepeta mussinii*). With Jekyll's superb touch, gray or silver plantings were firmly established as a garden genre.

Jekyll's Grey Walk at Hestercombe Gardens in Somerset, England, designed in collaboration with Lutyens and now restored, is a splendid example of her style. Heat-loving silvers planted against a terrace wall and bound by stone pavings benefit from the extra heat absorbed and retained by the stones. At the front, wide, cushiony mounds of *Santolina chamaecyparissus nana* combine with purple-blue— flowering dwarf *Nepeta mussinii* and an edging of *Stachys byzantina*. Behind, a mass of metallic *Eryngium* is backed by clouds of white, daisy-flowered *Erigeron karvinskianus* billowing from the stone wall itself, a characteristic Jekyll touch. Lavender, *Echinops*, and *Cerastium tomentosum* fill in between. (*Cerastium* was substituted for the white-flowering pinks of her original design.) Not only was her palette small, but she was not afraid to use common plants. Her genius lay in what she did with them.

It was, however, Vita Sackville-West and her White Garden at Sissinghurst Castle who launched what became known, ironically, as the "silver cult." Where Jekyll featured silvers and used white in a supporting role for luminous effect, Sackville-West did the opposite: she used silver plants as secondary luminaries to highlight whites.

Names like "Grey Garden" and "White Garden" may seem confusing when each type relies so heavily on the other for its fulfilment, but it seems reasonable to define them according to the dominance of one or the other type in the planting scheme. Sackville-West's enormous influence is attributable in part to her considerable following through her popular gardening columns in London's *Observer*. Regarded as an arbiter of taste *par excellence* among ordinary gardeners, she roused the gardening public.

White Garden, Sissinghurst Castle, 1953. A silver-leaved pear tree (*Pyrus salicifolia*) shelters a lead statue of the Virgin, with lamb's ears, artemisia, and white iris in the foreground. Photo by Edwin Smith, courtesy of Nigel Nicolson.

Even before 1930, when she and her husband, Harold Nicolson, bought a rundown castle called Sissinghurst in Kent, they had experimented with single-color gardens, but it was not until 1949–1950 that the White Garden was actually executed. Its stunning success was a collaboration of Harold's design genius combined with Vita's flamboyant, poetic use of garden plants. Where Jekyll depended on subtleties of color and form, Sackville-West went for a rich, lavish display, a flaunting visual imagery of robust roses—old and wild—combined with scented and wild flowers, unusual species, and climbing plants, all spilling over straight, rigid lines, creating lushness on a grand scale. An opponent of over-tidiness, she allowed flowers to self-seed and invited selected wildflowers to make themselves at home.

The unusual garden layout, composed of two dissimilar halves, has been commented on many times. One half is laid out as a formal parterre of box-edged, L-shaped beds, each containing a striking plant combination or a single, dramatic specimen. The other half—the one that comes to mind when Sissinghurst's White Garden is mentioned—is composed of two deep beds on either side of a path leading to a weeping silver pear tree (*Pyrus salicifolia*), one of the earliest plants in the garden. The White Garden is enclosed on two sides by a weathered brick wall, an ancient yew hedge on the third, with the box beds acting as a wall on the fourth side. Tall *Onopordum*, *Leucanthemella*, and swaying white *Cleome* provide the deep beds with a separate sense of enclosure and intimacy.

Now imagine the plants within: climbing white clematis, white lavender, white agapanthus, white double primrose, white anemones, white camellias, pale peach primulas, extravagant clouds of *Gypsophila paniculata* 'Bristol Fairy' and *Crambe cordifolia*, white weigelas on the garden wall, white pansies, white peonies, and white iris. Here and there are touches of shimmering silver, including the silver pear tree; metallic Arabian thistle (*Onopordum nervosum/O. arabicum*), with each giant leaf measuring 8 in. (20 cm) across and 20 in. (50 cm) long; and a massed sea of silvers and grays, including santolina, cineraria, southernwood (*Artemisia abrotanum*), and creeping yarrow (*Achillea ageratifolia*). A stand of pure white regal lilies (*Lilium regale*) rises above. The White Garden's intense romanticism is the source of its enduring popular appeal.

Both Jekyll and Sackville-West understood that the very presence of other colors among silvers and white—green, blush pink, pale peach, dusky red, pink, purple, even yellow—transforms what could be a sterile exercise into a horticultural tour de force.

The silver cult gained tremendously from the popularity of the White Garden at Sissinghurst. Gray gardens were established at London's Kew Gardens and at

Silver pear tree (*Pyrus salicifolia* 'Silver Frost') at The New York Botanical Garden.

Lynden Miller artfully combines silvers with other colors, in the tradition of Jekyll and Sackville-West, at The New York Botanical Garden.

Edinburgh's Royal Botanic Garden, and aficionados were able to find seeds and plants featured in catalogs and nurseries. Mrs. Desmond Underwood, who wrote one of the first books to focus entirely on silver plants, operated Ramparts Nursery in Colchester, England, a mecca for the faithful. In *Grey and Silver Plants* (1971), she pointed toward a new understanding of silvers that went beyond their aesthetic role in garden-making. Mrs. Underwood knew the beauty of silvers from intimate association and reminded her readers that they were practical plants, too, easy to grow and maintain *when they are matched to their preferred habitat* (our emphasis). This was something new. Never before in their long history in human affairs—when they had been cataloged in herbals, when later they were recommended for knot hedges, or when they were featured in the stunning gardens at Munstead and Sissinghurst—had their affinity for specific habitats been a matter of concern.

Mrs. Underwood told her readers how she came to see the light. She recalled that after World War II, with no help and frustrated by her inability to keep her garden tidy, she complained to her father that she would just grow a holly hedge "riddled with elm roots." Her father wisely advised her to abandon fancy, thirsty plants such as delphiniums and roses that require more care and water, and concen-

Silvers, including *Teucrium fruticans*, *Salvia leucophylla*, *Phlomis italica*, lavenders, *Teucrium marum*, marguerites, and olive trees, are easily grown when matched to their preferred habitat at Venzano, in Tuscany.

trate instead on plants that "knew how to withstand drought" and take care of themselves. She took this advice to heart, thinking about Mediterranean types she had seen growing in their native landscape, trying many of them as well as others over decades, and carefully observing their growth habits and needs. Her goal was to find plants that could grow with minimal care yet remain attractive all season. The era of grand, labor-intensive gardens of seasonal interest—a spring, summer, or fall border—was past, at least for most people. Ordinary gardeners, Mrs. Underwood pointed out, had small gardens with one border and wanted it to look its best all season, not just at certain times of the year, so it was necessary now to judge plants "not merely for their flowers but also for their general effect when not in flower." The fact that the vast majority of silver plants feature long-lasting foliage made them prime candidates for her discerning attention.

Grey and Silver Plants was a call to revolutionize the way we think about ornamentals in general. This original idea finally found full expression the 1990s, when *xeriscaping* or water-wise gardening, a concept developed in America, came of age by combining the practical with an aesthetic vision.

In America, the silver cult became subsumed in the herb revival of the 1930s, which itself was an offshoot of the Colonial Revival movement. The character of

The Sundial Herb Garden in Connecticut shows the formal pattern associated with herb gardens since the herb revival of the 1930s.

herb revival, still with us today, was greatly influenced by Montague Free's knot garden, designed for the 1939 World's Fair in New York. This herb cult, despite its small size, has had a major impact on herb garden design. Even today, the picture that comes to mind when we hear "herb garden" is of a formal, geometric layout of hedged beds with dissecting paths, loosely based on ancient forms, filled with gray and green foliage plants against a dark earth background (which helps to emphasize varied forms and subtle color variations), and often ornamented at its center with a sundial or statue. Within this genre, silver plants were considered very important visual elements for their contrast to shades of green.

Helen Morgenthau Fox, a pioneer in the movement and its most imaginative exponent, created beautiful gardens of estate proportions with a staff of gardeners at her elegant New York homes, Foxden I and II, and High and Low. Foxden II was her first laboratory for exploring the world of herbs at a time when no current literature on the subject and few sources for seeds and plants were available. Extraordinarily intelligent and cultured, Fox set out to learn everything she could about herbs, all their forgotten uses in the kitchen and household as well as their role in garden design. Her curiosity led her to try a wide variety of plants, including native types rediscovered today. Like Mrs. Underwood, Fox stressed that plants should always be matched to habitat, to conditions similar to the area of the world from where they came. Hairy herbs, especially, she warned, need a warm, even hot, exposure, with quick, sharp drainage—invaluable advice.

In *The Years in My Herb Garden* (1953), Fox set forth her firm belief that herbs look best in formal, rather than naturalistic, plantings, but unlike those who followed her and kept alive the flame of "classic herb garden design," she interpreted "formal" to mean plants that are for the most part allowed to grow naturally within well-defined, straight-edged boundaries. The effect was a restrained graciousness, a harmony of colors and forms. Black-and-white archival photos show a combination of herbaceous borders dominated by great lavender hedges and a formal layout of impressive stone steps leading to terraced beds of medicinal shrubs and fragrant plants. Always conscious of the entire landscape rather than a single planting, she used herbs throughout her gardens, with a few exceptions—kitchen herbs, for instance, were confined to rows in the vegetable garden.

In a chapter, "The Grayest Plants in the Garden," she devoted most of her comments to artemisias, of which she grew an astonishing range. Since gray is the dominant color or shade in the herb garden proper, she advised either planting for contrast with bright-flowering salvia, alternating gray with greenery, or planting the grays according to their shades, from nearly white beach wormwood (*Artemisia stelleriana*) to gray-green nepeta and horehound. This latter suggestion—a silver on silver garden—is difficult for most gardeners to achieve successfully, for it needs an artist's eye for subtle combinations of hues, forms, and textures.

One such practitioner was the late Adelma Grenier Simmons, whose Connecticut house, farm, and gardens, known as Caprilands, became a mecca for herb enthusiasts in the 1960s with the publication of her first major book, *Herb Gardening in Five Seasons* (1964), until her death in the late 1990s. Caprilands is still open to the public. Those who visited her in her garden often described their experience as "transforming," not surprising since Simmons was a charismatic figure who saw herself as an actress, rather than a teacher, on a stage she created. With its romantic atmosphere of artistically planned theme gardens, a tree-shaded gravel walk leading to a shop filled with the aroma of silvery wreaths, and a 1790 farm house, Caprilands was the setting for herbal luncheons that became the hallmark of a visit.

The metamorphosis of an abandoned Connecticut farm in the 1920s—when Simmons and her husband bought it—into a thriving herb business began in the 1930s, when Simmons planted her first herb garden near the house, featuring *Artemisia ludoviciana* 'Silver King'. It was an auspicious beginning, for she was so attracted to the genus and to silvery plants in general—their ethereal appearance appealed to her sense of romance—that the white farmhouse was repainted a dark, blackish red to show off the silver plants to advantage.

Three small but exquisite silver gardens exemplify Simmons's flair for design and drama. The Medieval Garden is a green-and-silver bed with wood chip walks and yew hedges. The Sunken Garden, with fieldstone-faced beds and walks, is backed by *Viburnum opulus* and has a central bed of bright purple and magenta-pink flowers. Tall species such as eucalyptus (wintered over in the greenhouse) and thistles combine subtly with silver junipers.

The Piper's Garden at Caprilands, 1980s. Photo by Nell Gardner.

The Piper's Garden—the most famous of her silver plantings—was composed entirely of silver plants. It featured granite chip walks, a silver juniper hedge, and a single Russian olive tree. No more than 20 by 21 ft. (6 by 6.5 m), the range of plants within its tiny boundaries was impressive. Raised 6 inches (15 cm) from the walks, the garden provided extra drainage for the silver plants. The statue *Piping Boy*, a harmonious note against surrounding silvery foliage, dominated a bed edged with clipped santolina in a cloverleaf design. The area around the cloverleaf was mulched in white crushed stone, which made a dramatic frame that drew the eye to the central figure and its immediate setting, and then to the eight surrounding beds, looped like draperies at the edges of the garden as a virtual stage set with silvers.

One of the "drapery loops" was composed entirely of artemisias, a fulfilment of Simmons's speculation that it could be done. Among them were fringed artemisia (*Artemisia frigida*), southernwood (*A. abrotanum*), western mugwort (*A. ludoviciana* and *A. ludoviciana* 'Silver King'), Roman wormwood (*A. pontica*), and common wormwood (*A. absinthium*), all edged with *A. schmidtiana* 'Silver Mound'. The success of this planting was its integration into the entire Piper's Garden, a detail that when combined with the whole, created the look she sought: an unearthly shimmering, magical place of muted shades, tones, and hues from nearly white to powder-blue, sparkling among purple, blue, pink, and pale yellow blooms. The range of plants within this tiny area expressed Simmons's sophisticated tastes, far beyond the usual classics. She traveled to Mediterranean regions and learned from these experiences to grow tender types in her greenhouse, among them the native flowering shrub *Conradina canescens*; *Euryops*, a large plant from South Africa; and *Dicliptera suberecta* from Brazil, with leaves like velvet.

Low maintenance was not a term in Simmons's gardening vocabulary. The choice of edging plants graphically illustrated her use of plants as instruments of her aesthetic vision, rather than as plants chosen for their suitability to habitat, for most of these were vigorous, even rampant types, such as bugle (*Ajuga reptans*) and snow in summer (*Cerastium tomentosum*), that could be kept within bounds only by a firm, guiding hand. When control was withdrawn, even for a short period, the garden was overrun. As an experienced gardener, she was well aware of the physical needs of the plants she cultivated, but she regarded them primarily for visual effect rather than as plants in their own right with a special affinity for certain growing conditions. In many ways, we are only just now catching up to pioneers Fox and Simmons, who explored the many artemisias (Simmons had more than 30), native silvers, choice shrubs and trees to use as focal points and accents, and a wide variety of frost-tender types from Australia, South Africa, and the tropics.

Silver plants were mostly confined to the herb repertoire into the 1980s. If you wanted to see the full range of silvers available, you would most likely find them in an herb garden or in a specialty herb nursery. Gradually, the wider horticultural world became aware of the extraordinary beauty and practical uses of silver plants through endeavors such as the Silver Garden in the conservatory at Pennsylvania's Longwood Gardens, which was planted entirely with silver, gray, and white foliage types. In 1988, the Geographic House conservatory was dismantled when its tall, overgrown specimens overshadowed the adjacent Acacia Passage. Silvers, it was felt, would be a good partner for the nearby acacias.

The design of the Silver Garden by California landscape architect Isabelle Greene reinforced the concept that silvers grow best when planted in an appropriate habitat. By using raised beds, paths, and huge boulders, she ingeniously recreated distinct silver plant habitats, including a low-lying desertlike environment and high, rocky outcrops. Native flora as well as plants from South Africa, South America, and the Mediterranean area are thus accommodated in a striking setting that highlights their beauty and caters to their special needs. Great pains were taken, by means of underground heating cables and an air-circulation system, to give them heat and light required for full, optimal growth. A variety of

The Silver Garden at Longwood Gardens.

unusual plants from desert, coastal, and high-altitude climates—from downy to waxy leaved types—can now be viewed without having to trek to their original habitats. Visitors can see the native century plant (*Agave americana*), with larger-than-life succulent leaves to 6 ft. (2 m) ending with hooked spines and a tall (to 15 ft. or 4.5 m) flowering spike of white, clustered blooms; South African blue chalksticks (*Senecio serpens*), a succulent blue ground cover; and old man cactus (*Cephalocereus senilus*) from Central Mexico, so covered with white hairs on its stem and spine that it looks like an overgrown beard.

The nearby Mediterranean Garden carries on the effort to display plants from around the world that create unique ecosystems, among them *Saliva discolour* from Peru, silvery and felty with purple-black flowers showing from silvery green calices; tall, dusty miller–like Catalina silver lace (*Eriophyllum nevinii*); and *Phlomis italica*, a shrubby silver member of the mint family from Spain's Balearic Islands. These plants all come from Mediterranean climates around the world from California to Australia, where plants thrive and flower in moist winter conditions before going dormant during the hot, arid summer. Designed by Ron Lutsko, of the California firm of Lutsko Associates, plantings center around a water display of small pools fed by drip fountains to represent water's central importance, and scarcity, to Mediterranean flora.

Nancy Webber's xeriscaped front yard in Austin, Texas, shows the rich diversity of plants with bold forms and textures that can be used in the garden while conserving water.

The idea of matching plants to habitat, so ingeniously illustrated in Longwood's Silver Garden, was an outgrowth of the xeriscape movement that began inauspiciously in the city of Denver, Colorado, when during a period of water shortage in the early 1980s, the city's Water Works launched a publicity campaign to convince the local public to save water. The word *xeriscape* (based on the Greek word *xeri*, meaning dry) was created during a brainstorming session, and a new concept in gardening was born. It stresses the reduction of turf and high water-use areas and selection of plants appropriate to the site, with an emphasis on using native flora, grouping plants in accordance with their water needs, improving soil conditions to lessen water needs, using mulch to reduce water evaporation, and capturing rainwater on the site.

While landscape architects, town planners, and concerned horticulturists embraced the new concept, it struck the vast gardening public then as an unappetizing way to go about creating a beautiful environment. Early examples were, in the words of one observer, "stark and scary" moonscapes of rocks and yuccas. But as droughts hit various parts of the country, the movement spread, gradually evolving into a highly sophisticated approach to gardening whose principles could be applied virtually to any climate and any region of the country, whether

Rose sage (*Salvia pachyphylla*), *Yucca neomexicana*, and *Ephedra equisetina* at the Dryland Mesa, Denver Botanic Gardens.

or not the style or technique was consciously linked to xeriscaping. "Naturalistic" and "low-maintenance" gardening, for instance, are ultimately derived from xeriscape standards.

Today xeriscape programs avoid negative stereotypes by emphasizing that xeriscaping is not confined to waterless, lawnless, flowerless landscaping restricted solely to native flora, but is simply about conserving, not eliminating, the use of water. Xeriscaped settings can be well-designed groupings of diverse and beautiful flora that may combine areas of higher water use with more self-sustained plantings. "Water-smart" gardening, a term coined by the Denver Botanic Gardens, showcases this approach in a series of beautifully designed gardens, among them the Rock Alpine Garden, Dryland Mesa, High Plains Perennial Garden, and the Water-Smart Garden itself. In all of these areas, the principle of matching plants to habitat is carefully observed without sacrificing aesthetics. The gardens provide color, diversity of forms, and interest for all seasons.

The xeriscape movement was the catalyst for a new interest in silvers for difficult habitats as Mrs. Underwood, ahead of her time, had suggested decades ago. Other silver fanciers, such as Australian botanist-horticulturist Roger Spencer, were prophets of the new silver movement. *Growing Silver, Grey and Blue Foliage Plants*, his 1987 work (now a collector's item), thoroughly explored the genre for Australian conditions. Some of the native Australian plants he described, such as *Plectranthus argentatus*, have since become well established in North American gardens.

A new generation of enthusiastic collectors has contributed plants from the Mediterranean region, Australia, South Africa, the tropics, and North America to extend the silver palette favored by Jekyll (although the plants she loved remain popular). A new silvery look in shade-loving pulmonarias, heucheras, and other types recently introduced into North American nurseries refutes the notion that silver plants are synonymous with a sunny, dry climate. No longer confined to herb gardens and herb plant nurseries, silvers are displayed in public gardens and at an increasing number of specialty and traditional plant nurseries.

As the marketplace for silvers expands, new kinds are finding their way into home gardens. *Helichrysum petiolare*, only recently introduced, now trails from nearly every window box and container throughout the land. Silvers have traveled a long way from humble herbs in the Old World apothecary to the forefront of a new gardening wave, where their practical and aesthetic possibilities are being fully explored.

Tender perennials *Plectranthus argentatus* and *Helichrysum petiolare* engulf their container.

Sun-loving, tender *Tradescantia sillamontana*, a downy silver, snuggles up to a waxy agave.

CHAPTER TWO

Sorting Silvers

SILVER TYPES

Although we call all of them *silvers*, their silveriness varies from near glittering white and absolute silver to green-gray, grays, and silvery blues, and from spotted and streaked leaves to types covered with a metallic sheen. Silvers can be found in most plant groups, although few true annual species exist, since these occur mostly in winter rainfall areas where conditions are unfavorable to silver adaptation. We think of many of the silvers, such as the dusty millers (senecios), as annuals, but they are actually shrubby perennials in their warm, native climate. Although silvers are represented in many families in the plant kingdom, they are especially well represented in the sun-loving family Asteraceae. Silver plants dominate some genera (green plants are the exceptions among artemisias), while in others, they are anomalies. Their natural habitats around the world range from dry deserts to rain forests, from treeless plains swept by searing winds and intense heat to frigid mountain tops, rocky cliffs, and salt-sprayed coastlines. Some silvers even grow in alpine bogs. They live and thrive in such forbidding conditions because they have adapted to their environment by becoming silver.

Silvers are of three types: downy, waxy, and variegated. With the recent introduction of new silvery pulmonarias, heucheras, ferns, and brunneras, variegated plants have assumed more importance. While downy and waxy types are predominantly sun-lovers, variegated silvers thrive in shade, so their inclusion in the silver palette greatly extends landscaping possibilities.

Silver plants encompass the spectrum from tiny, compact alpines to soaring evergreens. Leaves can be long and thick or small and dainty, curled, cupped, or needlelike, with textures from soft and velvety to hard and leathery. Some plants are deeply rooted to anchor them from the wind and to enable them to draw down, others spread wide (as in a desert) for moisture. Many silvers contain toxic sap, give off sharp aromas, or display forbidding thorns to discourage hungry animals, for silvers inhabit difficult terrain where it pays to be armed. The world of silvers is complex and can be confusing, but if you enter it with a basic knowledge of the general types and the special language used to describe them—the vocabulary of silvers—hunting for the right silver for the right place will be a rewarding endeavor.

DOWNY TYPES

Plants within this group, the largest of the three, spring to mind when we hear the phrase "silver plant." Leaves (in some cases, the entire plant) are covered with a protective layer of down or hairs over the plant's natural green. The length, density, and position (upright or flattened), and the plant's exposure to bright sun determines the plant's coloring through all the shades of silver from near white and sterling to green-grays. The function of down is to maintain a layer of humidity close to the plant's surface that protects it from extremes of heat and cold. The effect is to create an aura or glow around the plants as sunlight bounces off their hairs, causing them to look silvery. Such plants, tough by design and beautiful in their impact, exist and flourish in seemingly impossible conditions.

More than 200 species of artemisias cope very well with the dry, blazingly hot summers and cold, windy winters that characterize vast expanses of treeless sagebrush, steppe country, or seacoast around the world, from the American West to southern Russia and North Africa. We tend to think of downy types as *true* silvers, because they are so unequivocally silver in appearance. In addition to artemisias, plants that quickly come to mind are the stachys, helichrysums, verbascums, as well as aromatic herbs and flowering plants whose blooms complement silver foliage, such as lavenders, salvias, santolinas, and perovskia.

Salvia argentea, a downy silver.

Beach wormwood (*Artemisia stelleriana*) forms thick colonies on sand dunes, Cape Cod.

One way to learn about the cultural needs or appearance of a particular downy type is to learn to "read" the plant through its Latin description: *Thymus pseudolanuginosus* describes a type of thyme that is rather woolly, a rough translation of *pseudo* (rather) and *lanuginosus* (woolly). A rule of thumb is that the hairier the plant, the drier growing conditions it requires. From just a name, the gardener knows that woolly thyme is covered in thick down and needs sharp drainage. Other instructive Latin epithets in the downy vocabulary include *cinereus* or *cinerascens* (gray); *argentea*, *argenteus*, and *argentus* (silver); and *albi*, *albo*, and *albus* (white).

Some downy silvers, often the most striking ones, have silver-backed foliage characterized by a polished, silvery sheen. In this kind, collapsed hairs—seen only with a magnifying glass—form what is called *scale*. Depending on their shape, or degree of curling or cupping, the least rustle of wind can turn up the leaves' undersides, sending out dramatic waves of silvery shimmers that dominate the entire landscape, as in the swaying foliage of a poplar or the mass of upturned leaves on the lilting stems of a buddleia bush. Scale can also cover entire leaves, as in epiphytic tillandsias, where it plays a vital role in retaining and absorbing moisture and nutrients from the atmosphere.

WAXY TYPES

This versatile group's foliage, or the entire plant, is covered in a protective waxy layer in the form of powdery *bloom*. This creates a sleek appearance; a smooth, slippery texture; and a silvery blue, steel-blue, gray-blue, or powder-blue cast, depending on the nature of the powder. In some types, especially succulents, the heavier waxy coating is called *meal*. Just as you rub the bloom off a freshly picked plum before you eat it, bloom is easily rubbed off waxy silvers. Take a leaf of

Agave parryi, a waxy silver.

silvery blue dianthus or eucalyptus and gently rub your thumb across its foliage. As if by magic, the leaf now appears green. The waxy dusting or coating is thought to have the same function as down in protecting plants from the extremes of heat, cold, drought, wind, salt spray, and unrelieved sun in deciduous woodlands in spring and fall.

Just as with downy silvers, once these conditions do not exist, most plants lose their protective covering. Other waxy silvers include eryngiums, junipers, spruce, and several grasses. Some, such as agaves, yuccas, and euphorbias, are further adapted to dry desert conditions by hoarding juice or sap in their leaves and stems, giving them a swelled appearance. Needle-leaved conifers from cold, windy,

Eryngium yuccifolium, a waxy type, in Chicago Botanic Garden's Native Plant Garden.

mountainous regions are helped by the reduction of their foliage surface and restricted stomata, or transpiration holes, usually on the back of their needles. Useful epithets to know among this group include *caesius, glaucescens, farinosus, pulverulentus,* and *pulverulenta,* all of which mean powdery or mealy. *Glaucous* is a term used to describe foliage with a waxy coating that makes it appear blue-green or blue-gray, depending on the depth of wax or bloom.

Blue spruce (*Picea pungens* var. *glauca*) has reduced foliage (needles) and a protective waxy coating.

Heuchera 'Silver Scrolls', a variegated silver.

Pulmonaria 'Excalibur' has silver spots covering air pockets that provide protection from the sun.

VARIEGATED TYPES

Variegated plants are characterized by streaked, spotted, edged, frosted, or marbled leaves. They can be natural variants (sports) or the result of the breeder's art. It has been suggested that the pale spots and blotches that appear on the upper surfaces of the leaves of some pulmonaria cover air pockets, which prevent the lower layer of cells from overheating, an adaptation to unfavorable growing conditions in their mountain habitats. Similar in function to down or wax, such spotting in pulmonaria—and perhaps by extension in other types as well—is compared to a kind of sunscreen. In our own gardening experience, we have observed that thin-leaved, unspotted pulmonarias such as *Pulmonaria rubra* may dry up during extended periods of heat and drought, even when planted in deepest shade, while silvered types, though they may wilt during the hottest part of the day, rebound and survive. Pulmonaria fanciers should keep this in mind when choosing species or cultivars.

Among silvers, the vocabulary of variegated and striped types includes *maculatus* and *variegatus* (blotched) and *marginatus* (edged). Other silvers in this group include lamiums, ajugas, begonias, cyclamen, brunnera, and ferns. These types are dominated by shade-loving foliage plants and ground covers that thrive in moist conditions, allowing the gardener to create silver highlights in the darkest places.

Japanese painted fern (*Athyrium nipponicum* var. *pictum*), a shade-loving variegated silver.

CHANGES

No matter how well we learn to "read" them, when silvers are growing in a real garden under variable conditions, we soon discover that they change in appearance, becoming more or less hairy, waxy, or variegated in response to seasons, weather, site, or plant maturity. Downys such as senecios are dulled when their hair is flattened by summer rains, but their young, inner growth always remains dry and bright. Downys that appear so silvery in summer (cerastium and lamb's ears) may take on an attractive bluish cast in winter, while waxy Colorado blue spruce, iridescent on the coldest days of winter, loses some of its luster in warmer weather. Sun-loving downys, planted in shade and rich rather than dry, gritty soil, are less hairy, hence, not as silvery as plants grown in full sun in thin soil. The helichrysums that were light green in spring turn intensely silver in the long, hot days of summer, while waxy eucalyptus leaves, round and silvery blue in youth, are elongated and green in maturity. And depending on the source of seeds or plants, species and cultivars carrying the same name may vary considerably in appearance as well as hardiness. This phenomenon has been especially observed in the many seed-grown forms of *Serenoa repens* (saw palmetto), a variable plant in nature. While the most silvery forms are chosen for propagation, seedlings can vary in foliage color from green to nearly white or blue, with variations in between. Just as downy and waxy silvers change their appearance in response to conditions, variegated types also change with the season, climate, and degree of shade or exposure to unmediated sunlight.

ADAPTABILITY

Our goal is to encourage gardeners to create beautiful garden effects with silver plants. But if silvers are designed to grow in specific habitats around the world, we wondered how well they would adapt to the varied garden conditions found throughout North America—from the temperate Northeast, characterized by damp or snowy winters where drought is the exception, to the cool, moist Northwest; from the hot, humid Southeast to the arid Southwest; and to a wide range of soil conditions. Are some more adaptable than others? Which silvers are best suited to specific conditions? Since we have grown—and killed—many silver plants in various locations, we looked first at our own experiences.

In a garden on Cape Breton Island, Nova Scotia, officially designated Zone 6 but in practice Zone 4, we observed silvers over three decades. Although the climate was characterized by cool and moist summers, cold and heavy acidic soil, constant wind, and alternate freezing and thawing in winter—conditions anathema to many silvers—quite a few of the classics thrived in raised beds filled with compost soil. Successes included many artemisias, salvias, rue, stachys, dianthus, achilleas, sedums, and horehound. Plants that barely succeeded or failed completely included lavenders (species and cultivars of *Lavandula angustifolia*), perovskias, thymes (especially woolly thyme), the "never-fail" basket-of-gold alyssum (*Aurinia saxatilis*), and buddleia, all silvers with little or no adaptability to cold, wet conditions and heavy soil.

In the Adirondack Mountains of eastern New York, officially designated Zone 4 but in practice Zone 5, all the failed silvers, and many more, found a welcome home in thinner, fast-draining soil. Here summers are hot and often dry, and winters are snowy and frigid. Although the growing season is shorter than in Cape Breton, it is fast-paced, with plants shooting up and putting on growth with the first burst of spring. These conditions are especially favorable for shrubby perennial silvers such as lavender, which must produce woody growth their first season in the ground to survive over the winter. Cool shade- and moisture-loving plants, though, such as pulmonarias, previously grown in sun or shade in moisture-retentive soil, needed maximum shade in a constantly amended bed of deep, friable soil.

In a northwestern Connecticut garden officially classified Zone 5, cupped to the south-southwest and protected from north winds by the mountain to which it tenaciously clings, we have experienced several week-long chills of -25°F (-32°C), some winters with almost weekly blizzards, rainless summers with plant-rotting humidity and summers when it never seemed to stop raining, summers with temperatures mostly from 60° to 70°F (15° to 20°C), and summers with weeks of temperatures of 100°F (38°C) or more. Humus-rich, moisture-retentive soil, a precipitous slope, encroaching forest, underground water, microclimates created by garage-sized glacial boulders, and voracious deer are all factors that shape the garden. The most adaptable silvers, and among the very best plants in the garden, are *Buddleja davidii* 'Nanho Blue', *Nepeta* ×*faassenii* 'Six Hills Giant', *Salvia officinalis* 'Berggarten' and dwarf *S. officinalis* 'Compacta', *Pulmonaria* 'Excalibur', plain as well as fancy lamb's ears (*Stachys byzantina* 'Helene von Stein'), *Helictotrichon sempervirens* 'Sapphiresprudel', and *Euphorbia myrsinites*, a pernicious weed in drier habitats but here a welcome, modest self-sower that keeps its color all winter. The failures include silvers that can't take prolonged humidity, such as *Helichrysum petiolare*; overcrowding, such as *Veronica spicata* subsp. *incana*; or too much moisture in the ground, such as lavender; as well as those that need more moisture, such as *Ajuga reptans* 'Silver Beauty'; or those that are too attractive to voles, such as gazanias.

Our mountainside garden in Connecticut, where lamb's ears (*Stachys byzantina* 'Helene von Stein') and *Nepeta* ×*faassenii* 'Six Hills Giant' thrive in full sun with fast drainage.

Species lamb's ears (*Stachys byzantina*) appreciate shade in hot summer climates, as in Bill Harris's Maryland garden.

These experiences suggest that silvers vary considerably in their adaptability and that site, soil, and favorable microclimates are often more crucial than hardiness ratings. Sometimes unimproved species such as *Lavandula angustifolia* or *Stachys byzantina* may be more vigorous, hence more adaptable to less than ideal conditions than their cultivars, but the reverse may also be true. *Artemisia stelleriana* 'Silver Brocade', for instance, has proved more adaptable and less demanding of perfect drainage than the wild form. We also discovered that even in a cool summer climate, sun-loving silvers (lamb's ears and some artemisias) could be grown in partial shade if the soil bed is deep enough. In our efforts to determine the adaptability of silvers in other parts of the country, we talked to experts and observed silver plants growing in gardens, both public and private.

Bismarckia nobilis at Harry P. Leu Gardens, Orlando, Florida.

Winter-hardy *Juniperus horizontalis* 'Wiltonii' in a Minnesota garden.

Yucca rostrata at Peckerwood Garden in Texas.

Madalene Hill's raised bed for growing lavenders in her southern Texas garden.

Artemisia ×'Powis Castle', here growing with *Miscanthus sinensis* 'Morning Light', *Panicum virgatum* 'Prairie Sky', and moisture-loving *Lysimachia nummularia* 'Aurea', is more adaptable to moist soils and humidity than other artemisias. Design: Bill Harris.

We covered a lot of ground across this vast land and saw a wealth of silvers, often the same ones, growing in entirely different circumstances. Certain obvious themes emerged: silvers do best when matched to habitats similar to those in their country of origin; some species and cultivars within a genus are more adaptable to extreme conditions than others; soil, site, and microhabitat influence adaptability more than officially designated growing zones; and adaptability can be encouraged by clever cultivation. Artemisias and other classic silvers have become classics because they are so extraordinarily adaptable.

Common stalwarts, such as *Artemisia ludoviciana* 'Silver King', *A.* ×'Powis Castle', *A. abrotanum*, *Cerastium*, *Nepeta* ×*faassenii*, and *Achillea* 'Moonshine', combine drought tolerance with a hardy, undemanding constitution. We saw them growing well in places with harsh winters and short, cool summers; places with short winters and long, hot, muggy summers; and in all types of soil, from thin to heavy. So if you can't grow lavender, try poor man's lavender, or southernwood (*Artemisia abrotanum*). Like lavender, it is aromatic and woody, can be trimmed into a hedge, and looks lovely at the foot of an old rose.

A ribbon of silvers: *Helictotrichon sempervirens*, *Perovskia atriplicifolia*, and *Panicum virgatum* 'Heavy Metal' at Noerenberg Gardens, Minnesota.

CHAPTER THREE

Designing with Silvers

*Green is well and good, but it's even better when spiced
with the exotic sheen of silver-leaved plants.*

—Panayoti Kelaidis, *Fine Gardening,* 1994

WHETHER DESIGNING A LANDSCAPE from scratch or reworking a section
of a perennial garden, most gardeners can't wait to start acquiring plants. Walking
through the garden, snipping and digging, touching, smelling, noticing the sur-
prises and delights of our plants is the joyful heart of gardening. Plants with similar characteristics tend to harmonize with each other, creating a sense of
tranquility. The contrast of plants that are very different from each other adds

zing. Paying attention to the characteristics of our favorite plants—color,
shape, sheen, habit, texture, and other
qualities—helps us predict how they
will combine with plants that have
similar or different characteristics.

We started not with a theory of
color and design but with muddling
around in our own gardens, combining
plants until they "felt right." We
learned that compiling a bouquet while
strolling through the garden with snip-
pers or walking a plant around the nursery to see how it looks with other plants
inspires unanticipated combinations.
Serendipitous self-sowers instructed us
by making felicitous combinations on
their own.

A bouquet of lamb's ears and columbine, a
study in silver and white.

51

Self-sown
Viola tricolor weave
through spiky
*Helictotrichon
sempervirens*
'Sapphiresprudel'.

THE ART OF COMBINING SILVER PLANTS

Copying directly from other gardens is certainly fair game, but often it's the ideas, not the plants themselves, that take root in our own gardens. Liking the lovely tension between cool, bright *Artemisia ludoviciana* 'Silver King' and the chartreuse zinnias and nicotiana we saw flowering in sun at the Berkshire Botanical Garden, for instance, inspired us to pair chartreuse-flowering *Alchemilla mollis* with the gleaming silver blades of *Pulmonaria* 'Excalibur' in a shady spot. Wiry, nodding native delphiniums weaving their way up through bold, spiny-tipped Zone 8 yuccas in a Texas garden suggested contrasts with our own hardy *Yucca filamentosa*. Once we realize that we like a certain kind of combination—warm with cool or bold with delicate—we can extrapolate to other kinds of plants that will grow happily in our own gardens.

Chartreuse *Zinnia* 'Envy' and *Nicotiana langsdorfii* with *Artemisia ludoviciana* 'Silver King'.

COLOR

Color is often what we notice first. It sets the emotional tone of a garden. We are excited by flamboyant color combinations or soothed by subtle ones. Yet color is the most personal of choices. One person's subtle seems dull to another, vibrant crosses the line to tacky for some, and classic may seem tired.

Silver at its purest is not a color at all but the very essence of light. It is the chameleon of the plant kingdom, changing with light and season, hard to put your finger on. Silver can be a retiring background or the star of the show, garish or subtle, soothing or distinctly exciting. Some silvers are stunning on their own—an avenue of poplars, a solitary shimmering eucalyptus, a helichrysum topiary. Silver plants have a unique ability to intensify other colors or to knit

A background of *Artemisia ludoviciana* 'Silver King' infuses pastels with a refreshing radiance.

them together (sometimes at the same time). It is in relationship to other plants, whether blending or contrasting, that silvers, finding their strength, truly shine.

Silver as a peacekeeper

On a hot day, the shade of a silver tree seems cooler than shade from other trees. A silver passage in the garden provides respite. The many shades of silver, from gray-green, to gray, pewter, bright silver, or silver-blue, blend well with each other because of their shared tonal qualities. Silver gives white flowers a context that saves them from washing out in the sun. Silvers and grays have a special sympathy with pastel-colored flowers and the washed-out earth tones of plants such as New Zealand sedges. A drift of silver can buffer clashing colors, helping them blend together and giving our eyes a rest.

Some silver plants seem to look good with everything. We have seen Russian Sage (*Perovskia atriplicifolia*), lamb's ears (*Stachys byzantina* 'Helene von Stein'), blue oat grass (*Helictotrichon sempervirens*), and *Nepeta* ×*faassenii* 'Six Hills Giant' keeping the peace in gardens all over the United States. In a Connecticut garden, the nepeta edging a long allée knits together all the hues and tangle of a rose garden. In Minnesota, bright perennials are unified when displayed against a shimmering ribbon of spiky blue *Helictotrichon*, *Panicum virgatum* 'Heavy Metal', and *Perovskia*. In our own garden, *Stachys byzantina* 'Helene von Stein', with sparse silver hairs on gray-green leaves, is a fine bridge between plants on the green side and bright silvers. We suspect that whatever riot of color a garden might possess, a good dose of any of these four plants, or of any number of silver substitutes, would make sense of the chaos.

Nepeta ×*faassenii* 'Six Hills Giant' knits together the hues of a rose garden

Platinum palmettos (*Serenoa repens*) contrast with dark green coontie ferns (*Zamia floridana*). Design: Elizabeth Gillick.

Silvery *Caryopteris ×clandonensis* 'Longwood Blue' and *Artemisia* ×'Powis Castle' contrast with the dark foliage of *Colocasia antiquorum* 'Illustris' and *Phormium tenax* 'Atropurpurea' at the Norfolk Botanical Garden.

Assertive colors vibrate against silver lavenders, salvias, and rosemaries at Wave Hill.

Western native *Penstemon barbatus* glows against *Artemisia tridentata/Serphidium tridentatum* at the Denver Botanic Gardens.

Tree-scale silver and gold contrast: *Picea pungens* var. *glauca* 'Hoopsii' and *Chamaecyparis pisifera* 'Golden Mop', Twombly Nursery.

Silver contrasts

Peace in the garden is fine up to a point, but a garden that only blends and never contrasts gets dull. For gardeners seeking drama, pairing any of silver's tonal qualities with their opposite qualities creates excitement. If a silver is bright and light, try a dark companion. Silver and gold is another case of opposites attracting. Many silver plants—notably the senecios, helichrysums, achilleas, and santolinas—have yellow flowers, providing built-in warm contrast. The possibilities for dynamic combinations seem endless. If silver is cool, turn up the heat by pairing it with warm reds, russets, and oranges. If it is a dull gray, create a glow with more brilliant tones. If it is a clear, simple tone, surround it with complex or muted neighbors with purple-green leaves or mauve flowers. If it is on the blue side, pair it with oranges or yellows across the color wheel.

Textural contrasts within the silver range: *Crambe maritima, Stachys byzantina* 'Helene von Stein', and *Artemisia* ×'Powis Castle' at the Denver Botanic Gardens.

Texture

Combining plants with textures that are alike or different adds another dimension to garden vignettes. Texture is created by size and shape of leaves and by the feel or appearance of the leaves' surfaces. The lobed fans, deeply cut lace, or tiny, softly curling tendrils of artemisias contrast with linear grasses and with the round leaves of eucalyptus. It is difficult to appreciate the virtues of the many small-leaved nepetas, lavenders, origanums, helichrysum, and santolinas when they are all jumbled together, as they often are in herb gardens. These plants might not contrast much with each other, but their petite leaves make for big contrasts with *Verbascum bombyciferum*, agaves, yuccas, and other large-leaved plants. Contrasting the many surface textures of silvers—shiny, dull, fuzzy, pebbled, soft, hard, leathery, downy, powdery, smooth, and waxy—suggests many ways to enrich our combinations.

Dalea greggii, agaves, yuccas, and palm at Peckerwood Garden, Texas.

FORM

Paying attention to growing habit and silhouette (upright, laterally branching, curving, swirling, weeping, weaving, mound, mat, or spiky vase-shaped) gives us additional opportunities to make exciting garden pictures. A few silver plants— Scottish thistles, artichokes, and agaves—are so boldly architectural that they make striking contrasts with just about everything. Try juxtaposing spiky grasses with low scrambling, round-leaved plants; soft, low mounds with taller, more upright plants; or a hard architectural form with a frothy, indistinct outline.

DYNAMIC COMBINATIONS: ALIKE BUT DIFFERENT

Color, texture, and form do not exist in isolation. They interact—or fail to—all at once. The more ways they interact, the more satisfying the combination. A simple combination of lamb's ears and cushion spurge works exceptionally well, not just because it contrasts gold and silver, warm and cool, but because the spurge's rounded flowerheads and bracts, small and smooth leaves arranged on upright stalks, smooth surface, and modulated hues are strikingly different from the lamb's ears' mat of much larger bladelike leaves, very fuzzy texture, and uniform color.

Silver and gold: *Stachys byzantina* and *Euphorbia epithymoides*.

Begonia 'Looking Glass' and elephant ears (*Colocasia esculenta* 'Black Magic')—alike but different.

In a container planting of *Begonia* 'Looking Glass' and elephant ears (*Colocasia esculenta* 'Black Magic'), we can see that although the leaves have a similar shape, the elephant ears are much bigger. Leaves have a similar texture, but the begonia's surface sparkles in sunlight, while the elephant ears remain dull. Both have hanging leaves attached to stems in the same manner. Major veins of both are green, but the begonia is silver on the front and red on the back, shimmering and light in comparison to the dark, almost black, elephant ears. The plants' similarities are close and their differences extreme, adding up to a complex, resonant picture.

Topiaries in Cooperstown, New York, set into a bed of silver *Artemisia* ×'Powis Castle', *Helichrysum italicum* 'Nana', *Helichrysum petiolare*, and *Kalanchoe pumila*.

Formal squares of *Buxus* 'Green Velvet' and *Artemisia ludoviciana* 'Valerie Finnis' at the Chicago Botanic Garden.

STYLE

The very act of making a garden, of intentionally arranging plants and spaces, sets it apart from nature and from architecture. Yet the degree and manner in which the garden speaks to its surrounding buildings and landscapes and takes cues from them conveys a sense of place. Whether set into a green background or an architectural hardscape, formal gardens and landscapes are characterized by symmetry and geometry or an architectural framework or reference. Space and other formal design elements are usually more important than specific plants. Formal gardens can be extremely minimal or quite elaborate, with many parts and many kinds of plants. In a formal garden with parterres or clipped evergreens, nothing articulates the contrast between hedging material and filler like silver plants. One of the glories of Central Park's Conservatory Garden in spring (see page 15 in chapter one) is a swirling design of clipped *Santolina chamaecyparissus* filled with deep blue muscari. Here silver defines a pattern and a space with a filler that changes with the seasons.

Informal gardens and landscapes look more to nature for a model, whether by imitation of nature's infinite variety, planting patterns, plant communities, or landforms. Plants usually appear to be more important than formal design elements. Plantings may actually be even more carefully planned than those in a formal scheme, but they may appear to be more casual, more naturalistic. Cottage gardens informally integrate useful and beautiful plants of all descriptions. In our Adirondack combined kitchen and flower garden, bronzy red beet tops provide a pleasing partnership with *Artemisia ludoviciana* 'Silver King'; tomatoes on stakes, tall corn stalks, rows of blue-gray cabbage, and assorted lettuce from green to red are rimmed by a border of hardy roses, dwarf lavender, and the silvery blue mats of fragrant dianthus.

In Texas, garden designer Nancy Webber's naturalistic front yard informally reflects the countryside that the city displaced long ago. She is guided by her observations of the land, its light, plant communities, and spareness. Gravel paths meander around low-stacked walls and arrangements of porous local limestone. These support a colorful community of interesting plants that naturally grow in desert and limestone ledges. Large sculptural agaves, blue sotol (*Dasylirion wheeleri*), *Nolina nelsonii*, blue yucca (*Yucca rostrata*), and blue fan palms (*Brahea armata*) are scattered throughout her garden, spaced widely to avoid competition for scarce water, as they would be in nature.

For Lauren Springer, xeriscaping in the dry western United States is just sensible gardening. She advises that if you don't have a lot of water, work with plants that do well without a lot of water. Xeric plants look natural in dry places.

Nancy Webber's informal Texas front yard, based on natural plant communities.

Matching plants to habitat, the principle that drives all her work, she used an extraordinary variety of drought-resistant natives and introduced species tolerant of the clay conditions in her hillside garden. Here, silver plants have an important role doing what they were born to do: hang on through severe drought, burning sun, and wind. Her yard reflects her affinity with the spare surrounding landscape, blending right into it. Native red sandstone terraces, walks, and steps meander around the house, providing outdoor living spaces and garden areas densely planted with a colorful variety of dryland plants. More than 40 dwarf conifers throughout the gardens keep a low profile in summer, but in winter they tie the garden to chaparral-covered hills, dotted in conifers and silver native plants.

As the gardens move away from the house (and a water source) merging into the wild, plantings become spare, dominated by the toughest survivors—acantholimons, hardy yuccas, artemisias, apache plume (*Fallugia paradoxa*), and woolly, white plants from the Mediterranean. Although Springer groups plants using natural plant communities as her model, her artist's eye is always at work. She plays colors and textures off each other, highlights the sculptural quality of some plants, and makes the most of contrasts, weaving an enchanting tapestry.

Lauren Springer's informal planting includes silver *Dianthus ×allwoodii* 'Sops in Wine' seedlings, *Achillea ×kelleri, Hieracium villosum, Anacyclus depressus* (Mt. Atlas daisy), and *Antennaria parvifolia* 'McClintock'.

A garden doesn't have to be entirely formal or informal. Many gardeners use elements of both. The late Joanna Reed's herb garden near Philadelphia employs the best of both worlds. The formal pattern of this rectangular garden—divided by straight and curved bluestone paths, with a circle in the center—is enhanced by the informality of beds filled to overflowing with lavenders, salvias, nepetas, achilleas, santolinas, feathery blue sedum, Russian sage, spurge (*Euphorbia myrsinites*), and other herbs. The multitude of textures, leaf sizes and shapes, plant habits, and tones of silver play off the strong, simple design of the hardscape, keeping things interesting. The fragrance from sweet lavender and pungent salvias adds an engaging sensory element beyond the visual.

Lauren Springer's Colorado garden blends into the surrounding landscape.

Joanna Reed's informal plantings within a formal framework.

USING SILVERS IN GARDEN AND LANDSCAPE

Whether massed or spotted throughout a scheme, woven into other plants or standing separate, viewed up close or from a distance, acting as a buffer, blender, or contraster, silver plays many roles.

BEDS AND BORDERS

Perennials are the mainstay of traditional herbaceous beds and borders, but adding shrubs, ornamental grasses, annuals, bulbs, small trees, vines, and ground covers makes for a livelier mix and a longer season of interest. Beds and borders can be planted with only annuals for a seasonal scheme or with shrubs for a permanent, lower maintenance feature. Adaptable silvers such as *Artemisia ludoviciana* 'Silver King', *A.* ×'Powis Castle', and tender *Plectranthus argentatus* can hold their own in the rich, watered soils demanded by many familiar perennials. They add lightness and set a traditional border apart from a lush, green backdrop.

The O'Fallon Perennial Walk at the Denver Botanic Gardens appears as lush and floriferous as any traditional English perennial garden, but traditional thirsty perennials are replaced by water-thrifty plants. Springer's Colorado "hell strip" garden made famous in her book *The Undaunted Garden* (1994) took dryland perennial gardening to its extreme. The brilliantly flowering low mounds, set off by evergreen and silver-foliage plants, thrived in sun-baked, compacted alkaline soil between concrete sidewalk and street, out of hose's reach.

Whatever the plants, whatever the style, silvers work their magic in many ways. A shrub bed or border with a simple design and restrained plant palette can be refreshing. Outside San Antonio, Texas, Bill Bauer of Austin design firm Gardens

Juniperus scopulorum back a border containing *Picea pungens* var. *glauca* 'Montgomery', *Helictotrichon sempervirens*, *Echinops bannaticus* 'Taplow Blue', *Nepeta* ×*faassenii* 'Six Hills Giant', and *Lychnis coronaria* at the Denver Botanic Gardens.

Silver *Plectranthus argentatus*, *Artemisia* ×'Powis Castle', and *A. ludoviciana* 'Silver King' add a sense of lightness to Thyrza Whittemore's Connecticut garden.

Drought-tolerant *Artemisia versicolor*, *Sidalcea* 'Elsie Heugh', and *Penstemon* 'Red Rocks', Denver Botanic Gardens.

planted a silver shrub garden with masses of gray-leaved *Cotoneaster glaucophyllus*, Texas sage (*Leucophyllum frutescens*), and soft leaf yuccas (*Yucca pendula*), from which tall, blue-green pencils of Italian cypress (*Cupressus sempervirens*) emerge. The bed is evocative of desert rangeland, while standing out against surrounding green pastures. Beds and borders can be comprised entirely of grasses in an ever-moving array, in which silvers provide color contrast. Tom Bodnar of Twombly Nursery values silver-blue grasses and shrubs for their ability to create contrasts and harmonies. He likes to pull in blue-blooming *Caryopteris* ×*clandonensis* 'First Choice' to echo silver-blue/green *Schizachyrium scoparium* as well as the silver-blues of lower growing fescues and blue oat grass.

Lynden Miller uses every trick in the book in her Jane Watson Irwin Perennial Garden at The New York Botanical Garden. This series of garden rooms is lively with tones, textures, leaf shapes, and forms, contrasting and blending. Silvers are cooling and dazzling, working on many levels and in sequences that move the visitor through the garden's spaces. Miller flanks a passage between two garden rooms with a pair of icy silver-blue upright Arizona cypress trees (*Cupressus arizonica* var. *glabra* 'Blue Ice'). A silver-green *Elaeagnus* tree, *Perovskia atriplicifolia*, mounds of artemisias, and *Plectranthus argentatus* echo the blue cypress and play off more vibrant colors. She knits the garden together subtly by repeating silver's colors, forms, textures, and leaf shapes, making dynamic relationships with combinations that are alike but different.

THE SILVER SHADE GARDEN

Shade silvers brighten otherwise dark areas of the landscape. A wealth of silver variegated pulmonarias and heucheras have been introduced in recent years. Cyclamens, asarums, begonias, Japanese painted fern (*Athyrium nipponicum* var. *pictum*), and brunneras possess equally intriguing leaf patterns. Variegated silvers

Silver shrub border in Texas: *Cotoneaster glaucophyllus*, *Leucophyllum frutescens*, *Yucca pendula*, and *Cupressus sempervirens*. Design: Gardens.

Colors, forms, and textures blend and contrast with *Cupressus arizonica* var. *glabra* 'Blue Ice' at The New York Botanical Garden. Design: Lynden Miller.

Gleaming silver *Pulmonaria* 'Excalibur' shines against green companions.

benefit from nonsilver companions of decidedly different appearance, such as upright Solomon's seal (*Polygonatum* sp.) or broad-leaved golden hostas, and they associate beautifully with their nonsilver cousins. Pulmonaria leaves grow in importance as the season advances, becoming larger, tougher, and substantially more silver as they turn from welcoming the sun to protecting themselves from it. They become even more luminous at dusk. While we never intended to create a moonlight garden, a planting of shade silvers more than serves this purpose.

GROUND COVERS

We think of ground covers as low plants that form spreading mats or take root to form a colony covering the earth. They cool the ground, prevent erosion, and keep weeds from gaining a foothold. Ground covers can also be used to carpet the floor of a garden, providing a visual anchor and background for taller plants. *Ajuga reptans* 'Silver Beauty' and lamiums do this admirably in partly sunny to shady areas, as do veronica and lamb's ears in full, baking sun. Any perennial or shrub that holds its ground can be used as a ground cover if planted in masses. Native grasses—*Panicum virgatum* 'Heavy Metal', *Schizachyrium scoparium* (little bluestem), or *Sorghastrum nutans* 'Sioux Blue'—planted *en masse* bring a touch of their prairie origins into sunny areas. Silver sedges work in part shade, and rushes in damp soil.

Lamium maculatum 'White Nancy' grows as a ground cover under a hedge of *Syringa meyeri* 'Palibin'.

Dichondra argentea carpets the floor of an Austin garden. Design: Big Red Sun.

EDGERS AND WEAVERS

Low perennials or shrubs can be used to edge a garden, either loosely to add sub-tle definition to boundaries or as a short-clipped hedge or a dense barrier. Lamb's ears can be used to form a bright ribbon or planted in clumps alternating with hebe, as we saw in Portland, Oregon. Other good choices for sunny gardens are nepetas for a billowing edge, lavenders for clipped or unclipped low hedges that remain through winter, and dianthus, especially when it is allowed to flow over a stone path, softening the garden's boundary. Ever useful lamb's ears and low-growing Roman wormwood (*Artemisia pontica*), beach wormwood (*A. stelleriana* 'Silver Brocade'), and sea foam artemisia (*A. versicolor* 'Sea Foam') are good weavers for creating a soft transition in flower borders, while still defining their edges. For part shade, try lamium cultivars, and for deeper shade, pulmonaria, which when kept in bounds by mowing forms an impenetrable, upright herba-ceous hedge.

Clumps of *Stachys byzantina* alternate with hebe in a Portland, Oregon, garden. Design: Betty Rahman

Helichrysum petiolare edges and weaves through a Connecticut garden bed.

Hedges and screens

Hedges, like edgers but taller, serve to define garden spaces and boundaries. Taller hedges planted with shrubs or trees additionally serve as walls to garden rooms, as windbreaks, or as screens. A rigid-clipped hedge of brilliant silver-blue Arizona cypress might seem heavy-handed in a naturalistic, predominately green landscape—or it could be a stroke of genius—highlighting the difference between nature and human endeavors. Toned-down silvers like caryopteris for a loose, deciduous hedge or various upright junipers blend well with other garden plants and the larger landscape. Weeping blue Atlas cedar (*Cedrus atlantica* 'Glauca Pendula') can be trained over a frame to make a cascading curtain for a see-through divider. For the seashore, tough-as-nails sea buckthorn (*Hippophae rhamnoides*), with willowlike gray leaves and decorative yellow-orange berries, breaks the wind and flourishes in burning sun and salt spray. Tall, silver ornamental grasses such as *Miscanthus sinensis* cultivars look great screening a pool or play area.

Bold forms and contrasts within a container: *Salvia argentea*, *Centaurea cineraria* 'Colchester White', *Phormium* 'Bronze Baby', and *Scaevola aemula* 'New Wonder'. Design: Jan Axel.

Containers

A container planting is a distillation, a whole garden in microcosm. In designing containers, anything goes—but everything counts. The same principles that guide successful landscaping apply here. When planting mixed containers, using plants that harmonize or contrast with each other in more than one way maximizes their impact and subtlety. Instead of stuffing a mishmash of flowers into a container, consider using a combination of just a few flowering and foliage plants. Some plants are so vigorous—or exquisite—that they are better off in a pot by themselves. A single silver plant, well matched to its container and well sited, can be far more striking and memorable than a crowd of overfilled pots.

The phenomenal rise of container gardening over the last 10 years owes

much to the introduction of new tropical and subtropical plants, ornamental
grasses, and foliage plants, and to the
development of heat-resistant plants
that keep blooming from spring to
frost. A willingness to experiment, to
consider any kind of plant—perennials, annuals, herbs, grasses, foliage, and
flowering—makes this an exciting time
to garden if only in the space of a few
pots on a terrace or fire escape. It's
hard to go wrong with trailing or
upright helichrysums; the broad, vel-
vet-leaved *Plectranthus argentatus*; upright,
feathery *Centaurea cineraria* 'Colchester
White'; or spreading, fan-leaved
Artemisia stelleriana 'Silver Brocade'.

Containers can be grouped, setting
up a rhythm along a path, creating a
focal point, or furnishing a terrace.
They allow us to make a whole

Lotus 'Amazon Sunset' and *Eucalyptus
gunnii*, Longwood Gardens.

rearrangeable garden in a spot not suited to planting and to combine plants that
we couldn't otherwise grow together. Exquisite alpines, from the tiniest saxifrage
to miniature dwarf forms of juniper, firs, and false cypress (*Chamaecyparis*), that
could never survive in the rough and tumble of the garden, prosper among rocks
in a trough or similar container. Along with creating the aura of their natural

Alternating pots
of *Kalanchoe
pumila* and *Buxus
sempervirens*
'Antarctica'
topiaries,
Clark Foundation,
Cooperstown,
New York.

Dryland *Verbascum bombyciferum* grows next to *Canna* 'Tropicana' planted in water, in Garfield Park, Chicago.

Miniature alpine habitat with sharp-draining soil mix, rocks, and pebble mulch in hypertufa trough with *Saxifraga ×kinlayii* at Stonecrop Gardens.

Silver *Helichrysum italicum* and green *Myrtus communis* topiaries, the Chicago Botanic Garden.

habitat, rocks shield roots from heat, conserve moisture during drought, and help to drain away excess moisture during wet spells. Within a very restricted space you can create an entire miniature garden landscape of contrasting shapes—tight buns, spreading mats, and upright silhouettes—that exist in a world of their own.

TOPIARY

Any small-leaved, densely branched shrub or woody perennial lends itself to clipping into topiary. Topiaries—whether large shrubs in the landscape, strands of a knot garden, or small potted forms—always seem fanciful, especially if they are silver rather than the usual green. When grown in a tub and trained as topiary, even common wormwood (*Artemisia absinthium*) is transformed into an arresting accent.

TREES

As large elements in the landscape, silver trees can be powerful focal points—or they can stick out like a sore thumb. Any well-shaped silver tree can be a show-stopper when backed with a tall yew hedge or other dark background. We often see evergreens, particularly blue spruces, randomly scattered around green suburban yards, looking like awkward teenagers that don't quite fit in. To incorporate silver trees artfully, use them as part of a varied garden ensemble rather than stranded specimens or cluster plantings. Repeating related tones—a bluestone walk, gray house trim, a stone wall—or using masses of silver or gray perennials throughout the landscape helps silver trees look like they belong. Gardeners in extreme climates are wise to make silvers the backbone of the landscape, not only because they will survive, but because they look like they belong there.

ACCENTS AND FOCAL POINTS

Accents repeated throughout the border punctuate. Tall or bold, spiky accents like yuccas, agaves, and tall ornamental grasses are emphatic exclamation points. In the evening, silver accents become a series of beacons to follow down the garden path. A focal point is an even stronger statement, a point of reference that directs our gaze—and our footsteps—toward a culmination. The gigantic Scotch thistle (*Onopordum acanthium*) and cardoon (*Cynara cardunculus*) are architectural knockouts that seem to extend the vista when they are planted at the extremities of a border. A silver pear tree or a gigantic agave has a similar effect.

Silvers are luminous garden jewels with the power to transform a green-dominated world. Today's adventurous gardeners have found important uses for silvers throughout the entire landscape, beyond their traditional place in the herb garden. Gardeners are discovering that silvers' compelling visual qualities equal their ability to survive—and shine—in challenging sites and soils.

Cedrus atlantica 'Glauca' underplanted with *Artemisia* ×'Powis Castle' at the Norfolk Botanical Garden.

A gigantic pair of agaves is a focal point at Florida's Bok Tower Gardens.

Veronica spicata subsp. *incana* growing in optimum conditions in well-drained, gritty soil on a slope, with *Sedum sexangulare.*

Encyclopedia of Silvers from A to Z

W ITH SO MANY SILVERS IN OUR REPERTOIRE, we need to understand their cultural needs. The chief causes of success or failure in growing silvers are subtle (and sometimes not so subtle) variations in soil and site. Soil and site are where desire and reality meet. Selecting plants that want to grow in our conditions is the first step toward success. If we do not have the perfect growing conditions, we can amend soil to a certain extent and site plants to their best advantage.

Providing well-drained soil is the key to success with the majority of silvers. Well-drained soil is aerated with sufficient air spaces, so that moisture is absorbed and moves through the soil, becoming available to plants' roots with the excess draining off. Most silvers need some moisture at their roots, but any build-up at ground level, where stem meets soil—even for a brief period—can cause irreversible damage. Such conditions often occur during periods of fluctuating freezing and thawing or during a prolonged wet spell. With silvers, excess moisture is far more likely to be the culprit in winter deaths than low temperatures.

Santolina chamaecyparissus and heucheras thrive on an ancient sand dune, Cape Cod.

Salt and sun-resistant silvers: *Buddleias* in the intermediate zone between beach and yard are occasionally inundated with salt water. Lavenders, *Artemisia schmidtiana* 'Silvermound', and *A.* x'Powis Castle' get less salt. Design: Dickson DeMarche, Landscape Architect.

SUN SILVERS

Most silvers are sun lovers from hot and arid environments. They prevail in regions of intense sunlight, in well-drained to sharply drained soil high in mineral content and low in organic matter. In the garden, most are adaptable to a good basic soil of friable loam in which clay, sand, and organic matter are present in ideal proportions to encourage drainage. Such soil can be fine-tuned to meet the needs of a wide variety of silvers. Good basic soil is dark in color from the slow decomposition of organic matter such as compost, which produces *humus*; crumbly in texture; moderately enriched (many, but not all, silvers benefit from moderate enrichment); and acidic to neutral in the 6.5 to 7 pH range.

Good basic soil will by itself satisfy a wide range of silvers, but it is improved by adding a little grit for faster drainage and as a low-nutrient conditioner. *A convenient soil formula for most sun-silvers is two parts compost-enriched soil to one part grit and one part low-nutrient soil conditioner, such as rotted sawdust.*

Spring-blooming *Dianthus caryophyllus* in a raised bed with well-drained, gritty soil.

Good basic soil, however, goes only so far with certain sun silvers. If you have tried and failed with plants such as the helichrysums, gazanias, or woolly thyme—silvers that require extra-sharp drainage and also resent humidity—try planting them on a slope, on top of a stone wall, or in a raised bed where a lot of grit has been incorporated into the soil and is also available as a mulch on top of the soil. Sun silvers that need an extra boost of drainage will also need an open, sunny site. *Open* in this context means uncrowded, allowing sunshine and a flow of air around plants. If you have trouble keeping the downiest, most silver plants—silver sage (*Salvia argentea*) or *Artemisia schmidtiana* 'Silver Mound'—alive or in healthy condition, plants may be overcrowded. When this happens, moisture collects in basal foliage, leading to rot. Clearing space around the plants and thinning overgrown plants should help. We discovered this simple secret when over-wintering *Aurinia saxatilis*, when we trimmed basal foliage clumps in the fall. Once established, most sun silvers need little extra watering except in extended drought, when most benefit from a deep soaking every week or two.

SHADE SILVERS

Shade silvers need a heavier, more nutrient-rich, moist growing medium. For these, increase the humus content and eliminate the grit. When grown in shaded beds in soil built up to 6 in. (15 cm) with top-quality compost, such plants can withstand prolonged periods of drought combined with high heat, especially if they are also mulched with wood chips, grass clippings, old straw, or other organic matter (dampness at ground level is desirable here). *A useful soil formula for*

Heuchera and Japanese painted ferns in rich, moist woodland soil, mulched with bark chips.

shade silvers is two parts good basic soil to one part finished compost. For shade silvers such as cyclamens that need dry shade conditions, the best site is under deciduous trees where tree roots absorb extra moisture.

ALPINES

While many common rock garden plants—from seacoast, desert, forest, or other habitats—can be accommodated by an ordinary raised bed and soil, alpines are more demanding. Originally from high mountain areas, they require open, airy conditions; porous soil; and protection from blazing summer sun and wet winter conditions, either of which guarantees early death. In nature they grow between rocks and in sloping crevices, where they stay dry in winter and during rainy weather. Most of the alpines listed here need dry scree conditions; others need a moraine, which provides moisture from an underground water source. A simulated scree can be built in sun or shade and should be at least 3 ft. (1 m) deep and filled with broken slate, rocks, or broken bricks. Then soil and a gravel mulch is added on top. Such a built-up bed is very useful, not only for alpines, but for keeping silvers dry where heat and humidity usually do them in, especially in the southern United States.

Stonecrop Gardens recommends the following for alpine soil mix, enough to work with in a wheelbarrow (one part equals a large scoop or shovelful): *four parts humus, nine parts sand, two parts peat (sifted through a 0.25 in. or 0.5 cm screen), two parts perlite, two parts vermiculite, and a cup of 5-10-3 alpine fertilizer mix called Electra.*

Some dedicated rock gardeners build beds of stone and pure sand, 6 in. (15 cm) deep, for fussier alpines. Others swear by a mound or wall composed of tufa, a porous rock that holds moisture. Seedlings grow well in their small holes, seeds germinate in their cracks, and as it ages the tufa gains character. In arid parts of the country, silvers may need more than the natural moisture that collects between rocks in a wall. David Salmon of High Country Gardens suggests that when building

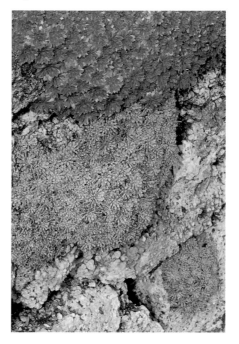

Encrusted saxifrage (*Saxifraga crustata* 'Vochinensis') thrives in a porous tufa stone wall at Stonecrop Gardens.

and backfilling a stone wall, it is important that drip tubing be installed with emitters that reach plant roots, or gravel-filled lengths of perforated PVC pipe be installed vertically behind the areas where plants will be placed. He says that

Raised stone beds at Stonecrop Gardens. Walls were planted as they were built.

watering from behind the plant will more thoroughly wet the root ball than watering face-on with a hose.

DESERT SILVERS

For gardeners who don't live in a desert area but pine to grow statuesque agaves, yuccas, and other succulents, the right environment can be created in a dry garden bed. Yucca Do Nursery in Texas advises its customers to build a mound on top of the soil, raising it as high as possible. The mound is composed of recycled construction material, such as broken bricks, tiles, and concrete, combined with rocks, 2 to 4 in. (5 to 10 cm) wide, or pea gravel.

For the soil mix, combine two parts (10 gal.) ground pine bark, one part (5 gal.) coarse concrete sand, and one part (5 gal.) pea gravel. Add to this 1 gal. 6-2-4 organic fertilizer rich in minerals and microorganisms (its own mixture is called "Yucca Doo-Doo"), supplemented with 1 cup bat guano, 0.5 gal. kelp, and 0.5 gal. dolomite lime for every 20 gal. of soil. Top dress the soil surface with pea gravel or crushed granite to shade roots, collect heat during the winter, and help prevent weeds. According to Yucca Do, keeping desert plants high and dry with this constructed dry garden bed helps them to grow, even thrive, in high rainfall and low temperature areas even as far north as Boston.

CONTAINERS

Soil should be tailored to meet the needs of different types of silvers:

For most silvers, use ⅔ potting mix to ⅓ compost soil with a couple handfuls of perlite mixed in.

For shade silvers, increase the compost component.

For alpines, succulents, and rock garden plants, decrease the compost component and add a few handfuls or more of grit to the mix.

For planting in stone or hypertufa troughs, confine the soil mix to pairing peat with perlite or coir (from coconut fiber) with sand.

GRASSES AND GRASSLIKE PLANTS

Grasses and grasslike plants—sedges and rushes—constitute some of the most adaptable and useful plants on earth. For millennia they have been used for grain (the staff of life), for fiber (clothing, baskets, and mats), and shelter (think of prairie sod houses). Widely dispersed around the world, mostly in temperate climates, they are adapted to a variety of habitats, some very harsh, on wind-swept prairies, in meadows, along beaches, on cliffs, and on mountain peaks. In the Victorian era, the taste for growing unusual or exotic foliage plants as ornamentals fueled the collection of grasses from the Americas, Europe, and Asia. Those with tall, overblown forms, such as *Miscanthus sinensis*, or with unusually colored foliage, such as *Festuca glauca* (blue fescue), became popular for their special effect in the garden. But when the rage for big forms and strange foliage passed from the gardening scene, grasses declined in popularity. They had no role to play in the new suburban garden dominated by turf grass or the flower-dominated border.

More recently, grasses have been rediscovered, not because they are exotic or strange. On the contrary, they have sparked our horticultural imagination precisely because they seem more natural and less artificial than other ornamentals. They have a starring role to play in what is dubbed "the new American garden." Tom Bodnar of Twombly Nursery advises applying the same principles of successful landscaping to grasses. Repeating favorite plants throughout a landscape ties borders together and unifies a garden. For greatest impact, keep the design simple by limiting the number of different plants used in a planting scheme. Consider ornamental grasses as a unique and softening texture to the garden.

The majority of silvers in this group are true grasses belonging to the grass family Poaceae (*Festuca*, *Helictotrichon*, *Panicum*, and *Schizachyrium*). Others are from the Cyperaceae, or sedge family (*Carex*), and Juncaceae, or rush family (*Juncus*). Silvers among them are waxy types (with the exception of miscanthus), ranging in coloring from silver-gray and silver-blue to powder-blue. In mild climates, foliage is mostly evergreen. Individual flowers are very small, often growing in large, delicate-stemmed clusters that freely move in the slightest breeze, thus assuring the successful dispersal of their seeds. Except where noted, those featured here are mostly slower growing grasses that form single clumps or densely bunched clumps that form tussocks. Others are more vigorous spreading types whose above-ground stolons or underground rhizomes establish colonies if not controlled by yearly chopping out with a sharp spade or by mowing. Grasses from hot, dry-climate summers are triggered into fresh growth by the cool rainy season in fall or early winter and are referred to as *cool-season growers*. The majority we describe are *warm-season growers* that regrow in the spring, really get going in warm summer temperatures, and then bloom by midsummer, late summer, or fall. Matched to their preferences, grasses and grasslike plants are rarely subject to diseases or insect infestations, but there are exceptions. Most grasses are resistant to drought and deer browsing, but not to gophers and voles.

TRUE GRASSES

Now that they have been in our repertoire for a while, gardeners have discovered that some grasses can be highly invasive and difficult to eradicate. When grown in too favorable conditions, they may proliferate to form unwanted colonies. To avoid contributing to environmental problems (in your own yard as well as in the surrounding area), plant potentially invasive grasses in habitats that are somewhat different from those from which they came. Wetland grasses, for instance, should be grown in drier conditions, and those that originate in a sandy soil will be slowed down by clay soil conditions. Choose cultivars whose flowers are too late blooming to set viable seed in your area. If you are undecided, consult your local agricultural extension service or visit the USDA Plants Database web site and read about invasive flora (see Bibliography).

RUSHES

Rushes are grassy plants native to wet or moist regions of the temperate world, with fine, stiff, smooth, and cylindrical foliage that grows up from hairy roots to form clumps. Some spread by rhizomes as well as by self-seeding. Flowers are small, delicate, and generally insignificant. They grow in sun or shade and moist conditions, even shallow water.

SEDGES

Sedges are found in varied habitats around the world from maritime to alpine. In contrast to rushes, sedge stems are solid and three-angled, rather than round and jointed—sedges have edges. Unlike grasses, which grow mostly in sun, sedges do well in shade, thereby extending the use of grasses and grasslike plants to shade gardens.

Artemisia schmidtiana 'Silver Mound' keeps its neat cushion shape if cut back before flowering.

MAINTENANCE AND PROPAGATION

Maintenance is a vital aspect of growing silver annuals and perennials. Where foliage is more desired than flowers, it is important to cut back the flowering stalk at first sign of growth to maintain a compact form, as with artemisias. Perennials, such as the achilleas, whose flowers are an important feature, should be deadheaded for repeat bloom. Potentially invasive silvers such as *Onopordum* or *Cynara* should be deadheaded or cut back soon after bloom to prevent seeding. Nepetas, which bloom *en masse*, can be sheared back all at once for repeat bloom after blooms are spent.

For grasses, split and replant divisions in early spring or summer when they are congested or die out in the middle. Grasses such as fescues and helictotrichons, grown in leaner soil than others, should not be cut back. Renew them in the spring by running your finger through them to draw out dead foliage. Divide fescues every two to three years in spring.

Hard-prune subshrubs such as lavender and perovskia to a growing point in the spring, but don't be impatient or you may severely delay or even destroy the possibility of new growth by cutting back too early. In cooler climates, do *not* cut

Enjoy *Perovskia atriplicifolia's* silvery stems all winter; then cut them back in the spring to rejuvenate.

back woody perennials in the fall, since this may encourage soft growth more susceptible to frost. When maintaining or working around sharp and spiny plants, such as agaves and yuccas, follow Nancy Webber's advice: wear snug and long sleeves, jeans and boots, eye protection, and gloves for protection against snagging and puncture wounds.

Trees and shrubs require careful siting because you don't want to have to move them. Most conifers languish with less than five to eight hours of sun a day, but too much sun and wind may cause burn or dehydration, especially in winter. In their first year, give newly planted trees or shrubs a soaking once a week during summer unless rainfall is abundant. Most pruning carried out when trees and shrubs are dormant can be confined to taking out dead, damaged, or excessive growth. Conifers can be pruned at their tips to encourage new growth.

Silvers are resistant but not immune to disease and insect infestations. Evergreens can be attacked by aphids, spider mites, and scale, which suck juices from their foliage. In late summer under dry conditions, some pulmonarias are prone to powdery mildew. To discourage fungal rot, botrytis, or slugs, it is important to groom silvers by removing debris and dead leaves around the base of the plant, especially in late fall before cold, wet conditions set in. By choosing the right silver for the right place, you can avoid untimely deaths. Woolly silvers, for instance, do poorly in urban environments where dust and dirt are caught in their furry coats.

Raising silver plants from seed is an economical way to grow a number of plants for bedding or containers (cultivars should be increased vegetatively). It may be the only way to grow obscure natives and alpines. Seeds that need fluctuating temperatures for germination should be sown in pots, mulched with grit, and stored outdoors in a protected area over the winter. Simple division is the easiest way to increase herbaceous silvers such as achilleas and lamb's ears. An easy way to propagate fleshy rooted silvers such as eryngiums and verbascums is to make root cuttings in the fall. Succulents such as agaves produce offsets that can be removed from the mother plant and replanted. Layering is a simple way to propagate shrubby silvers with long, flexible basal branches, such as lavender or santolina. Tip cuttings of woody or shrubby silvers can be made whenever sufficient growth occurs, usually by midsummer. This method works well with non-woody tender perennials such as helichrysums, senecios, and *Centurea cineraria* 'Colchester White'. Dianthus, in a group by itself, is increased by pulling, not cutting, a young shoot or pip from a stem joint or node and growing on as a tip cutting. Soft-stemmed tender perennials such as plectranthus or begonias are easily increased by rooting stems in water.

Silver Korean fir (*Abies koreana* 'Horstmann's Silberlocke').

ABIES

Common name: fir
Family: Pinaceae, pine
Description: waxy tree
Origin: mountains; Asia, Spain, western United States
Site and soil: sun or light shade; moist, well-drained, slightly acidic
Height and width: 30–75 ft. (9–23 m) tall; 15–30 ft. (4.5–9.0 m) wide
Hardiness: Zones 4–8

These high-altitude evergreen conifers—most familiar as the archetypal Christmas tree—thrive in cool mountain habitats where they attain great size. Many are native to North America. They are stately in appearance, with dense whorls of rigid horizontal branches that spread out from a straight trunk to form a strong pyramidal form, most perfect in younger specimens. As trees age, they may lose their lower branches, which never regrow. Firs are distinguished from other conifers by their flattened leaves and erect cones. Needles are soft to touch with a pleasant, resinous aroma. They are ovate to rounded in form and dark green, gray, or bluish on top, often with silvery stomatal banding on their undersides that gives the entire tree a silvery aspect. Colorful, erect cones are showy; often purple-blue, violet, brown, or gray-blue; and borne at the tree's highest branches in early summer. In the wild, more silvery forms stand out among greener types, suggesting landscaping possibilities. Although of limited landscape use because of their specific requirements (high atmospheric moisture and cool temperatures) and very tall, stiff forms, they are unrivaled as majestic specimens, screens, or in a background grouping. Shorter and dwarf forms are very desirable in mixed borders and in rock gardens.

On north-facing forest slopes in southern Oregon, California, and the southern Rocky Mountains, white fir, *Abies concolor*, may reach more than 100 ft. (30.5 m). In favorable garden conditions—rich, moist, well-mulched soil—it generally grows 30–50 ft. (9.1–15.2 m) tall by 15–20 ft. (4.5–6.0 m) wide, gaining 1.5 ft. (0.5 m) in height in a single season. It is the best fir for the American Northeast and is widely grown for its desirable qualities. It has silver-blue needles—at 2 in. (5 cm), the longest of any fir. Especially light in new growth, it holds its dense lower limbs longer than other types and endures hot, dry conditions. The tree's overall appearance is enhanced by a smooth, light-gray trunk and branches. *A. concolor* 'Argentea'/'Candicans' is a selection of outstanding beauty with vivid bluish white needles throughout the summer and winter. 'Compacta' is a dwarf form, to 6 ft. (1.8 m) tall, irregularly shaped in maturity. 'Dwarf' is similar, but shorter. 'Violacea', similar to the species in height and width, has bluish white foliage, especially silvery in new fresh growth. White fir, considered a good substitute for blue spruce (*Picea pungens* var. *glauca*), is hardy from Zones 4 to 8.

Korean fir, *Abies koreana*, 30 ft. (9.1 m) tall and 20 ft. (6 m) wide, is a popular garden subject for its slow growth; compact conical form; short, dark green, radially spreading needles, which are very white on the reverse; and handsome, deep-purple cones, even on very young trees. The choice 'Horstmann's Silberlocke' is especially desirable for its short needles that twist and curve to show brilliant silver undersides. 'Silver Show' is shorter with a more spreading habit; 'Starker's Dwarf' grows into a dense, flat-topped 2 ft. (0.6 m) tall mound and prefers shade. Korean firs are suitable for bonsai and hardy from Zones 6 to 8.

Slow-growing Spanish fir, *Abies pinsapo*, 75 ft. (22.8 m) tall and 15–25 ft. (4.5–7.6 m) wide, has a dense, symmetrical form and blue-gray leaves, and it can be grown in dry, alkaline soil. In southern California, where it is slow-growing, it is a dwarf tree reported to reach only 25 ft. (7.6 m) in 40 years. 'Argentea' has the most silvery white undersides.

Western native blue noble fir, *Abies procera* 'Glauca', also slow-growing, grows best in the western United States, where it grows to 200 ft. (61 m) or taller. It has distinctive powder-blue needles (bluer than blue spruce) that are short and upward pointing and large cones; 'Glauca Prostrata' is a prostrate form. Blue noble fir is hardy from Zones 5 to 8.

Veitch's fir, *Abies veitchii*, 50–75 ft. (15.2–22.8 m) tall and 25–30 ft. (7.6–9.1 m) wide, is a very hardy, fast-growing fir, most ornamental in young growth, with soft, glossy, upturned green foliage that reveals intensely silvery white undersides. Its unusually long needles, crowded together, give the tree a very dense form that is enhanced by large purplish to blue-gray cones from 2 to 3 in. (5.0 to 7.5 cm). Veitch's fir is hardy from Zones 3 or 4 to 8.

ACACIA BAILEYANA

Common name: golden mimosa, Cootamundra wattle
Family: Leguminosae, pea
Description: waxy tree
Origin: Southeast Australia
Site and soil: sun; well-drained
Height and width: 15–25 ft. (4.5–7.6 m) tall; 10–20 ft. (3–6 m) wide
Hardiness: Zones 9–11

Of the many trees and shrubs in this huge genus of more than 700 species, golden mimosa is the most cultivated one in warmer regions of the American West. It is a shallow-rooted, evergreen tree that can reach 30 ft. (9.1 m) in height, with a graceful, spreading form. Its arching branches are clothed in finely divided, feathery leaves, gray to waxy blue with a silvery overcast. Branchlets as well as seed pods have the same coloring, adding to the silvery appearance. In late winter or early spring, the tree is embellished by small, fluffy, and fragrant golden flowers, crowded together in dense clusters. Grown as a street tree in southern California, golden mimosa is especially beautiful when massed on banks as a multi-stemmed, shrublike tree. To achieve this form, remove the lead shoot.

Acantholimon, unknown species, in bloom (pink) with *Marrubium incanum* and grass (*Aristida purpurea*) in Lauren Springer's Colorado garden.

ACANTHOLIMON
Common name: prickly thrift
Family: Plumbaginaceae, leadwort
Description: waxy perennial
Origin: high arid regions; Middle East, Mediterranean, Asia
Site and soil: sun; sharply drained scree or raised bed
Height and width: 4–10 in. (10–25 cm) tall; 8–18 in. (20–46 cm) wide
Hardiness: Zones 3–9

Acantholimons form perfect rosettes, as if cut from a machine, but they are well-armed with needle-sharp tips. Panayoti Kelaidis, who has extensive experience growing acantholimons, considers them prickly but not nearly as sharp or as dangerous as agaves. Plants in this genus of about 150 species form fiercely armed evergreen tufts or cushions from green to silver, usually slow-spreading, that are effective as barriers. Early summer flowers, five-petaled and borne from a funnel-shaped calyx, are small-headed and stemless or held on wiry stems. The genus name is based on the Greek *akanthos* (a thorn) and *limonium* (sea lavender), the latter a reference to the decorative papery bracts left behind after flowers fade, similar to those of *Limonium* or *Statice*.

One of the easiest silver acantholimons is *Acantholimon venustum*, native to Turkey. Its long, needlelike, silvery leaves form a 10 in. (25 cm) tall and 18 in. (46 cm) wide cushion that grows up from a woody base. Open sprays carry at least 20 pink flowers on each wiry stem. Even better armed, *A. acerosum* forms 8 in. (20 cm) tall and 18 in. (46 cm) wide hard cushions of thick, silver-gray, daggerlike foliage to 1 in. (2.5 cm) long. Pink flowers bloom on arching stems. Two for troughs are *A. ulicinum/androsaceum* and *A. araxanum*. *A. ulicinum*, native to dry hillsides in Crete and the Balkans, is a variable plant 4 in. (10 cm) tall and 8 in. (20 cm) wide, one of the smallest acantholimons. In its most desirable form, it grows as a tight, rounded, gray-green pin cushion topped by stemless, bright-pink flowers in summer, held in white, papery calyces. *A. araxanum*, a favorite with trough enthusiasts for its very silvery needlelike foliage 2 in. (5 cm) long, reaches 6 in. (15 cm) tall in favorable growing conditions, spreading 12 in. (30.5 cm) wide. Many bright pink flowers on 7 in. (18 cm) stems are produced in early summer.

ACHILLEA

Common name: yarrow
Family: Asteraceae, aster
Description: downy perennial
Origin: mountains, meadows, waste places; Europe, Asia, Mediterranean regions
Site and soil: sun; sharply drained
Height and width: 6 in.–5 ft. (15 cm–1.5 m) tall; 12 in.–3 ft. (30.5 cm–1.0 m) wide
Hardiness: Zones 3–10

Plants in this genus of about 85 species are low and mat-forming or upright, but all grow by spreading roots, some proliferating more vigorously than others. Aromatic foliage is usually deeply cut, from ferny to toothed. Leaf coloring depends on the density of hair and ranges from high-wattage silver to more subtle grays and gray-greens. Flat-topped flowerheads 3 in. (7.5 cm) or more wide

Achillea 'Moonshine'.

are composed of closely packed, clustered florets. Individual florets of dwarf types are generally larger than those of taller forms and grow in neat, clustered heads or as single daisies from 0.5 to 1.0 in. (1.5 to 2.5 cm). Blooms in the pale lemon to bright gold and white range from spring through summer are perfectly designed foils for the spreading foliage. Flowers as well as foliage release a pleasant, somewhat spicy or medicinal aroma when the plant is brushed or bruised. The genus takes its name from Achilles, who is supposed to have used yarrow to treat the wounds of his soldiers. As with any popular group of plants, nomenclature can be confusing.

Dwarf achilleas are among the easy-to-grow alpines. Flowers are characterized by tight clusters of short-rayed daisies, yellow or white, on the basic flat-topped flowerhead. The most often grown dwarf is *Achillea tomentosa*, woolly yarrow, a European species to 6 in. (15 cm) tall. It has whitish leaves, as its Latin epithet and common name suggest, and carries canary-yellow, clustered flowerheads that bloom from late spring to midsummer with repeat bloom in late summer if plants are cut back. *A. tomentosa* 'Aurea' is similar, with rich, golden flowers. Both are hardy from Zones 3 to 8, but neither do well in hot, humid conditions. *A. ageratifolia*, Greek yarrow, forms a low, tight mat of small, lance-shaped silver leaves covered with tiny, white-petaled daisy flowers with off-white centers on 4 to 6 in. (10 to 15 cm) stems. It blooms from late spring to early summer and is hardy from Zones 5 to 9. *A.* ×*kelleri* is sturdy and compact, 8 in. (20 cm) tall and wide, with silver, filigreed foliage and yellow-centered, crisp, white flowers from spring to early summer. Hardy from Zones 6 to 9, it is a tough little plant, able to take coastal winds yet remain fresh all summer. *A.* ×*lewisii* 'King Edward', 6 in. (15 cm) tall and 18 in. (46 cm) wide, is one of the most popular dwarf forms, loved for its ability to carpet the ground with gray-green foliage and for its pale, lemon-yellow flowers in dense corymbs to 4 in. (10 cm) wide from late spring to early summer. It is hardy from Zones 4 to 9. *A.* ×*wilczekii*, 12 in. (30.5 cm) tall and wide, is lauded by rock garden and alpine guru Baldassare Mineo of Siskiyou Rare Plant Nursery for its wide, woolly, silver-gray foliage—saw-edged rather than feathery—and nodding, white flowers from late spring to early summer. It is hardy from Zones 5 to 9. *A. clavennae*, silvery yarrow, forms mats of chrysanthemum-like, silky, silvery foliage and bears large, flat-topped, white flowerheads on 6 to 10 in. (15 to 25 cm) high stems. Hardy from Zones 3 to 9, it is short-lived. *A. umbellata*, to 6 in. (15 cm), forms a cushiony mound of silver, filigreed foliage, nearly covered by small, white daisy flowers. 'Weston' is more silvery with snow-white flowers. A plant pointed out to us as *A. heireichii* in a friend's garden is a very attractive ground cover. Growing to 8 in. (20 cm), its gray-green foliage forms a low mat topped by light yellow flowers in summer. These are all hardy from Zones 4 or 5 to 9.

Achillea 'Moonshine' is the premier representative of the border achilleas. Growing to a compact 2 ft. (0.5 m), it bears ferny gray foliage, lightly frosted with silver. Flowers throughout the summer are sulphur yellow in wide, flat clusters (those that bear flowers of a different shade of yellow are impostors). Deadheading encourages continuous bloom. While not an aggressive spreader, it should be divided every two or three years to maintain its compact form. It takes heat (but not prolonged, deep heat combined with humidity, as in the southern United States) and cold, and is hardy from Zones 3 to 10.

AGAVE

Common name: century plant, woody lily
Family: Agavaceae, agave
Description: waxy succulent perennial
Origin: Americas
Site and soil: sun to shade; sharply drained
Height and width: 1.5–10 ft. (0.5–3.0 m) tall; 2.5–10 ft. (0.8–3.0 m) wide
Hardiness: Zones 5–10

Agaves are striking plants found in every possible climatic niche, from dry tropical coastal zones to alpine forest conditions where they are subject to moisture and snow. The silvery agaves originate in the American Southwest and Mexico, where they epitomize the landscape. Rosettes of rigid, fleshy, swordlike leaves, from narrow to wide, pointed and arching or perfectly rounded, are sleek and smooth or textured. Many have toothed margins, some with spines, and vicious leaf tips with an elongated point that is fearsome in some species. Silvery agaves range in color from gray to powder-blue, and their forms vary from relatively small to monumental, from 12 in. (30.5 cm) to 20 ft. (6 m) across, with flowering spikes up to 40 ft. (12 m) in the air. Lilylike flowers, pollinated by bats, moths, or hummingbirds (depending on their type), bloom in terminal umbel-like clusters, racemes, or panicles on leafless stems. The genus name from the Greek *agavos* means noble, a reference to this spectacle, while the common name is based on the monocarpic habit of many agaves to flower infrequently—but it is misleading. Smaller species are faster growing and may bloom when they are 3 or 4 years old; slower growing, larger types may take 40 to 50 years to bloom, but not a century. Agaves flower only once, and then the plants die but leave progeny (offsets or pups) behind.

Nancy Webber warns that weeds should never be allowed to get started around agaves (they will be very difficult to eradicate), so avoid planting in lawn areas and follow her advice regarding self-protection when in the vicinity of or handling agave plants. For millennia, agaves have sustained native people with food, fiber, drink, and medicinal preparations. The commercial and illegal overharvesting of agaves has led to concerns about the destruction of their habitat. Diseases and insects include root rot in poorly drained soil, scale insects and mealybugs on young growth, and agave snout weevil on mature plants. Treat with grub killer according to directions. Natural variations among species results in taxonomic uncertainty—for instance, apparently identical plants may have different names.

Agave americana, American century plant, 6 ft. (2 m) tall and 8–10 ft. (2.5–3.0 m) wide, has the archetypal monumental form. A fast-growing type with wide, gray leaves, it is adaptable to a range of conditions, including those of humid coastal climates. Flowers on very tall stalks are bright golden yellow. *A. americana* var. *protoamericana*, the fastest growing of the hardier agaves, is distinguished by its variability of form and leaf color. The one offered by Yucca Do is for the silver collector: upright, compact, 4 ft. (1.2 m) tall and wide, with wide, textured, blue-gray foliage. These agaves are subject to the agave snout weevil. They are hardy from Zones 8 to 10.

A handsome, gigantic spreading and suckering plant with blue-gray to powder-blue, nearly white recurving (backward-bending) leaves to 6 ft. (2 m) in length and 12 in. (30.5 cm) wide, *Agave franzosinii* grows 10 ft. (3m) tall and 15 ft. (4.5 m) wide and is of unknown origin. Its flowering spike, to 30 ft. (9 m) in the air, bears yellow flowers in late summer. It grows best in full to partial sun.

Agave harvardiana, Harvard's century plant, 3 ft. (1 m) tall and wide, has medium-size rosettes, densely packed with stout, spiny, blue-gray leaves. It is native to rocky, grassy slopes from Texas to Mexico and is relatively cold-hardy from Zones 5 (maybe 4) to 9. At higher elevations give it full sun; in low deserts give it a little shade. It occasionally produces offsets. Asparagus-like flower spikes are produced in summer (but don't hold your breath). In cold areas, protect from winds and moisture.

Powder-blue *Agave lophantha* var. *coerulea*, 3 ft. (1 m) tall and wide, was introduced by Yucca Do via Sean Hogan. Its beautiful coloring recommends it for the garden, but its daggerlike foliage should be kept far away from paths. It is hardy from Zones 8b to 10, surviving to 12°F (-11°C) with minor leaf damage.

One of the most highly prized agaves for its compact, gray-green, rounded foliage—like a perfect artichoke heart—Parry's agave, or mescal, *Agave parryi*, is native from central Arizona and New Mexico south to Mexico and is hardy from Zones 6b to 10. It is relatively small, growing to 20 in. (51 cm) tall and 3 ft. (1 m) wide, but a single plant soon produces colonies of offsets. Creamy yellow flowers, pink or red-tinged in bud, are borne on 15 ft. (4.5 m) high stalks. *A. parryi* var. *parryi* is a medium-sized agave, 3 ft. (1m) tall and wide, with light gray to blue-green, wedge-shaped leaves and dramatic black spines at their tips. Because of their wide natural range, plants are very adaptable to soils and sites. They are said to be susceptible to weevils. *A. parryi* var. *huachucensis*, 2 ft. (0.6 m) tall and wide, is silver-blue with fiercely spine-tipped foliage. It is more robust than the species with larger leaves and larger bunches of flowers. Found in oak and pine woodlands, it does best with the moisture associated with this habitat. *A. parryi* subsp. *neomexicana*, New Mexican mescal, 1.5–2 ft. (0.5–0.6 m) tall and 2 ft. (0.6 m) wide, is a relatively dainty specimen by agave standards and very hardy. It has small, light gray leaves, sometimes nearly white, in flat-topped rosettes that sucker freely to produce large clumps. It grows best in partial sun and needs additional watering in the hottest days of summer. It is hardy to Zone 7. *A. parryi* var. *truncata* has a dense, symmetrical form with wide, blue-gray leaves, which sets it apart from the other types. Plants grow 2 ft. (0.6 m) tall by 4 ft. (1.2 m) wide in full sun (partial shade will spoil its form) and may produce offsets more than 5 ft. (1.5 m) across; heavily watered plants will grow much larger. This agave is also amenable to pot culture and is hardy at least to Zone 8.

AJUGA REPTANS

Common name: bugle
Family: Lamiaceae, mint
Description: variegated ground cover
Origin: garden
Site and soil: partial shade; evenly moist
Height and width: 5–9 in. (12.5–23.0 cm) tall; 2–4 ft. (0.6–1.2 m) wide
Hardiness: Zones 4–9

Introduced from Europe but naturalized in North America, *Ajuga reptans* is a creeping plant, as the epithet *reptans* suggests. It grows by short rhizomes that produce rosettes of downy, outward-spreading, oval leaves, 2 to 4 in. (5 to 10 cm) long, often crinkled and tinged with bronze, purple, pink, cream, and silver. The early spring flowers are sky blue to deep blue, almost purple (rarely white), and are borne in dense terminal spikes, with the small flowers arranged in whorls around erect, square-sided stems. Typical of the mint family, they are double-lipped and very inviting to foraging bees and butterflies. The odd name "bugle" is explained by some as a corruption of *Ajuga* (not yoked), a reference to the shape of the flower's calyx. Carpet bugle is a very descriptive common name, for during the growing season, the plant sends out runners with paired leaves, which at intervals develop roots. These effectively nail down the carpet to create a growing mat of dense foliage. Over the winter, the older plants die out, but the next season, young plants develop and send out more runners. Bugle is an ancient medicinal based on its astringent properties. It was regarded as an "all-heal" because it was used for outward and inward complaints, ranging from wounds to coughs and liver disorders. In crowded growing conditions, especially in the southern United States, crown rot may be a problem.

We love ajugas for their beautifully colored crinkled foliage, bright spring bloom, and tight carpeting habit, so useful where it is needed in corners and edges and byways, wherever grass is difficult to mow. *Ajuga reptans* 'Silver Beauty', by far the most popular silver bugle, has rounded, gray-green foliage edged silver-white and bears bluish violet flower spikes. The silver-gray foliage of 'Silver Carpet' has a metallic sheen that is enhanced when it is paired with bluish violet to purple spikes of bloom. 'Grey Lady', a rare (in North America) English cultivar, is worth seeking for its smaller leaves, pale blue flowers, and vigorous habit. 'Silver Princess' has silvery, gray-green foliage, with irregular white variegation and pink highlights. Its flowers are blue. 'Arctic Fox', to 4–6 in. (10–15 cm), is different for its wavy-edged foliage, gray-green in the center, ringed by bright cream, and finished off with a dark green edge.

ALYSSUM

Common name: madwort
Family: Cruciferae, crucifer
Description: downy perennial or subshrub
Origin: rocky, mountainous; Europe, Asia
Soil and site: sun; sharply drained
Height and width: 6–18 in. (15–46 cm) tall; 18–24 in. (46–61 cm) wide
Hardiness: Zones 3–9

Alyssums belong to a large genus of about 150 species widely distributed in open, rocky ground at high altitudes. In North America, the silvery ones are miniatures, with trailing woody stems densely clothed with short, usually pointed, silver-gray leaves and long-lasting spring flowers—from soft to bright yellow—in dense corymbs. Each little flower is four-petaled, in the form of a cross, a characteristic preserved in the family name from the Latin *crucis* (cross). The common name is based on the old folk belief that alyssums cure madness from rabies. Alyssums are preeminent rock garden, scree, and ground cover plants, perfect for nestling between rocks, in rock crevices, and between pavings, or for growing in troughs. When they are in bloom, the foliage will be virtually obscured, but after flowering, the silvery leaves are all-season highlights.

The most familiar of the miniature alpines is *Alyssum montanum*, similar to *Aurinia saxatilis*/*Alyssum saxatile*, known familiarly as basket-of-gold. Some gardeners rate the smaller form a better plant for its longer bloom and more attractive foliage and habit. It has a semi-prostrate form, 6–8 in. (15–20 cm) tall and 12 in. (30.5 cm) wide, with bright yellow flowers over dense, gray-green foliage.

'Mountain Gold' is an even more diminutive, 4 in. (10 cm) tall and 15–18 in. (38–46 cm) wide, with similar flowers and foliage. It is hardy from Zones 4 to 8. Other tiny alyssums that combine silver foliage with yellow flowers but offer something new include *A. idaeus*, 3 in. (7.5 cm) tall and 18 in. (46 cm) wide, with rounded, grayish white, hairy foliage and soft, yellow flowers, recommended for scree plantings; *A. propinquum*, only 2 in. (5 cm) tall and 30 in. (76 cm) wide, with pale yellow flowers, choice for troughs; and *A. tortuosum*, 3 in. (7.5 cm) tall and 12 in. (30.5 cm) wide, aptly named for its contorted stems, covered with silver-gray foliage and the usual yellow flowers. These are hardy from Zones 4 to 10.

AMORPHA CANESCENS

Common name: lead plant
Family: Leguminosae, pea
Description: downy shrub
Origin: Great Plains from Canada to Texas
Site and soil: sun; infertile, alkaline, well drained
Height and width: 2–4 ft. (0.6–1.2 m) tall; 3 ft. (1 m) wide
Hardiness: Zones 2–8

Lead plant (*Amorpha canescens*).

Called lead plant because it was thought to point to deposits of lead, this is a tough, underused shrub from high, mountainous, prairie regions. It is a very deep-rooted and deciduous legume, conspicuous for its silver-gray pinnate foliage that is small and hairy on both sides. Masses of small, pealike flowers—violet-purple with orange eyes—are arranged in thin, terminal spikes by late summer. Flowers are very attractive to bees and butterflies in search of nectar. Lead plant grows best where it is put to the test in a dry, windy, exposed site, although it benefits from deep soaking every couple of weeks. It does not do well in low desert heat. It will grow in most soils but suffers in wet clays. In colder regions, it may die back to the ground but will grow back up from its roots. In warmer regions, and whenever necessary to keep plants compact, lead plant should be cut back to 1 ft. (30.5 cm) in late autumn. Once its needs and virtues are understood, it is a positive asset in the prairie landscape for its shrubby form and distinctive long-season foliage (silver-gray in spring, gray-green in summer) among prairie flowers and grasses.

ANAPHALIS

Common name: pearly everlasting
Family: Asteraceae, aster
Description: downy perennial
Origin: clearings, waste areas, mountains; Asia, North America
Site and soil: sun or partial shade; lean, dry to moist, well-drained
Height and width: 4–24 in. (10–61 cm) tall; 18–24 in. (46–61 cm) wide
Hardiness: Zones 3–8

Plants in this genus of about 100 species can be recognized by their white foliage, often gray-green on top and woolly underneath, and from 1 to 6 in. (2.5 to 15 cm) long, in spreading mats. Clustered white buds, like little pearls, on woolly white stems are held in papery white, petallike bracts. Open flowers resembling miniature straw flowers are small—to 0.25 in. (0.5 cm) wide—and globe-shaped with prominent ray-flower yellow centers. Carried in dense

Pearly everlasting (*Anaphalis margaritacea*).

corymbs to 6 in. (15 cm), their effect is magnified. The stiffness of the petals and the dried nature of the entire plant suggest its suitability for dried bouquets. Most species grow rapidly by rhizomatous roots to create colonies in the wild on the poorest soils. Pearly everlasting has a history of use as a tobacco substitute (rabbit-tobacco and ladies' tobacco are common names) and as a healing herb for various common complaints. In enriched soil, plants grow fast and need thinning to achieve their best form.

Among the several species for the garden, none is more popular than *Anaphalis margaritacea*, a wildflower across Canada and throughout New England into the mountains of Virginia, west to Ohio, and north to the Dakotas. An erect clump, 24 in. (61 cm) tall and wide—shorter in the wild—with lance-shaped, silver-green leaves, woolly underneath, it grows best in full sun and is more tolerant of drought conditions than other species. Small, white, nearly pompom flowers, from midsummer to early fall, are typical of the genus. 'Neuschnee' (new snow), an improved garden form from Germany, is more compact, 18 in. (46 cm) tall and wide. The variant *A. margaritacea* var. *yedoensis*/ *A. yedoensis* from Japan is shorter with narrow, woolly white leaves. *A. triplinervis*, a Himalayan species with spoon-shaped, silver-gray leaves, bears its dense, domed flowerheads from midsummer to late summer; foliage turns soft gray-green by early fall. 'Sommerschnee' (summer snow) has pure white flowers, and 'Sulphur Light' has pale yellow flowers with deeper yellow centers. These are hardy from Zones 3 or 4 to 8. *A. alpicola*, a miniature pearly everlasting for troughs from the mountains of Japan, is 4–8 in. (10–20 cm) tall and 24 in. (61 cm) wide and grows in most soils except dry. Its leaves are woolly gray, and its small flowers are reddish brown at their base. It is hardy from Zone 6 to 9.

ANDROSACE

Common name: rock jasmine
Family: Primulaceae, primrose
Description: downy perennial
Origin: mountains; Asia
Site and soil: sun; sharply drained
Height and width: 5–6 in. (12.5–15.0 cm) tall; 18 in. (46 cm) wide
Hardiness: Zones 3 or 4–8

"To the inveterate rock gardener," observed rock gardening expert H. Lincoln Foster (1968), "the androsaces are the joy and despair of his heart." These cool-climate alpines are part of a large genus of about 100 widely dispersed species that seem to grow directly from rocks. Growing as tufted or mounded cushions or trailing mats, they produce rosettes of foliage, sometimes covered with silky hairs that give them a well-defined silvery presence. Rose, pink, or white flowers, usually eyed, are stemless or borne on short stems, to bloom in primula-like clusters in spring and summer. Some types are lightly fragrant; all are variable. Where winters are wet and snowless, plants turn to mush by spring, and where summers are very hot and humid, they can turn sodden and moldy. At Millstream House, the Fosters' Connecticut home and unique rock garden habitat, androsaces were grown on an open site on a sunny slope in sharply drained, gritty scree or moraine conditions, where the top of the plant was kept dry with a stone-chip mulch, but where roots could reach deep and find moisture. The easiest is *Androsace lanuginosa*, a trailing mat, 6 in. (15 cm) tall and 18 in. (46 cm) wide, that can spread to 3 ft. (1 m) wide. Its leaves, to 0.75 in. (2 cm), are covered with silky white hairs as its Latin epithet suggests. Rounded clusters of variable, lavender-pink, white-eyed flowers, produced at the ends of reddish trailing shoots, bloom over summer. It is hardy from Zones 4 to 8. *A. sarmentosa* var. *chumbyi* is ideal for pavings. A spreading, tufted, silver mat, 5 in. (12.5 cm) tall and 18 in. (46 cm) wide, with hairy leaves 0.5–2 in. (1–5 cm) long, it produces pink flowers in spring and is hardy from Zones 3 to 8.

ANTENNARIA

Common name: pussytoes
Family: Asteraceae, aster
Description: downy perennial
Origin: dry fields, rocky slopes; Europe, Asia, North America
Site and soil: sun or partial shade; fertile to poor, well-drained
Height and width: 2–16 in. (5.0–40.5 cm) tall; 12–18 in. (30.5–46.0 cm) wide
Hardiness: Zones 3–8

About 45 species of antennaria are characterized by rounded silvery foliage that forms basal rosettes. Off-white or pinkish flowerheads, soft and fuzzy, appear as solitary heads or in tight clusters on short, woolly stems in summer. The tight clusters of flowerheads, shaped like a cat's paw, gave rise to the common name. Pussytoes have also been used as a tobacco substitute, as recorded in common names, such as Indian tobacco and ladies' tobacco. Growers report best results using sharply drained soil with a sand or gravel base, or planting directly in gravel. In cooler climates, give plants full sun, but where summers are very hot, protect plants from the full force of blazing sun by giving them partial shade.

Tuck plants into rock crevices and troughs, between pavings, or to trail over border edges.

One of the most popular pussytoes is *Antennaria dioica*, a gray-green mat, 2 in. (5 cm) tall and 18 in. (46 cm) wide, of spoon-shaped, gray-green foliage to 1.5 in. (3.5 cm) long, with corymbs of small, white or pale pink flowerheads on short stems to 0.75 in. (2 cm) in early summer. It is distributed throughout Europe, northern Asia, and North America in mountainous habitats. The most interesting forms of this species are those with colored flowers: 'Nyewood Variety', 3 in. (7.5 cm) tall and 12 in. (30.5 cm) wide, is distinguished by its dense mat of silver foliage and cherry-red flowers; 'Rosea', 4 in. (10 cm) tall and 24 in. (61 cm) wide, has pink flowerheads. 'Minima Rubra' is an exquisite miniature creeping carpet; it forms a 2 in. (5 cm) tall and 6 in. (15 cm) wide mat of silver-green foliage and carries small, rosy flowers on very short stems. *A. parviflora*, one of the most drought-tolerant, is a wildflower on the western plains of the United States, 2 in. (5 cm) tall and 9 in. (23 cm) wide. Sparsely blooming 'McClintock' is a highly praised selection, grown mostly for its attractive low foliage. *A. neglecta*, wild in the Gaspe Peninsula (Quebec, Canada) and in dry fields and open slopes, is a slow-growing silver mat with tiny leaves and pink flowers in the spring.

ARCTOTIS

Common name: African daisy
Family: Asteraceae, aster
Description: downy annual, perennial
Origin: coastal meadows, deserts; South Africa
Site and soil: sun; well-drained
Height and width: 12–24 in. (30.5–61.0 cm) tall; 12 in. (30.5 cm) wide
Hardiness: Zones 8–11

African daisies are one of several South African daisy flowers, like gazania, that erupt in a colorful mass to carpet the veldt during the brief, cool, rainy season before the onset of hot temperatures. And like the others, African daisies are built along rugged lines. Anchored by strong, underground woody rhizomes that allow them to withstand wind and rain, plants spread to send up deeply lobed, elliptic foliage to about 5 in. (12.5 cm) from green on top, white-felted beneath, to intensely silver-white on both sides. Flowers are large, varying in size from 2 to 5 in. (5.0 to 12.5 cm) wide and carried on thick, succulent-looking stems. Their colors range from rich orange and creamy white to pink, reds, and apricot-

Arctotis ×venidium, Harlequin hybrid in container, Denver Botanic Gardens.

yellow among hybrids, sometimes with a darker inner ring. The original species close in the afternoon and on cloudy days, but the hybrids stay open longer. The genus name is from the Greek *arctos* (bear) and *otus* (ear), a reference to the scales on the outer seed heads, supposed to resemble a bear's ears. Once established, they withstand drought and dry, hot, sunny weather, but they do better along the coast where a cooling breeze is present. When grown in high heat combined with high humidity, they are subject to botrytis and gray mold. Otherwise, they are relatively free of diseases and pests.

These daisies carry their own color-coordinated ensemble of bright shades, set off by silvery foliage. One of the most striking is 'Zulu Prince', a cultivar of *Arctotis fastuosa/Venidium fastuosum*, cape daisy or monarch of the veldt. In the species, foliage is deeply lobed and silver-white, and flowers of 4 to 5 in. (10.0 to 12.5 cm) are rich orange. The cultivar is also large-flowered. It carries its creamy white flowerheads—each adorned with a black and orange inner ring—on tall stems to 24 in. (61 cm), spreading to 12 in. (20.5 cm).

Seed strains resulting from interspecific breeding, mainly between *Arctotis venusta* and *A. fastuosa*, broaden the range of colors to include pink, carmine red, purple, apricot-yellow, cream, and red, some darker ringed. Flowers are from 3 to

3.5 in. (7.5 to 9 cm) wide; deeply cut foliage, handsome in its own right, varies from silver-green to silvery gray, on plants 18–20 in. (46–52 cm) tall and 12 in. (30.5 cm) wide. Hardiness varies. Thompson and Morgan rates its T & M Hybrids hardy from Zones 8 to 10. Those in the Harlequin Hybrids series are rated hardy from Zones 9 to 11.

One of the best, originally introduced as a cultivar rather than as a seed strain, is *Arctotis* ×*hybrida* 'Flame'. Of trailing habit and especially free-flowering, its fiery orange daisies are carried over silver-felted foliage. Mature plants withstand temperatures to 35°F (2°C). Another cultivar, *A.* ×*hybrida* 'Wine', is hardier. Also trailing, it is a rapid grower with burgundy-colored flowers over silver-gray leaves, hardy to 20°F (-7°C). It shows unusual drought-tolerance. Logee's recommends both for container culture, where they are dwarfed to 6 to 8 in. (15 to 20 cm). For best performance, both should be deadheaded regularly.

Blue-eyed African daisy, *Arctotis venusta*/*A. stoechadifolia*, is unusual for its central, steel-blue disk florets surrounded by creamy white petals backed lavender, above woolly gray foliage. Plants grow 24 in. (61 cm) tall and 16 in. (40.5 cm) wide and are rated hardy to 41°F (5°C). *A. venusta* var. *grandis*, developed as a cut flower, is especially lovely. Its daisies, from 4 to 5 in. (10.0 to 12.5 cm) wide above silvery leaves, grow on more compact plants to 18 in. (46 cm).

ARTEMISIA

Common name: wormwood, sage brush
Family: Asteraceae, aster
Description: downy perennial, subshrub, shrub
Origin: deserts, dry fields, mountains, steppes; Northern Hemisphere, South
    Africa, western South America
Site and soil: sun; dry, well-drained
Height and width: 5 in.–4 ft. (12.5 cm–1.2 m) tall; 12 in.–4 ft. (30.5 cm–1.2 m) wide
Hardiness: Zones 3–10

Named for the goddess Artemis, the genus is dominated by subshrubs, many evergreen or nearly evergreen. As plants with a long history of use as medicinals to treat a variety of complaints, they have always been represented in herb gardens. Gardeners value them for their beautifully cut foliage in the sterling to gray range, versatility of forms from ground-hugging to tall shrubs, and dependability. Bitter properties, present to some degree in all artemisias, are due to the chemical thujone, which gives them their characteristic bracing aroma and medicinal value as a vermifuge. Some have an important place in traditional Chinese

Artemisia stelleriana 'Silver Brocade'.

medicine, and many are choice for crafts (especially wreaths). Taxonomic confusion abounds among artemisias: species are shifted around, plants are sold under names that have no botanical standing, and plants with the same names may bear little resemblance to one another (while plants with different names appear very much alike!). Herb and regional nurseries are the best places to find rarer sorts. *Artemisia cana*, now *Seriphidium canum*, and *A. tridentata*, now *S. tridentatum*, are listed here for convenience. Most artemisias benefit from cutting back just before or after flowering to prevent them from sprawling.

Gray-green *Artemisia abrotanum*, southernwood, named for its uncertain southern European origin, grows 30 in. (76 cm) tall and wide. It is one of the toughest artemisias, willing to grow in every soil except wet. A favorite of the proverbial English cottage garden, it has branches and sprigs of feathery leaves with a strong scent of lemon-camphor. Its various folk names, from old man to maiden's ruin, refer to its use in ointments to promote beards and prevent baldness and its use as a love charm. Besides serving as an attractive, shrubby foil for roses in the same way as lavender, it is invaluable for covering hard soil in an exposed, sunny site where little else will grow. If left untrimmed, southernwood will grow into a sprawling bush that is effective in an informal garden with most perennials. Almost any piece of stem taken near the base of the plant will grow

Artemisia versicolor weaving through *Sedum reflexum, sempervivums,* along a stone walk in Lauren Springer's Colorado garden

to bush size over two seasons when inserted directly into weed-free, well-drained soil. *A. abrotanum* 'Silver', silver southernwood, is a desirable variant, less upright and more silvery. A citrus-scented form, sometimes offered as 'Tangerine', or tree southernwood, is a striking columnar plant that grows to 6 ft. (2 m) and is well worth looking for in specialty herb nurseries. *A. abrotanum* is ironclad hardy from Zones 4 to 8 or 9; the cultivars may be less hardy.

Famed as a vermifuge (for expelling intestinal worms) and an important ingredient in absinthe, *Artemisia absinthium*, wormwood, is a subshrub from Europe, 3–4 ft. (1.0–1.2 m) tall and 3 ft. (1 m) wide, hardy from Zones 4 to 8 or 9. Its aroma is pleasantly medicinal in small doses, but it can cause a headache, is potentially poisonous to consume, and is very bitter to taste. Growing from a woody base, wormwood's stems bear deeply lobed, gray, velvety leaves. Several plants, spaced 2 ft. (0.6 m) apart and left untrimmed, will form an attractive, loose hedge. The hybrid *A.* 'Huntington'/*A. absinthium* 'Huntington', a selection from Huntington Gardens in Pasadena, California, is a large shrub with deeply cut, silvery leaves, listed as hardy from Zones 6 to 9. *A. absinthium* 'Lambrook Silver', marginally hardy to Zone 5 and willing to grow to Zone 9, is an attractive, more compact form, 18–32 in. (46–81 cm) tall, with luxuriant, deeply divided foliage, that tolerates clay soil. Wormwood is hardy from Zones 4 to 8 or 9.

A much reclassified clump-forming cultivar, *Artemisia alba* 'Canescens'/ *A. canescens*/*A. splendens*, 20 in. (51 cm) tall and 12 in. (30.5 cm) wide, is a singularly different artemisia in appearance, more like a santolina with silver-gray, curling foliage on erect, silvery stems. It is used as a low hedge or edger or as ground cover and is hardy from Zones 4 to 8.

An upright, rounded shrub from the Mediterranean, *Artemisia arborescens*, tree wormwood or silver wormwood, is 3 ft. (1 m) tall and 2.5 ft. (0.8 m) wide, with silky, fernlike foliage especially brilliant in summer. Plants can be dwarfed to 2 ft. (0.6 m) in a container, and they need to be overwintered indoors. Tree wormwood is hardy from Zones 8 to 9.

A native, many-branched shrub for naturalizing, *Artemisia californica*, California sagebrush, needs sharply drained, dry soil and grows 3–13 ft. (1–4 m) tall and 3–6 ft. (1–2 m) wide. Once established, it needs little or no water and tolerates alkaline soil, sand, and clay. Its finely dissected, stemless leaves—entire or lobed—are silver-gray, soft, and hairy, and they give the entire plant a very silvery appearance. 'Montara', a natural hybrid between *A. californica* and *A. pycnocephala*, has been called a native "Powis Castle." It grows from 12 in. (30.5 cm) tall and 2–3 ft. (0.6–1.0 m) wide and tolerates seaside and clay conditions. California sagebrush is hardy from Zones 7 to 10.

Artemisia cana, silver sage, grows as far north as Oregon and into Canada. It has narrow, silvery green leaves, is fragrant, and is entire to lobed. Some consider it the most silvery of the western sagebrushes. A relatively little bush, it can reach 3 ft. (1 m) in the favorable conditions of full sun and dry, sharply drained soil. Regarded in its own country more as a plant for animal browse, British gardeners think it is a fine ornamental. Las Pilitas Nursery in California carries *A. cana bolanderi* for the rock garden. Silver sage is hardy from Zones 4 to 10.

Artemisia capillaris, Japanese wormwood, from river banks and seashores in Asia, is a great boon to gardeners in the southern United States because of its high tolerance of heat combined with humidity. It is a low, wide, juniperlike bush that forms a dense mat, 3–4 ft. (1–1.3 m) tall and 1 ft. (30.5 cm) wide, of silky, silvery green, finely cut foliage. Tony Avent rates it hardy from Zones 7 to 9 but says he's "just guessing." It grows in the nursery's Juniper Level Botanic Garden in scree conditions.

Another western native, *Artemisia filifolia*, sand sage or silvery wormwood, is 3 ft. (1m) tall and 30 in. (76 cm) wide and very tough; it is adapted to extremes of heat, cold, and wind, yet it makes a fine garden plant in rather ordinary conditions. It has very narrow, threadlike foliage, sterling silver in appearance, on stems that swirl from the plant's base. It will grow in both sandy and clay soils.

Artemisia frigida, fringed wormwood or fringed sagebrush, is mat-forming and 14 in. (35.5 cm) tall and wide. It is a western native subshrub with soft, finely cut, gray-white foliage; arching stems; and trailing form—similar to *A. schmidtiana* 'Silver Mound' but a little more upright and easier to grow in the arid conditions of the American Southwest. In a genus of drought- and heat-tolerant plants, it is exceptional. Lauren Springer says it performs better in the western United States than *A. schmidtiana* 'Silver Mound'. It is a Royal Horticultural Society Award of Garden Merit (RHS AGM) winner, hardy from Zones 3 to 8 or 9.

No species in the genus has been surrounded with more taxonomic confusion than *Artemisia ludoviciana/A. palmeri/A. purshiana*, western mugwort, also known as cudweed and white sage. It was collected in Missouri by the Lewis and Clark Expedition, but it also grows naturally in Utah, Texas, and Arizona. Though seldom grown in its original form, it is worth understanding its general appearance and habit to distinguish it from its several offspring: it is a tall, sprawling plant, at least 3 to 4 ft. (1 to 1.2 m) tall and 2 ft. (0.6 m) wide, with gray stems that bear lance-shaped, gray-white, felty foliage, sometimes with a bluish tinge; its lower leaves are more noticeably cut and hairier on the undersides, and its upper leaves are more pointed and entire. Plants begin to sprawl as panicles of small yellow flowers, heavily borne on stem ends, begin to bloom. All types have fast-running roots, but some of the cultivars are somewhat better behaved.

Artemisia ludoviciana 'Peach' is reported to be a compact silvery form to 2 ft. (0.6 m) and a moderate runner in friable soil, less so in clay. *A. ludoviciana* 'Purshiana' has been pushed around, taxonomically speaking, and is now recognized as a cultivar. We like it for its extraordinary adaptability to moisture and ability to grow in partial shade. It is a sprawling form with segmented grayish leaves all along its stems, rather than just at its base, wider and less silvery than those of 'Silver King' (leaves have a bluish cast when grown in less than full sun). *A. ludoviciana* 'Silver Bouquet' is reported to be similar to 'Peach', but taller, 2 to 3 ft. (0.6 to 1 m), and aggressive. *A. ludoviciana* 'Silver King'/*A. ludoviciana* var. *albula* is the tallest variant and the one that is widely used in wreaths. It grows from 2 to 3 ft. (0.6 to 1.0 m) or more in richer soil, has more rigid stems than the species, and narrower, less segmented leaves, except at the bottom of the plant, that are are whitish year-round. The foliage is silvery green on the upper side and pure sterling on the underside. Its upfacing leaves give the entire plant a light grayish, almost white cast (it is also called ghost plant). Although it is an aggressive root-runner, we find it invaluable for its narrow, upright form and gray-white color all season, even in winter. It needs to be reduced every season without fail.

Artemisia ludoviciana 'Silver Queen', to 2 ft. (0.6 m), may be offered in two forms. Gertrude Foster, who studied the phenomenon in depth, claimed that the U.S. 'Queen' has weaker stems and the cut segments on its felted leaves noticeably curve outward. The U.K. plant has broader, light gray leaves divided 2 in. (5 cm) from the base of the plant. Highly prized *A. ludoviciana* 'Valerie Finnis' is a great, spreading mat of broadly cut, felted leaves on stems to 18 in. (46 cm) that weaves itself among neighboring plants to delightful effect.

Artemisia pedmontana/A. caucasica from the high mountains of southern Spain is an alpine plant that forms a tight mat, 4 in. (10 cm) tall and 18 in. (46 cm) wide, of silky, filigreed, silver foliage. It is hardy from Zones 3 to 7 or warmer.

One of the ingredients in vermouth, *Artemisia pontica*, Roman wormwood or old woman, from southern Europe, is a little plant that forms a light gray, loose mound to 12 in. (30.5 cm) of frothy, soft, lacy foliage, amenable to most soils except wet. The richer the soil, the looser, more sprawling its growth. Because it is amenable to clipping, it is effective in knot gardens, where its thready, gray leaves contrast well with green-leaved plants, but it needs a firm hand: cut back and chop out extra plants in the spring, and by midsummer give it another clipping, or let it run as a ground cover. It is hardy from Zones 4 to 9.

Discovered at Powys Castle in Wales, *Artemisia* ×'Powis Castle'/*A. arborescens* 'Brass Band', Powis Castle artemisia or silver sage, is thought to be a cross between *A. absinthium* and *A. arborescens*. It is a gray-blue subshrub, 24 in. (61 cm) tall and 30 in. (76 cm) wide, loved for its dense mound of lacy foliage, its tolerance for both drought and humidity, and its rapid growth. Its height is variable, depending on conditions. In the American Northeast, it generally grows to 30 in. (76 cm) or less, while in warmer, more favorable regions it reaches its maximum height of 3 ft. (1 m) tall and 4 ft. (1.2 m) wide; it does not do well in clay soil. It is hardy from Zones 6 to 9.

Native to coastal California, *Artemisia pycnocephala*, sand sage, 24 in. (61 cm) tall and 16 in. (40.5 cm) wide, has a mounding habit and silver, filigreed foliage. It is especially suited to coastal conditions in California, but it is also being promoted as a desirable replacement for 'Silver Mound' artemisia where that is difficult to grow. 'David's Choice', a selection of the wild form, is best trimmed to about 12 in. (30.5 cm).

Aptly named for its perfect silver ball shape, *Artemisia schmidtiana* 'Silver Mound' originated in the coastal and mountainous regions of northern Japan, where its creeping roots spread out in bare soil. In cultivation, it grows 12 in.

(30.5 cm) tall and 18 in. (46 cm) wide, its stems and feathery foliage on soft gray stems are shimmering silver, and its little nodding, round flowers are silvery cream. Much in demand for its form and color, it withstands wind and grows best in light soil but is adaptable. It can be grown (though not easily) in the hot humidity of the American South by planting it in a raised rock bed, on a sunny hillside, or in a clay container kept on the dry side. *A. schmidtiana* 'Silver Bouquet' is reported to be a more substantial form to 24 in. (61 cm). Both are hardy from Zones 4 to 9.

A silvery native tundra plant for the dry rock garden, *Artemisia scopulorum*, Rocky Mountain sagewort, is only 7 in. (18 cm) tall and 6 in. (15 cm) wide. It bears little gray ball flowers on short stems. It is hardy from Zones 3 to 8.

Sprawling patches of beach wormwood, *Artemisia stelleriana*, 5 to 8 in. (13 to 20 cm) tall and wide-spreading, with lobed foliage similar to chrysanthemums, are such a familiar sight on beaches throughout the northeastern United States that it is regarded as native, yet it actually originated on sand dunes in Japan and Korea. In the United States, its virtues as a garden plant are only now coming into their own, but it has long been cultivated in England, where Gertrude Jekyll urged gardeners to grow it instead of frost-tender senecios 'Silver Brocade'/ 'Boughton Silver', an improvement over the species, with wider lobed leaves and a more compact form, has been raised to the status of a high-fashion plant for containers with colorful tropicals. Beach wormwood must have light and perfectly drained soil or it will expire over the winter in a hint of dampness. It is hardy from Zones 3 to 7.

Artemisia tridentata, big sagebrush or great basin sage, is the archetypal sagebrush of Western romances and is the plant, *par excellence*, evocative of the landscape of the American Southwest. It usually grows to 3 to 4 ft. (1 to 1.2 m), or to 6 ft. (15.2 m) in its northern range, but it can reach 15 ft. (4.6 m). It is many-branched, with closely packed, stiff, narrow gray leaves 0.75 in. (2 cm) long, toothed at their tips, and very aromatic. It is hardy from Zones 4 to 9.

Lauren Springer introduced *Artemisia versicolor* into the wholesale nursery trade in 1989–90 from cuttings she brought from England. It is the same as the cultivar 'Sea Foam', which produces silver-gray, curled foliage, similar to lichen in appearance, on plants that grow in a soft, spreading mat, 6–12 in. (15.0–30.5 cm) tall and 18 in. (46 cm) wide, with a fragrance similar to southernwood. It was designated Plant Select for 2004. (The Plant Select program developed by Denver Botanic Gardens and Colorado State University promotes the best plants for the dry conditions of the western United States.) Grown as a ground cover, it can be left to sprawl around rocks in a hot, sunny, exposed site. In the

American West, it grows in well-behaved, irregular mounds, but according to some growers in the Northeast it can be rampant. The best strategy is to grow it in low-fertility soil. It is rated hardy from Zones 4b to 8.

In 1996 the Chicago Botanic Garden, in USDA Hardiness Zone 5b, undertook a four-year comparative study of garden artemisias to determine the best ones for gardens in the American Midwest. Twenty-six species, cultivars, and garden hybrids were rated for winter hardiness, cultural adaptability to soils and the conditions of the evaluation site, disease and pest resistance, and ornamental attributes, which included foliage and habit quality, plant size, floral display, and spreading potential. Plants were grown in a site exposed to wind from all directions in well-drained, clay-loam soil amended with composted leaves. Maintenance was kept to a minimum: water was provided as needed, no fertilizer was used, and faded flowers and lodged stems, mainly after flowering, were not removed or cut back. A mulch of shredded leaves and wood chips was placed between growing plots to suppress weeds as well as for looks. In early November, hemlock boughs were placed over plants to shed water off crowns during the winter months. In 1995 and 1996, all plants were cut back to the ground after flowering to rejuvenate growth.

Among those we have described, *Artemisia* 'Huntington' died during the trial and was not replanted; *A.* ×'Powis Castle' died the first winter, was replanted, and succumbed the following two winters; and *A. capillaris* was removed after two years "due to a lack of ornamental qualities and a weedy nature." Lack of cold-hardiness was the primary cause of the death of *A.* ×'Powis Castle'. Those that suffered crown meltdown from high humidity and heat during late summer for at least a single season or more were *A. absinthium*, *A. absinthium* 'Lambrook Silver', *A. frigida*, *A. ludoviciana* 'Silver Queen, *A. schmidtiana* 'Silver Mound', *A. stelleriana*, and *A. stelleriana* 'Silver Brocade'. Stem regeneration was noticed within a few weeks of damage. *A. frigida* did not hold up as well as *A. schmidtiana* 'Silver Mound' in hot, humid weather, nor was it judged as highly as 'Silver Mound' in terms of habit and health. Excessive winter moisture rather than cold temperatures caused the decline and death of *A. frigida*, *A. pontica*, *A. stelleriana*, and *A. stelleriana* 'Silver Brocade'.

Among western mugworts, *Artemisia purshiana* was unaffected by rain or humidity. *A. ludoviciana* 'Valerie Finnis' was judged the best, most vibrant cultivar in this group for its silvery leaf color; broad, lance-shaped foliage; and less aggressive habit of growth. While other types occasionally became loose and open, losing their form when about to flower, this was not a significant characteristic of 'Valerie Finnis'. The overall top-rated artemisias were *A. absinthium* 'Lambrook Silver', *A. alba*, *A. ludoviciana* 'Valerie Finnis', and *A. schmidtiana* 'Silver Mound'.

ASARUM

Common name: wild ginger
Family: Aristolchiaceae, birthwort
Description: variegated perennial
Origin: woodland; Asia, North America
Site and soil: partial shade or shade; rich, well-drained
Height and width: 4–6 in. (10–15 cm) tall; 2 ft. (0.6 m) wide
Hardiness: Zones 5–9

Asarums are slow-growing, low-clump–forming or creeping woodland plants valued for their beautiful foliage. They are distributed mainly in eastern Asia and the southeastern United States with a few species in the northern states and in Europe. Leaves, mainly evergreen, are usually heart-shaped, from 2 to 5 in. (5 to 13 cm) wide, often glossy and exquisitely patterned or marbled in silver. Small spring flowers, virtually hidden under the plant's foliage, are urn- or pitcher-shaped (similar to the flowers of Dutchman's pipe) and brown, purple, or flesh-colored. In Japan, where asarums have been cultivated for centuries and enjoy a cultlike following, many have been selected for their silvery markings and are grown in containers so they can be enjoyed at close range. The foliage, when crushed, exudes a sweet scent, not at all like ginger.

Undervalued native asarums, hardy from Zones 5 to 9, are gaining interest for their beauty of form, adaptability to local and regional conditions, and extra hardiness. *Asarum naniflorum* 'Eco Decor', to 3 in. (7.5 cm), is a cloned cultivar of a rare, endangered species from the American Carolinas. Its small, rounded, dark green leaves—1.5 in. (4 cm) wide and beautifully marked with silver veining—most resemble cyclamen foliage. *A. virginicum* var. *virginicum* 'Silver Splash', to 6 in. (15 cm), is clump-forming. The original species grows from West Virginia to South Carolina on wooded slopes and boggy sites. The cultivar bears 2 in. (5 cm) wide rounded, dark green leaves, a contrasting background for dramatic silver veining. *A. shuttleworthii* 'Carolina Silver', to 6 in. (15 cm), from an Appalachian species, has large, heart-shaped leaves 4 in. (10 cm) wide, heavily marked with silver. 'Callaway' is a quicker grower, 4–6 in. (10–15 cm) tall and 2 ft. (0.6 m) wide, with small, exquisitely patterned leaves. The most popular of the Asian types is *A. splendens/A. magnificum* from China, hardy from Zones 6b to 9, with large, rounded, spear-shaped, dark green leaves marked in symmetrically blotched gray patterns. It is unusual for its vigor and 2 in. (5 cm) showy purple flowers. It forms large colonies in loose, humus-rich soil. Asian asarums are choice. *A. asperum* is a clump-forming type with pointed, heart-shaped leaves veined and spotted silver. *A. takkaoi* is a variable species, hardy from Zones 5 to 9, with plain or patterned leaves. Either clump-forming or creeping, it is distinguished by small leaves and is reported to be easy and vigorous. *A. takkaoi* 'Ginba' is a variant whose leaves are entirely covered with a silvery wash. *A.* 'Gosho Zakua', a Japanese classic, is hardy from Zones 6 to 9. It is unusual for its blue-green leaves, washed with silver-gray and marked with dark blue-green patches.

ATHYRIUM NIPPONICUM

Common name: Japanese fern
Family: Polypodiaceae, fern
Description: variegated fern
Origin: woodlands; Japan
Site and soil: partial shade or shade; moist
Height and width: 12–30 in. (30.5–76.0 cm) tall; 2–3 ft. (0.6–1.0 m) wide
Hardiness: Zones 4–9

In a genus of more than 180 species, Japanese ferns stand out for their unusual leaf coloration. This, like pulmonaria's spotting, is not really variegation but is caused by protective air pockets that insulate and reflect light. Growing up from creeping rhizomes, graceful fronds to 14 in. (35.5 cm) are triangular shaped, composed of lance-shaped segments notched or lobed at their margins. Coloring varies from gray-green to mid-green with reddish purple veining along the leaf's midribs. The most widely cultivated variant is *Athyrium nipponicum* var. *pictum*/ *A. goeringianum* 'Pictum', Japanese painted fern, which differs from the species in its more pronounced silver-gray leaves, zoned with gray and dark green. The midribs of each leaflet are burgundy, and the main stem varies from green to burgundy, depending on the plant's maturity. Plants grow 18–24 in. (46–61 cm) tall and 2–3 ft. (0.6–1 m) wide, with 18 in. (46 cm) long leaves, which spread slowly in arching clumps. The silver and burgundy theme may be variable even on the same plant. Named 2004 Perennial Plant of the Year by the Perennial Plant Association, it is the hardiest and most adaptable of the variants, willing to grow in gardens across the United States except in the desert and the coldest areas of Zone 3. Japanese painted fern has best color in partial shade (a half day of sun or less in hot, dry regions), in deep humus-rich, evenly moist soil. It does not suffer from any serious diseases or insect pests, and in our experience it cheerfully recovers from the "move-its" at nearly any time during the growing season if it is well watered.

Several cultivars have arisen from this variable plant. 'Silver Falls' and 'Ursula's Red' are both similar in habit to 'Pictum'. 'Silver Falls' has a pinkish red midrib and reddish purple veining that stands out on silvery fronds. Coloring gains in intensity throughout the season. 'Ursula's Red' has iridescent silver-white foliage on top and wine-red coloring on the leaf underside. 'Burgundy Lace', to 12 in. (30.5 cm), is striking for its purple coloring and silver stripes along the leaf's veins and tips. It matures to silver-green with purple midribs and is reported to be hardy from Zones 5 to 8. 'Ghost' is a departure from the familiar Japanese painted fern form. A hybrid of *Athyrium nipponicum* var. *pictum* and *A. filix-femina*, southern lady fern, it grows upright to 30 in. (76 cm), bears very silvery, elegantly cut, gray foliage, and is invaluable for dry shade.

ATRIPLEX

Common name: saltbush
Family: Chenopodiaceae, goosefoot
Description: downy shrub
Origin: coastal areas, deserts worldwide
Site and soil: sun; sandy to clay, dry to moist, well-drained
Height and width: 8 in.–10 ft. (20 cm–3 m) tall; 10 in.–6 ft. (25 cm–2 m) wide
Hardiness: Zones 4–9

Members of this genus of about 100 species are highly appreciated for their willingness to thrive both in saline soils and in drought conditions. This is of great importance in the western United States, where such conditions exist together. In nature, species are found in sparsely vegetated deserts, near salt water in almost brackish conditions, and in a range of soils from acid to alkaline. On evergreen or nearly evergreen shrubs and subshrubs, branches and narrow foliage are covered with minute scales or vesicular hairs that give them a silvery cast, nearly white in some types. The genus name is based on the Greek for orache or mountain spinach (*Atriplex hortensis*). The leaves of all species are salty and have been used for food and forage for millennia. From a horticultural standpoint, the most important native saltbush species is *A. canescens*, four-wing saltbush, whose range extends throughout the American West in high and low desert areas where winters are cold and summers are hot and dry, and where the annual rainfall varies from 6 to 16 in. (15 to 30 cm). Found in desert flats, gravelly washes, on ridges, slopes, and even sand dunes, it is fast growing, to 4–6 ft. (1.2–2 m) tall and 3–4 ft. (1–1.2 m) wide, and is one of the most silvery saltbushes. Dense scales on its branches and on both sides of its narrow leaves give the entire bush a whitish gray appearance. Paper-thin fruits with four wings, chartreuse at first and then brown, are a favorite food of birds and wildlife. Once established, plants need no further watering.

Several cultivars have been developed for site rehabilitation and are especially suited to certain growing conditions: 'Rincon', a very fast-growing type from New Mexico, grows best in the Intermountain region of the United States on sagebrush, pinyon-juniper woodland, and mountain brushland sites; 'Wytana', a very tough customer, was developed to grow on old mine sites in Wyoming; 'Marana', from southern California, is a hot desert plant used in southern Arizona to western Texas. All are hardy from Zones 4 to 7, except for the cultivar 'Marana', hardy only to Zone 7.

Atriplex gardneri, Gardner saltbush, is a fleshy-leaved subshrub, almost white in appearance, that grows only 8–12 in. (20–30 cm) tall and 10 in. (25 cm) wide. It is drought-resistant, tolerates both clay and saline soils, and is hardy from Zones 4 to 7. *A. lentiformis*, quail bush, is a large bush, 6–10 ft. (2–3 m) tall and 4–6 ft. (1.2–2 m) wide, with silver-green foliage over an intricate pattern of branches, and is considered very drought-tolerant. It is hardy to Zones 6 or 7 to 10.

Atriplex halimus, saltbush or sea orache, is striking in the wild, where it grows as a dense, silver-gray bush along the Mediterranean coast of southern Europe and is sometimes found naturalized in Britain in coastal sands and salt marshes. The species name means maritime. Leaves and stems are covered with vesicular hairs filled with a saline solution in their early growth. By the heat of summer, when hairs dry out, shrubs appear quite silvery. In garden conditions, plants grow 5–6 ft. (1.5–2 m) tall and 3–4 ft. (1–1.2 m) wide and are especially suited to coastal gardens fully exposed to sea winds, but they can be grown inland, too. They make a great hedge, trimmed or untrimmed, and plants respond well to pruning. Current research on its medicinal value suggests that an extract from *A. halimus* may help control diabetes. It is hardy from Zones 7 to 9.

AURINIA SAXATILIS

Common name: basket-of-gold
Family: Brassicaceae, mustard
Description: downy perennial
Origin: rocky mountains; Mediterranean, Turkey, Russia
Site and soil: sun; sharply drained
Height and width: 3–12 in. (7.5–30.5 cm) tall; 12–24 in. (30.5–61.0 cm) wide
Hardiness: Zones 3–7

Basket-of-gold is a traditional rock garden plant better known by its former name, *Alyssum saxatile*. No matter how common, it is always pleasing in spring when its downy gray, spoon-shaped foliage is crowned by a mass of 0.25 in. (0.5 cm), bright golden flowers in compact clusters on plants 8–12 in. (20.5–30.5 cm) tall and 12 in. (30.5 cm) wide. There is nothing quite like it for tumbling down a bank or over a rock wall. Beware of overcrowding, which causes rot.

The most enduring cultivar is 'Citrina'/'Citrinum', grown since the late 1800s and a recipient of the RHS AGM. It is similar in form to the species but its flowers are lemon to primrose yellow. 'Compactum', a dwarf form about 6 in. (15 cm) tall with medium-light yellow flowers, is also an old cultivar from the late 1800s. 'Dudley Neville', or more likely 'Dudley Nevill', has rich, butter-yellow flowers. The variegated form, 'Dudley Neville Variegated', 8 in. (20.5 cm) tall and 18 in. (46 cm) wide, bears pale apricot flowers against gray leaves edged in white. 'Golden Queen', 9–12 in. (23.0–30.5 cm) tall and 12 in. (30.5 cm) wide, a seed-propagated strain, has light yellow flowers. 'Goldkugel' (gold ball) is a very compact form, 8 in. (20 cm) tall and 24 in. (61 cm) wide, with deep golden flowers. 'Mount Hood Sunburst' has gray leaves margined creamy yellow, an improvement over 'Variegatum', a weak grower. 'Plenum' is unusual for its double flowers, but like many other doubles, it is not as vigorous as the single-flowered type. Its blooms are bright yellow, long-lasting, and sterile. 'Silver Queen' has distinctive silver-green foliage, grows to about 10 in. (25 cm), and has creamy yellow flowers. (G. S. Thomas suggests this is identical to 'Citrina'.) 'Sunnyborder Apricot', to 8 in. (20 cm), has pale, apricot-gold flowers against gray foliage. 'Tom Thumb', great for crevices or small spaces between rocks, is smaller in every way. It grows 3–4 in. (7.5–10.0 cm) tall from a mound of small, silvery leaves and bears golden flowers, smaller than the species.

BALLOTA PSEUDODICTAMNUS

Common name: false dittany
Family: Lamiaceae, mint
Description: downy subshrub
Origin: rocks, rough and waste ground; Greece, Crete, Turkey
Soil and site: sun; dry, well-drained
Height and width: 2 ft. (0.6 m) tall and wide
Hardiness: Zones 7–9

"As with people, so with plants, " observed Mrs. Underwood (1971). "There are some who do not impress at first sight, but who gradually worm their way into one's affections and make themselves indispensable." *Ballota pseudodictamnus*, she proclaimed, is such a plant, the only one in a genus of about 35 species that is especially garden-worthy. This species is an example of the way silver plants

Ballota pseudodictamnus.

respond to excessive heat and strong sun. In spring, rosettes of roundish, pale-green leaves grow from a woody base. As the season warms and the plant's woolly stems grow taller, lower leaves remain apple-green, but upper leaves, in response to the sun's intensity, become so clothed in hairs that they appear white. Tiny, two-lipped, tubular flowers typical of the mint family—white or pinkish white in color—appear in leaf axils held by a showy, pale-green calyx, useful at this stage in dried arrangements. The effect of the entire plant is quite silvery. The genus name is from the Greek *ballote* (to reject), and refers to the disagreeable odor and taste of *B. nigra*, the medicinal species. The most common cause of plant death is exposure to excessive moisture in winter and spring. In the garden, false dittany looks best among rocks in association with sun-baked Mediterranean flora.

BEGONIA

Common name: begonia
Family: Begoniaceae, begonia
Description: variegated tender perennial
Origin: garden
Site and soil: indirect sun indoors, partial shade or shade outdoors; well-drained
Height and width: 5 in.–3 ft. (12.5 cm–1 m) tall; 9–24 in. (23–61 cm) wide
Hardiness: to 50°F (10°C)

Begonias are widely distributed in tropical and warm-temperate climates found mainly in South America and Asia. They are a large group of plants, grown for their dramatic foliage and showy flowers. With an estimated 1300 species and as many as 10,000 hybrids, classification is sometimes difficult, but for the silver collector, the problem is reduced to manageable proportions. Most silver-leaved begonias are found among Angel-wing and *Begonia* Rex Cultorum Hybrids, which belong to the cane begonia group, so-called because of their thick, woody, bamboolike canes or stems that grow from fibrous roots. Angel-wings are vigorous—*B.* 'Lucerna' reaches 7 ft. (2 m)—with dramatic winglike foliage, to 8 to 12 in. (20 to 30 cm) long; usually deeply toothed and lobed, their edges waved or feathered, green or olive in color; often marked, speckled, and spotted with silver, with flushed maroon undersides. Flowers bloom in heavy, dangling clusters of cherry-red, red, orange, salmon, pink, and white. Rex begonia hybrids grow mainly from rhizomatous roots. They arose from the discovery in 1856 of *B. rex*, an Indian species, 10 in. (25.5 cm) tall and 12 in. (30.5 cm) wide. Since then, *B. rex* has been the focus of intense breeding between it and Asian species, producing plants with large, spectacular foliage, including dwarf types no taller than 5 in. (13 cm). The essential ovate, green leaf, usually to 8 to 12 in. (20.5 to 30.5 cm) long, is nearly forgotten in brilliant markings and overlays of colors that include red, pink, lavender, maroon (nearly black), bronze, and silver. Those hybrids crossed with tuberous begonias tend to be winter dormant (they are not truly rhizomatous). Several important silver begonias are often placed in the Fibrous group, a catch-all of fibrous-rooted types, including cane Angel-wings, grown for fancy foliage and/or for flowers.

Jessica Chevalier, formerly with Logee's Greenhouses, recommends growing begonias in clay pots. She keeps the soil light and fluffy—on the dry side—and every time she waters she uses a dilute amount of fish emulsion. Begonias fertilized with fish emulsion, she maintains, have a healthier root system, stronger growth, and more vibrant colors than those fertilized with a salt-based fertilizer.

Officially begonias require 60°F (16°C) nighttime temperatures with an ideal daytime temperature of 70° to 75°F (21° to 24°C). They are reported to survive short periods exposed to 50°F (10°C), but most leaves will drop. Unofficially, begonia aficionados such as writer Elvin McDonald have observed that Angel-wings are tougher (maybe others, too). When he lived in Houston, Texas, he saw that they grew all year in the ground along the Gulf Coast, and that when subjected to the occasional brief freeze they died back to the ground, but when they grew back from their roots they were stronger than ever (*Traditional Home*, July 2002). Indoors, provide sunny, indirect light in the spring, fall, and winter months—a bright east or west window is recommended. In the summer outdoors, site for morning or late afternoon sun or partial to full shade to avoid leaf scorch. Diseases and pests include botrytis, powdery mildew, mealybugs, aphids, and red spider mites.

Among the antique hybrids are 'Comtesse Louise Erody', a still popular Rex from the 1800s. It is smaller than most with spiraled foliage, the silvery sheen marked with olive veining, and its slightly ruffled edges outlined in pink—a charming ensemble. 'Green Gold' is a Rex with spiraled foliage that does well indoors or outside. Its large leaves are strikingly silver-white with deep green veining. Older leaves are blushed pink; newer leaves have a greenish gold hue. 'Lalomie', a Rex hybrid, is an easy grower, distinguished for its lush, very ruffled, metallic silver leaves with deep green veins and pinkish edging. 'Curly Silver Sweet', a spiral-leaved Rex, is different for its rounded leaves arranged neatly in tiers.

Our other choices each have different attributes to recommend. 'Connie Boswell' is a perfect choice for beginner growers. A fibrous-rooted type, it is upright in habit with intricately cut, metallic silver foliage deeply veined with lavender. Its color shows best in an east or west window in partial shade. 'Fireworks' is a large-leaved Rex with deep wine-red veining over silver leaves widely edged with purple-raspberry. 'Fortune Cookie' is a compact Rex with metallic silver foliage, like an oversize maple leaf, delicately veined dark green with reddish edging. The 'Fortune Cookie' surprise is the flowers nestled in the center of the plant, small and white petaled with golden stamens. We are pleased with 'Guy Savard', a fibrous hybrid introduced in the early 1990s, different for its long, lancelike, sharply toothed leaves, silver-pink with forest-green veining and maroon undersides. It usually grows no taller than 12 in. (30.5 cm). It is something like a larger version of the dwarf 'Kismet', a favorite Logee hybrid. 'Kismet' is a beautifully striped Angel-wing with 3 in. (7.5 cm) ruffled, silver foliage, veined a deep green. Young foliage is pinkish red. Our favorite Angel-wing is 'Looking Glass', a vigorous beauty 3 ft. (1 m) tall and 18 in. (46 cm) wide, considerably shorter in a pot. It has big, slightly ruffled leaves to 6 in. (15 cm), appealing satiny texture (inviting to touch), olive midrib and veins, and purple-pink undersides. 'Two Face', a fibrous type, is altogether different. Its mounds of pointed, bristly leaves, densely metallic silver with hair-thin green veins are vibrant rose-burgundy beneath. 'Silver Dollar', also bristly and fibrous rooted, has leaves with puckered splotches of metallic silver on an almost black background with vibrant rose-burgundy undersides. We cut back overwintered plants to 6 in. (15 cm) in the spring or early summer before we put them outdoors.

Look out for these beauties: 'Little Brother Montgomery', a cane type with Rexlike leaves, and most intriguing, fragrance in mature specimens with large foliage, sparkling silver with bronze and green-speckled veins. 'Raspberry Swirl' is a strong Rex grower with spiraled, large leaves, raspberry-red in their center, merging to silver and green. 'Uncle Remus', a dwarf Rex, is 6 to 10 in. (15 to 25 cm) tall with oversized maplelike leaves, green, dappled with silver and red shades ranging from crimson and rose to pink, then fading to blush. Its deeply cut leaves are edged with ebony-green. 'Silver Wings' is an Angel-wing with maroon foliage (on top and beneath), generously splashed with silver spots. *Begonia hatacoa* 'Silver', from Nepal, is rhizomatous, grows 12–16 in. (30.5–40.5 cm) tall, with narrow, elongated foliage, slightly puckered between its veins and painted like dull metal.

BISMARCKIA NOBILIS

Common name: Bismarck palm
Family: Palmae, palm
Description: waxy palm tree
Origin: grasslands; Madagascar
Site and soil: sun; sandy, well-drained
Height and width: 40–70 ft. (12–21 m) tall; 10–15 ft. (3.0–4.5 m) wide
Hardiness: Zones 9 or 10–11

This spectacular tropical palm, the only species in its genus, has green-leaved and blue-leaved forms. Each produces a heavy, stout, upright trunk that can reach more than 100 ft. (30.5 m) in its home ground. Palmate fronds emerge from the trunk in spiraling fans at least 10 ft. (3 m) wide. These are composed of 10 to 25 or more, 3 ft. (1 m) long spreading fingers or blades on 6 ft. (2 m) stems. Since a tree generally bears 20 to 30 fans, the effect is of a giant canopy that is electrified in the blue form by leaves more silvery than blue in appearance. Although the green and blue forms are structurally the same, the blue version performs better in very hot conditions because of its heavily waxed leaves. White flowers, male and female on separate trees, look like catkins nestle among leaves on 4 ft. (1.2 m) stalks and then produce fleshy, round fruits that are speckled brown and 1 to 3 in. (2.5 to 7.5 cm) in diameter. Immature trunks carry old leaf bases, 12 to 18 in. (30.5 to 45.5 cm) wide; mature trees still bear leaf scars on smooth, dark gray trunks.

The cultivar 'Silver Select' is reported to be hardier and more consistently silver than others. This is an asset in a group of plants reproduced by seed, a process that inevitably produces variations in color, form, and hardiness. These gorgeous giants grow best in a climate that is similar to the one they came from: cool, dry winters and hot, wet summers—that means southern Florida, protected sites of central Florida, extreme southern Texas, and parts of southern California, inland, where it is hotter, rather than on the coast, where the green form is a better choice. Testing hardiness limits has become a popular pastime among Bismarck palm aficionados and data is routinely shared on the Internet. Generally considered hardy to 28°F (-2°C), palm lovers report 50 percent leaf burn after exposure to 22°F (-6°C) on a tree grown over two winters in sandy, well-drained loam, in a protected site with surrounding tree canopies. Although some of the older leaves died off over the next two months, none of the tree's newer leaves were damaged.

BRUNNERA MACROPHYLLA

Common name: Siberian bugloss
Family: Boraginaceae, borage
Description: variegated perennial
Origin: garden
Site and soil: partial shade or shade; moist, humus-rich, well-drained
Height and width: 12 in. (30.5 cm) tall; 15 in. (38.0 cm) wide
Hardiness: Zones 2–8

Three species in the genus, distributed from eastern Europe to northwestern Asia, are rhizomatous, spreading plants grown for their flowers and foliage. *Brunnera macrophylla* is normally green. The cultivar 'Jack Frost' has oversize, heart-shaped foliage to 8 in. (20 cm) long and nearly 8 in. (20 cm) wide near its base, crisply cut and slightly cupped. The green leaves are painted with an overlay of metallic silver etched with green veining and rimmed with a narrow band of green. The green veining breaks up the silver coating into intricate stylized webbing. Sprays of tiny, deep-sky-blue flowers appear over the foliage, creating an appealing combination of silver and blue. As the flowers fade, the foliage swells in importance, transformed into a stack of oversized silver hearts. *B. macrophylla* 'Silver Wings', a sport of *B.* 'Langtrees', is distinguished from 'Jack Frost' by the thin, white margin that frames the silver-netted leaf, creating a winged effect. The species' common name, bugloss, is derived from Greek for ox tongue, because of the shape and texture of the leaves. Silver cultivars look best in a woodland setting, where they steal the show. Watch for seedlings that may vary. These beautiful, tough, low-maintenance, vigorous plants with few diseases or pests are among the most exciting shade silvers introduced in recent years.

BUDDLEJA

Common name: butterfly bush
Family: Buddlejaceae, butterfly
Description: downy shrub
Origin: riversides, rocky areas, and scrub; Asia, southwestern United States
Site and soil: sun; fertile, well-drained

Buddleja alternifolia 'Argentea'.

Height: 3–20 ft. (1–6 m) tall; 4–15 ft. (1–5 m) wide
Hardiness: Zones 4 or 5–10

These old-fashioned shrubs are favored for their long, fragrant flower trusses so attractive to butterflies; their tolerance for drought conditions; and their ability to grow up to 6 ft. (2 m) and just as wide in a single season from their roots. They are enjoying a renaissance of interest with the introduction of more compact, less weedy forms and a color range beyond the ordinary lilac-purple, including dark purple, reddish, blue, and pink flowers. For the silver fancier, there is the added allure of types with intensely silvery leaves, a coloration that heretofore has been merely suggested in silver-backed foliage. The bush's form is wide and arching, loosely and irregularly vase-shaped, or compact in the newer dwarf types. (In butterfly bush parlance, the term "dwarf" is relative, since some of these may grow up to 6 ft., or 2 m, tall.) Flowers of the Asian species discussed here are small and tubular, carried in dense pyramidal or conical heads, sweetly scented like honey, and sometimes marked with a darker eye. Leaves are often lance-shaped and willowy, dull green above and silvery below. In some types, leaves appear entirely silver in their early growth. Named for an English botanist, Adam

Buddle, the Latin genus name is spelled with a *j* as in *Buddleja*, but the common name form is spelled *buddleia*. You will find both spellings in the trade.

In climates with colder winters, buddleias may die back to the ground in the same way as an herbaceous perennial, but they are fast growing and will come back from their roots amazingly fast when warm weather sets in to produce flowers by midsummer to late summer on full-grown bushes. Early-flowering bushes like *Buddleja alternifolia*, which produces flowers on previous year's growth, are thinned out after flowering and then pruned hard after frost. Later flowering types such as *B. davidii*, which produces flowers on the current year's growth, are pruned back to about 12 in. (30.5 cm) or more just as new growth begins. If stems are left to 2–3 ft. (0.6–1.0 m), bushes will bloom about the same time as if they were hard-pruned, but hard-pruning has the advantage of keeping bushes shorter and more compact. Even in warmer regions, where shrubs do not die back, they should be hard-pruned to maintain a dense shape.

Buddleja alternifolia, fountain buddleia, from 10 to 20 ft. (3 to 6 m), is loose and congested with long, trailing branches clad in dull-green leaves, gray underneath, and bright, lilac-purple flowers in dense clusters by spring. In 'Argentea', a 1998 Plant Select, leaves have a silvery sheen from a covering of silky hairs. For a stunning effect (and to take up less room), it can be trained as a standard with a head of long, pendulous branches. It is hardy from Zones 5 to 9.

Buddleja davidii, old-fashioned butterfly bush or summer lilac, has been reinvented as a compact form, often with striking silver foliage and good flower colors. A stalwart type, adaptable and fast-growing, it grows well in moist, loamy soil (even on the alkaline side); takes heat; and tolerates drought once established. If it becomes overgrown, cut it back hard and fertilize to promote fresh growth. Most forms have green-grayish leaves, but among those with really silver leaves are the "dwarf" sorts in the jasmine-scented Nanho series, all rounded and compact with horizontal, lilting branches. *B. davidii* 'Nanho Blue'/'Petite Indigo', 3–4 ft. (1.0–1.2 m) tall, has deep lilac-blue flowers with an orange bee. Although less silver than *B. alternifolia* 'Argentea', we like the way we are able to train it as an arched, vase shape. It keeps its willowlike silver leaves all winter and in our experience is never touched by deer. 'Nanho White', 4–5 ft. (1.2–1.5 m), is an all silver-white ensemble. In our experience, 'Nanho Alba', white flowering with a yellow eye, is not the same as the more silvery 'Nanho White'. There is, of course, the usual variation in the trade, with similarities between plants of different names as well as differences between plants with the same name. We once admired a very silvery dwarf form of *B. davidii* 'Empire Blue' in a Rhode Island garden, where in February its leaves were intensely silver. 'Empire Blue' is usually offered as a taller, upright form to 6–8 ft. (2.0–2.5 m), but the dwarf one is worth looking for. Hardiness ranges from Zones 4 or 5 to 9.

Among the newer silver-leaved hybrids is late-spring–blooming *Buddleja* 'Indigo Pink', a bush of dense habit and fast growth, 5 ft. (1.5 m) tall and 4 ft. (1.2 m) wide, with gray-felted foliage and rich, pink flowers, hardy from Zones 6 or 7 to 10. Summer-blooming buddleias include *B.* 'Summer Beauty', with flowers of a reddish hue (something new for buddleias) on plants to 4 ft. (1.2 m), hardy from Zones 5 to 10; and *B.* 'White Ball', 3 ft. (1 m) tall and wide, desirable for its compact size. It is rated hardy from Zones 5 to 9. Less hardy, but very desirable for its silvery foliage, is white-flowering *B. fallowiana* 'Alba', an arching shrub 6 ft. (2 m) tall and 10 ft. (3 m) wide, which unlike the species retains its woolliness all season. It blooms in late summer and is hardy from Zones 8 to 9. A hybrid offspring, 'Lochinch' (*B. fallowiana* ×*davidii*), with lavender-blue tresses, is a great asset for its inherited silver foliage and hardiness to Zone 5, perhaps even Zone 4 in a protected site. Michael Dirr has observed two forms in the trade, a large form, 12–15 ft. (3.5–4.5 m) tall and wide, and a more compact form half that size, the one with which we are familiar. 'Silver Frost'/'White Frost', a Dirr selection from 'Lochinch', has its parent's silvery foliage and upright, white blooms.

Several buddleias are grown more for their woolly or felted foliage than for their flowers. Among them are *Buddleija nivea*, to 6 ft. (2 m), with huge, woolly leaves and small clusters of lilac flowers that bloom in late spring. *B. nivea* subsp. *nivea* is similar, with white-felted leaves and stems. *B. nivea* var. *yunnanensis*, from 8 to 15 ft. (2.5 to 4.5 m), has felted leaves, 12 in. (30.5 cm) long on woolly stems; it prefers poor soil and is hardy to Zone 6. *B. salvifolia*, as its epithet suggests, has sagelike foliage, gray-golden in color, on felted stems. As a bonus, in midsummer, fragrant lavender flowers are wrapped in wool. It is hardy to Zone 8.

The native species, *Buddleja marrubifolia*, woolly butterfly bush, 5 ft. (1.5 m) tall and wide, from southwestern Texas to New Mexico, grows in limestone canyons and arroyos. In full, exposed sun with sharp drainage it will grow into a dense bush with little pruning, and it is tolerant of extreme heat and drought. Foliage is soft and silver; flowers, nearly everblooming, are small, ball-shaped, and orange, and they bloom most heavily in spring and summer when they attract flocks of butterflies. Fragrance is slight compared to Asian species. It is hardy from Zones 7 to 9.

CALLUNA VULGARIS

Common name: heather
Family: Ericaceae, heath
Description: downy shrub
Origin: moors, lowlands; Europe, Asia Minor
Site and soil: sun; acid, well-drained
Height and width: 6–24 in. (15–61 cm) tall; 12–24 in. (30.5–61.0 cm) wide
Hardiness: Zone 4–8

In heather's natural range it grows as a spreading cover over miles of otherwise barren ground and in highland and lowland habitats. It provides food and cover for grouse, deer, smaller mammals, reptiles, and insects. Long recognized for its beauty, poets have sung its praises and ordinary people have turned it to practical use. The genus name, based on the Latin *kalluno* (to clean), refers to heather's use as a broom or brush. Growing on unused and discarded land, burned-over forest, and poor soil, heather forms a dense, evergreen mat, upright or spreading, of tiny, scalelike foliage of overlapping pairs, most often smooth and fleshy, in shades of green from light to dark and sometimes gold, chartreuse, or russet. Of interest to the silver fancier are the downy silver-gray sorts, of which there are many fine examples. In winter, leaves may be tinged dull chartreuse or purple. Plants produce one-sided spikes of small, bell-shaped flowers in racemes of varying length, from 0.5 to 4 in. (1 to 10 cm)—in white, red, and shades of pink and purple—on stems 6–8 in. (15–20 cm) long. It is the presence of colorful sepals, before the plants bloom and after the flowers have faded, that gives heather its singular visual beauty, especially when massed. Heathers produce phenomenal quantities of seed that quickly establish a multitude of plants in favorable conditions. Anyone who has visited Scotland's heaths and witnessed vast, undulating stretches of rose and purple heathers and heaths (distinguished by their darker purple flowers) can appreciate this phenomenon and its impact on the imagination and daily lives of people living within its natural range.

Heather has been used for animal fodder, fuel, plant dyes, ropes, thatching, to stuff mattresses, and as medicinal preparations. Flowers are a source of nectar for butterflies and bees, and heather honey, used in the ancient drink mead, is still highly prized. Heather is also called *ling*, derived from the Norse *lyng* (lightweight, as in a lightweight fuel). These little shrubs do best wherever cool, humid summer conditions prevail, as in coastal gardens in New England and the American Northwest, but they may also be grown inland. Plant them deeply with their lower foliage touching the soil in an open, sunny site, in humusy, acidic soil

Calluna vulgaris
'Silver Knight'.

amended with sand and peat. Over-fertilizing produces leggy, unhealthy plants. Ground that supports blueberries and rhododendrons should also grow heathers.

Early-blooming silver cultivars include *Calluna vulgaris* 'Anthony Davis', upright to 18 in. (46 cm), with gray-green foliage and long spikes of white flowers from midsummer to late summer. 'Silver Queen', an RHS AGM winner, has a broad, spreading habit, 8–12 in. (20.5–30.5 cm) tall and 18–22 in. (46–56 cm) wide, with lilac-pink flowers from midsummer to early autumn. The deservedly popular 'Sister Anne' grows into a low, dense, mounding mat, 6 in. (15 cm) tall and 18 in. (46 cm) wide, of downy gray foliage that turns a dull bronze or purplish in winter, great for lining walks or filling rock crevices. Its flowers are bright shell-pink in short racemes from midsummer to early autumn.

Later bloomers flower from late summer to autumn. These include 'Alison Yates', a vigorous, compact form, 18 in. (46 cm) tall and 24 in. (61 cm) wide, with silver-gray foliage and long-stemmed clusters of white flowers. 'Beoley Silver', 12–18 in. (30.5–46.0 cm) tall and 18–24 in. (46–61 cm) wide, has white flowers over downy silver foliage and is considered one of the best silver heaths because it retains its leaf coloring in winter. 'Dainty Bess', with lavender flowers, is useful for filling rock crevices because of its small mat, 2–4 in. (5–10 cm) tall, of tiny gray leaves. 'Jan Dekker', with downy gray foliage, has a mounding form, 6 in. (15 cm) tall and 12 in. (30.5 cm) wide, and mauve flowers. 'Kerstin', 12 in. (35.5 cm) tall and 18 in. (46 cm) wide, has mauve flowers, too, but its downy gray foliage is tipped pink and yellow. 'Schurig's Sensation' has silver-gray leaves, an upright form 20 in. (51 cm) tall and 24 in. (61 cm) wide, and dark, double-pink flowers that bloom over a long period from late summer to mid-autumn. 'Silver Cloud', whose hairy foliage remains silver-gray even in winter, is a low, spreading mat, 4–6 in. (10–15 cm) tall and 18–24 in. (46–61 cm) wide, with pale purple flowers. 'Tomentosa', a spreading form 18 in. (46 cm) tall and 24 in. (61 cm) wide, has gray-green foliage and lavender flowers. 'Velvet Fascination', a highly praised variety by David Small of the Heather Society for its enduringly silver-gray foliage, is upright to 18 in. (46 cm), with pure white flowers.

'Silver King', 'Silver Knight', and 'Silver Rose' share downy, silver-gray foliage and upright forms: 'Silver King', 10 in. (25 cm) tall and 15 in. (38 cm) wide, has white flowers; 'Silver Knight', so named because it is said to stand straight up like a knight in armour, is 18 in. (46 cm) tall and 24 in. (61 cm) wide, with mauve-pink flowers, and its foliage turns purplish in winter; 'Silver Rose', an RHS AGM winner, is 16 in. (41 cm) tall and 20 in. (51 cm) wide, with lilac-pink flowers.

Carex albula 'Frosted Curls' / 'Frosty Curls'.

CAREX

Common name: sedge
Family: Cyperaceae, sedge
Description: waxy perennial
Origin: wet to dry fields; New Zealand, Europe, North Africa
Site and soil: sun or part shade; wet to dry
Height: 6–12 in. (15.0–30.5 cm)
Hardiness: Zones 5–9

Of the nearly 1000 species in the genus *Carex*, a few are of interest to the silver collector. Confusion surrounds the nomenclature of *C. albula*, frosty or frosted curls sedge, native to New Zealand, which is usually marketed as *C. comans* 'Frosted Curls' or 'Frosty Curls'. It grows up to form dense, compact tufts of swirling leaves, like a mop of finely textured, long hair, 6–12 in. (15.0–30.5 cm). This is a terrific silver for sun to part shade in average to moist soil. Aptly named, its frosted, minty green leaves curl and twist, ending in an iridescent, whitish tip. Foliage turns yellow by fall and buff by winter. Small, cylindrical, green flower spikes bloom from early to late summer. Frosty curls looks best on a slope or in a tall pot, singly or in masses, where its trailing foliage shows off well with almost every other plant with different foliage and form. It is hardy from Zones 6 (with protection) to 9. *C. flacca/glauca*, blue sedge, is a variable, slow-creeping sedge from wet to dry fields in Europe and North Africa and is naturalized in eastern North America. Its blue-gray leaves are 0.25 in. (0.5 cm) wide and 6–12 in. (15.0–30.5 cm) long, forming a mat that competes well with tree roots. It is often used as a ground cover and filler. Blue sedge tolerates light to medium shade and is hardy from Zones 5 to 9.

CARYOPTERIS

Common name: bluebeard
Family: Verbenaceae, vervain
Description: downy shrub
Origin: dry slopes, woodlands; Himalayas, East Asia
Site and soil: sun; sharply drained
Height and width: 18 in.–4 ft. (46 cm–1.2 m) tall; 2–6 ft. (0.6–2 m) wide
Hardiness: Zones 5–9

The bluebeards belong to a genus of six deciduous shrubs, the most important of which is the hybrid *Caryopteris* ×*clandonensis* (*C. incana* × *C. mongolica*) introduced to the United States by 1933. A resourceful nurseryman is credited with popularizing it by inventing the name "blue mist," now a generic term for all the hybrids in this group. They bear small, aromatic, silver-green foliage, 1–2 in. (2.5–5.0 cm) long, slightly toothed, green above and white beneath, on upright, rounded shrubs decorated with a multitude of fringed lavender to violet-blue to vivid-blue flowers in late summer and fall. The combination of blue flowers above a mound of silver foliage is appealing at any time, but especially so in the late summer when fresh blooms are scarce. Aromatic flowers lure bees and butterflies in the last hurrah of the season. At the limit of their hardiness range, plants die back like herbaceous perennials, but they grow back up from their roots the following season. Although short-lived, they self-seed and layer themselves. Where they are marginally hardy, it's a good idea to protect the crown with boughs, straw, or even compost, as you would protect a marginally hardy perennial. The most silvery of the blue mist group are 'Dark Knight', 2 ft. (0.6 m) tall and 3 ft. (1.0 m) wide, a distinctive form with dark blue flowers against silver foliage; 'Kew Blue', a compact form with strong lavender-blue flowers; and the popular 'Longwood Blue', chosen at Longwood Gardens for its neat, upright shape, 18–24 in. (46–61 cm), and true-blue flowers over silvery gray foliage. A new introduction, 'First Choice', was selected for its earlier bloom, compact habit, 2–4 ft. (0.6–1.2 m) height, and its deep blue flowers matched to gray-blue foliage. One of blue mist's parents, *C. incana*, or silver bluebeard, is a significant silver shrub in its own right. It is a larger bush, at least 4 ft. (1.2 m) tall and 3 ft. (1.0 m) wide, with gray-felted leaves and violet-blue flowers in summer. 'Nana' is a dwarf form; the lovely 'Candide' has pure white flowers.

CEDRUS

Common name: cedar

Family: Pinaceae, pine

Description: waxy tree

Origin: forests; North Africa, Himalayas

Site and soil: sun; acidic to alkaline, moist, well-drained

Height and width: 8 in.–60 ft. (20.5 cm–18.3m) tall; 30 in.–40 ft.(16 cm–12.2m) wide

Hardiness: Zones 6b–9

Several trees are commonly called "cedar," perhaps because of their aromatic wood, but depending on the authority, only three are true species, all from the genus *Cedrus*. They are forest conifers with needle foliage that grows in spraylike clusters on short shoots. In nature, trees attain great size, 60–80 ft. (18–24 m) or taller in maturity. Cone-shaped when young, they become flat-topped in maturity, when their horizontal branches may spread 40 ft. (12 m) or more. Erect male cones are yellow and most noticeable when they spill out their yellow pollen in the fall. Most cedars, except for dwarf types, need plenty of room so they can spread out to show off their magnificent form. Where they are marginally hardy, plant them on hillsides rather than in colder lowlands.

Cedrus atlantica 'Glauca', blue atlas cedar, from the Atlas Mountains of north-west Africa, is very popular for its electric-blue needles in early growth on upward-pointing branches and for its fissured, silvery gray bark. Pyramidal and sparsely limbed in youth, after six years it develops a denseness of growth, fol-lowed by the development of wide, sweeping, horizontal branches. Over the next three or four decades, it may reach 40–60 ft. (12–18 m) tall and 30–40 ft. (9–12 m) wide, when as Michael Dirr (1997) observed, "In a crowd, this form shouts for attention." Mark Weathington, horticulturist at the Norfolk Botanical Garden in Virginia (Zone 8a), says it grows very well there in the humid, coastal Mid-Atlantic region without any special attention other than moist, well-drained soil. It does well in the similar conditions of the U.S. Gulf Coast and West

Cedrus atlantica 'Glauca'.

Coast. Give it plenty of room. 'Glauca Fastigiata', with strictly ascending branches, takes up less room but still has the desired "blue" look. 'Glauca Pendula', weeping blue atlas cedar, can be trained to any shape (even maintained as a small tree), draped over a wall or against it as an espalier form.

Cedrus deodar from the Himalayas also does well in hot, humid areas. It is a faster growing tree than blue atlas cedar, attaining 2 ft. (0.6 m) or more a year in its early growth. It is very graceful, with soft, bluish needles on horizontal branches that bend down at their tips, the lower branches themselves falling to the ground before growing back upward. Trees can be pruned in late spring to maintain the desired shape. 'Silver Mist', with soft, whitish needles, is a dwarf form 3–4 ft. (1–1.2 m) tall, but it can be kept to a small mound, 18 in. (46 cm) tall and 30 in. (76 cm) wide, in a rock garden. It grows well in sun or partial shade. 'Snow Sprite', another with whitish foliage, is a slow-growing, conical form that reaches 4–5 ft. (1.2–1.5 m).

CENTAUREA CINERARIA/CENTAUREA GYMNOCARPA

Common name: dusty miller
Family: Asteraceae, aster
Description: downy tender subshrub
Origin: rocky habitat; Corsica, Capri
Site and soil: sun; well-drained
Height and width: 30 in. (76 cm) tall;
   15 in. (38 cm) wide
Hardiness: Zones 8–10

In a genus of 500 species that includes several very silver "dusty miller" types, only one is just becoming familiar in North America (it is popular in England). *Centaurea cineraria* resembles the familiar gray-white bedding plant *Senecio cineraria*, which is also known as dusty miller. *C. cineraria* is larger than *S. cinerarea*, with hard stems and vigorous, spreading, fibrous roots. As stems shoot upward, they flare outward in sprays, then cascade downward, creating a very pleasing form. Stems are well

Tender perennial *Centaurea cineraria* 'Colchester White'.

clothed in deeply indented, filigreed foliage, precisely cut like a silver fern. Mauve flowers in sprays bloom from early to late summer.

Centaurea cineraria 'Colchester White' is a selection from England that was popular in Mrs. Underwood's time. It is vegetatively reproduced and tends to be larger and hardier than the species. Mature plants can take repeated hard frosts to 28°F (-2°C). This is an exceedingly handsome houseplant and very low maintenance. To winter indoors, dig it up and repot, cut back if you're short of room, or make stem cuttings in midsummer to late summer. Unlike other silvers that are overwintered indoors where light levels are low compared to summer sun, it retains its light gray–colored foliage. Depending on maturity, plants remain upright with cascading foliage or become quite lax, but they hold on to life until repotted, cut back if desired, and placed outdoors in early summer. 'Colchester White' is a superior plant that should be on every silver-lover's wish list. Grow it in the ground as a striking border shrub or in a container with tropicals. It pairs well with equally vigorous Wave petunias.

CERASTIUM

Common name: snow in summer
Family: Caryophyllaceae, pink
Description: downy perennial
Origin: rocky slopes, arctic and mountains south, temperate regions; Europe, Asia
Site and soil: sun; well-drained
Height and width: 2–8 in. (5–20 cm) tall; 18 in. (46 cm) wide, or indefinite
Hardiness: Zones 2–10

In a genus noted for its weedy members such as chickweed—naturalized over a good part of the world—the cerastiums stand out as prominent garden plants. Plants grow by running roots to produce a mat of trailing stems clothed in a mass of small, sharply pointed leaves—a soft, silver-gray—topped in late spring or early summer by a complementary mass of tiny, white, star-shaped flowers that resemble a cover of snow, as the common name so graphically suggests. If unchecked, plants spread far beyond their original site. Their value, however, outweighs their troublesome nature. *Cerastium tomentosum* is unsurpassable among rocks and cascading over a wall. It is as adaptable to desert heat as it is to frigid cold. Its mound grows to about 2–3 in. (5.0–7.5 cm) tall and spreads indefinitely. To control, shear back plants when bloom is just beginning to fade to obviate self-seeding and freshen foliage. Check root spread in the spring and fall (or more often if necessary) and pull plants out of bounds (roots pull out easily).

Several cultivars of the species are offered: a seed strain of *Cerastium tomentosum* 'Silver Carpet' forms a 6–8 in. (15–20 cm) mound that spreads 2 ft. (0.6 m) wide its first season and is reported to do well in dry sites as well as in partial shade. *C. tomentosum* 'Olympia' grows to 12 in. (30.5 cm) with more upright flower stems and a neater, less sprawling habit than the species. In tight plantings with little spreading room, try *C. tomentosum* var. *columnae*, hardy from Zones 4 to 10. A dainty specimen, 4 in. (10 cm) tall and 18 in. (46 cm) wide, it produces intensely silver-leaved rosettes that form a tight, round carpet. It produces its white star flowers from spring through midsummer. Alpine mouse ear, *C. alpinum* subsp. *lanatum*, is even more restrained, best grown as a crevice plant.

Cerastium tomentosum.

Growing 4 in. (10 cm) tall and 12 in. (30.5 cm) wide, it bears intensely woolly foliage and short-stemmed, white, star flowers. Like many alpines, it suffers in muggy weather and does not like baking in the hot sun. But when planted in the cool, earthy spaces created by a rock crevice, it will thrive. It is hardy from Zones 3 to 8.

CHAMAECYPARIS
Common name: false cypress
Family: Cupressaceae, cypress
Description: waxy tree
Origin: forests; Asia, North America
Site and soil: sun or partial shade; moist, well-drained
Height and width: dwarf to 4–50 ft. (1.2–15.2 m) tall; 4–20 ft. (1.2–6.1 m) wide
Hardiness: Zones 4–8

False cypresses are variable evergreen conifers from forest habitats, where they can reach more than 100 ft. (30.5 m). Species that originate in North America prefer the cool, moist conditions of the Pacific Northwest, while those that originate in Asia are more adaptable to climatic variations of wet to dry that prevail throughout the U.S. Northeast and Midwest. All have flattened, scalelike leaves in flat branchlets, soft in texture, sometimes ferny in appearance, from dark green and blue-green and yellow to silver-blues and gray-blues. Cones are usually small and reddish brown, as is the exfoliating tree bark. Slow-growing types are grown in rock and trough gardens and then replaced as they overgrow their allotted spaces. Many dwarf kinds have arisen from the few species that can be grown in the United States, and because of their variability they present a taxonomic puzzle.

Chamaecyparis lawsoniana, Lawson false cypress, is native from southwest Oregon to northwest California. It is a slender, broadly pyramidal tree that can reach more than 100 ft. (30.5 m), but cultivars are considerably shorter. 'Allumii', Sarah Lawson cypress, has a columnar form 20–50 ft. (6–15 m), with steel-blue foliage. 'Nana Albospica'/'Argentea Compacta' is a dwarf compact form, oval in shape, with silvery white growing tips that shows best color when the tree is well fed; it reaches 10 ft. (3 m) tall and wide. 'Ellwoodii' has an upright, narrow, columnar form with blue-gray foliage, and it grows 6–9 ft. (2–3 m). We have grown it in a container for years in our kitchen greenhouse window; by root pruning, we keep it dwarfed to 30 in. (76 cm). 'Pembury Blue', to 50 ft. (15.2 m), is silver-blue, best in full sun and moist soil. 'Silver Queen' is a unique silver-green, brightest in new growth, with an upright, pyramidal form that reaches 10 ft. (3 m) tall and 4 ft. (1.2 m) wide in 10 years.

Chamaecyparis pisifera, Sawara false cypress, is a narrowly pyramidal tree from Japan. It is horizontally branching, with silvery underside leaves, growing to 150 ft. (45.7 m). Many cultivars are desirable, most notably blue moss chamaecyparis ('Boulevard'/'Cyanoviridis'). It is slow-growing, with soft, silver-blue foliage, beginning as a small mound in early growth that eventually becomes a fat pyramid to 8 ft. (2.4 m) tall and wide over 20 years. It is intensely blue where soil is acidic and magnesium levels are high. Older, dead foliage should be removed from the center of the plant to allow light and air circulation. This is an excellent larger subject for bonsai. 'Baby Blue' is a slow-growing, very hardy, small upright and rounded form to 6 ft. (1.8 m), with silver-blue, twisted leaves, that grows only 6–8 in. (15–20 cm) a year. 'Curly Tops' has even curlier silver-blue foliage on a small, round, ball-like form, 4–5 ft. (42.0–1.5 m) tall.

CISTUS

Common name: rock rose
Family: Cistaceae, cistus
Description: downy shrub
Origin: deserts, scrubland, dry woodlands; Mediterranean to Caucasus
Site and soil: sun; dry, sharply drained
Height and width: 1–5 ft. (0.3–1.5 m) tall; 2–6 ft. (0.6–1.8 m) wide
Hardiness: 6–10

Rock roses belong to a genus of about 20 small to medium aromatic shrubs, mounding and spreading, and viscous from the gumlike resin on their leaves, the source of biblical ladanum (Genesis 43:11). Foliage is oblong to lancelike, often wrinkled, veined, covered with silky hairs above and woolly beneath, and undulate or wavy-edged. In the heat of the day, under a burning sun, the whole plant sparkles with resin. Short-lived flowers, 1–2 in. (2.5–5.0 cm), from late spring to summer, are similar to those of the rugosa rose, hence its common name. Five papery, rounded petals, some with basal spots, are spaced around prominent golden stamens to form a saucerlike bloom. Flowers possess a sweet floral scent and attract butterflies. The genus name is based on the Greek *kiste* (box), a reference to the shape of the plant's seed capsules. Today rock rose gum is used as a fixative or fragrance in perfumes, soaps, and toiletries.

These willing shrubs are used to harsh conditions in their native habitat and will be happiest on the coast where they are subject to wind, salt spray, poor alkaline soil (they grow in acidic soil, too), heat, and drought. They do very well in the Mediterranean-like Pacific coast area. Where plants are borderline hardy, give them a site sheltered from wind. Plants need perfect drainage, so plant on a slope, especially in clay, or in a raised bed for best results. Since they do not respond to heavy pruning, discard plants when they become woody and raise new plants from seed in the spring or from softwood cuttings in the summer. *Cistus* thrive in natural rocky outcrops, rock gardens, at the base of stone walls, and in places where other plants would languish, as in paved areas. Site them where you can enjoy their fragrance.

Cistus 'Peggy Sammons', one of the least hardy (from Zones 8 or 9 to 10), has a bushy, upright form 4–5 ft. (1.2–1.5 m) tall and 4 ft. (1.2 m) wide; oval, gray-green leaves; and white-spotted, purplish pink flowers in profusion. *C. albidus*, a compact form to 6 ft. (1.8 m), is densely hairy, almost white, its flowers rose-pink to lilac with yellow basal spots; *C. albidus* 'Albus' has pure white flowers. *C. crispus*, a hairy, rounded shrub to 2 ft. (0.6 m) tall and 4 ft. (1.2 m) wide, has wavy-edged, veined leaves with purple-red flowers. The cultivar *C.* 'Anne Palmer'

(*C. crispus* × *C. landanifer* subsp. *latifolius*) is rose-pink. One of the most silvery rock roses, *C. incanus*, is 3–5 ft. (1.0–1.5 m) tall and 3–3.5 ft. (1 m) wide, has ovate leaves densely covered with down, and bears purple-pink flowers. *C. incanus* ssp. *corsicus* has flat leaves and densely woolly stems. *C. incanus* subsp. *creticus* has undulate, veined foliage and rose-pink to purple flowers with yellow basal spots. *C. parviflorus* grows to 3 ft. (1 m) and has woolly gray leaves and pink flowers. *C. salvifolius*, sageleaf rock rose, grows to 2 ft. (61 cm), has very hairy young growth, gray-green wrinkled foliage, and white flowers with yellow basal spots. *C. salvifolius* 'Prostratus' is a small-leaved, low-spreading form 1 ft. (0.3 m) tall and 6 ft. (1.8 m) wide. *C.* 'Silver Pink', a real beauty, forms a low mound, 1–2 ft. (0.3–0.6 m) tall and 2 ft. (0.6 m) wide, of narrow, dark gray leaves that show off large, white-centered, silver-pink flowers with prominent golden stamens. *C.* ×*skanbergii*, 2–3 ft. (0.6–1 m) tall and 3–4 ft. (1–1.2 m) wide, has narrowish gray-green leaves, slightly wavy, and bears profuse, pale-pink flowers. All of these are rated hardy from Zones 8 or 9 to 10.

Hardier sorts (to Zone 7) are *Cistus* ×*pulverulentus* (*C. albidus* × *C. crispus*), a dense, low shrub, 2–3 ft. (0.6–1.0 m) tall and 2–3 ft. (0.6–1.0 m) wide, with downy gray, wavy-edged leaves and purple-pink to rose flowers. *C.* 'Sunset' has rose-pink flowers and *C.* 'Warely Rose' is cerise. *C. purpureus*, 4 ft. (1.2 m) tall and wide, has gray-green oblong leaves and dusky purple flowers spotted with chocolate at their base. *C.* 'Betty Taudevin', 4 ft. (1.2 m) tall and wide, has gray-green foliage and deep rose-pink flowers on purplish stems. The hardiest of all, to Zone 6, is *C.* 'Grayswood Pink', 3 ft. (1 m) tall and wide, mound forming, with silvery pink, white-centered flowers.

CONVOLVULUS CNEORUM

Common name: silverbush
Family: Convolvulaceae, morning glory
Description: downy shrub, subshrub
Origin: rocky scree; southern Europe
Site and soil: sun; sharply drained
Height and width: 2–4 ft. (0.6–1.2 m) tall; 3–4 ft. (1.0–1.2 m) wide
Hardiness: Zones 8–10

The silverbush is well named, for the entire plant—compact, round, and bushy—radiates a metallic, shimmering aura from the presence of silky hairs that cover its lance-shaped foliage. Flowers are in the morning glory form, borne in clusters and funnel-shaped to 1.5 in. (3.5 cm) wide, pink in bud, touched with pink in bloom, with yellow centers. When they open in late spring, the foliage is obscured but it returns to center stage after flowers are spent.

Mrs. Underwood observed that some things in life are worth working for, and silverbush is one of them. Like Adelma Simmons, who managed to grow it in her famed silver garden by carrying it over indoors in winter, Mrs. Underwood paid close attention to its needs and tried to mimic them in a garden situation. The first thing to bear in mind is that silverbush grows naturally in limestone rock crevices by the sea. In the garden that translates into a natural rockery—or lacking that, gritty, unenriched soil—Mrs. Underwood's own method was to set young plants between two bricks stood up on end in the soil. Then she filled the gap between them with gritty soil. Wherever it is grown, silverbush cannot abide cold subsoil with even a hint of dampness. Propagation techniques, also closely observed by these silverados, include tip cuttings (with bottom heat, they take up to six weeks to establish roots) and layering in midsummer. Sow seeds in the spring. Some authorities advise pruning plants severely to prevent legginess, but Mrs. Underwood advises pruning with caution; otherwise plants may be irreversibly damaged. This is understandable where silverbush may grow only to 18 in. (46 cm). In warm areas where silverbush feels at home and attains its full growth, less caution is required. Rust and leaf spot result from less than ideal conditions.

CUNNINGHAMIA LANCEOLATA 'GLAUCA'

Common name: blue China fir
Family: Cupressaceae, cypress
Description: waxy tree
Origin: garden
Site and soil: sun or partial shade; moist, well-drained
Height and width: 75 ft. (23 m) tall and 30 ft. (9 m) wide
Hardiness: Zones 6 or 7–9

A blue form of the species that originates in the forests of China, blue China fir is a tall conifer with the looks of an exotic tropical tree. Narrow to broadly upright, conical in shape with a rounded dome, its widespread branches bear ranks of lance-shaped foliage to 3 in. (7.5 cm), somewhat curved and pendulous, of a soft blue with a whitish bloom, with white bands on its undersides. Its ovoid to conical cones are greenish brown, and its shaggy, exfoliating brown bark reveals a red inner bark. It is another conifer that does well in the humid Mid-Atlantic region (U.S. northeast). At the edge of its hardiness range it grows only to 20 ft. (6.1 m) and can be kept even smaller by careful pruning. If cut back to the ground, it sprouts from the trunk, suggesting the possibility of coppicing. Where it is marginally hardy, it should be well protected from wind. If the top of the tree should freeze and die back, look for new growth coming up from its roots. We have heard of a stunning container planting that featured two tubs of blue China fir flanking either side of the doorway of an historic house, creating an effect that was both formal and exotic. Blue China fir is a good substitute for blue spruce (*Picea pungens* var. *glauca*) in areas too warm to grow the latter.

CUPRESSUS

Common name: cypress
Family: Cupressaceae, cypress
Description: waxy tree
Origin: dry hillsides, forest; western, southwestern United States
Site and soil: sun; dry, well-drained
Height: 30–50 ft. (9.1–15.2 m) tall; 12–15 ft. (3.7–4.6 m) wide
Hardiness: Zones 7–9

The word *cypress* brings to mind tall, perfectly straight trees silhouetted against a very blue Mediterranean sky, but cypresses are also native to the American West and Southwest, where they bring their special characteristics to an equally blue, cloudless sky. All are fast-growing, evergreen conifers—in this case, trees characterized by a typical narrow, conical shape, with overlapping, pointed foliage of silver-blue or gray-green, so tightly packed together that twigs resemble braided twine. Resinous glands on the leaves, responsible for foliage fragrance, appear as white specks. Bark is exfoliating, and cones (both male and female on the same tree) are small, round, or spherical. They are ideal for drought conditions, since they do not need supplemental watering once established, but they should be protected from cold, drying winds. Species can be grown from seeds or cuttings. To reproduce cultivars, make root cuttings in late fall or early winter. When perfectly sited and grown in the mild, hot, dry climates of their natural habitat, they have few disease and insect problems. Native cypresses can be grown in the southern and southeastern United States, too, but there they are usually short-lived. Arizona cypress, *Cupressus arizonica*, is important in the Christmas tree trade. In the landscape, native cypresses are arresting single accents, hedges, or silver screens.

The 30 or so cultivars of *Cupressus arizonica*, Arizona cypress, are grouped under *C. arizonica* var. *glabra*, smooth or blue Arizona cypress. Foliage in dense sprays well marked with white resinous glands varies in color from bright silver-blue to silver-gray. Bark exfoliates in purple-red papery layers. Although the majority of cultivars have been developed in Australia and New Zealand, the most outstanding one, *C. arizonica* var. *glabra* 'Carolina Sapphire', was developed in America. Its distinguishing features—a steely blue color; dense, lacy foliage; and a floral aroma between lemon and mint—were recognized in its registration by the RHS in 1987. 'Silver Smoke', another important cultivar in this group, is intensely silver, but the most silvery of all is *C. arizonica* var. *glabra* 'Blue Ice'/'Blue Pyramid'. It is tolerant of wind and cold and reported hardy to Zone 5. Other silver cypresses include *C. arizonica* 'Glauca', whose young foliage is

Cupressus arizonica var. *glabra* 'Blue Ice'.

especially silver-blue; *C. arizonica* var. *nevadensis*, or Piute cypress, from California, with handsome shredding red bark, apparent even on its upper branches, and bright gray-green leaves well dotted with resinous glands; and *C. bakeri*, or modoc cypress, from northern California, which is fast-growing, with a more open habit than most, reddish gray bark, and conspicuous resinous glands on its soft, gray-green foliage. It is reported hardy to Zone 5.

CYCLAMEN
Common name: cyclamen
Family: Primulaceae, primula
Description: tuberous variegated perennial
Origin: scrub, rock crevice, woodland; Mediterranean to Middle East and central Asia
Site and soil: partial shade, shade; dry, well-drained
Height and width: 2–5 in. (5.0–12.5 cm) tall; 4–6 in. (10–15 cm) wide
Hardiness: Zones 5 or 6–9

About 20 species of cyclamen are distributed mainly in the Mediterranean region from southeastern France to northern Turkey. The genus name is based on the Greek *kyklamenos* (circle form), perhaps a reference to the plant's rounded, bun-shaped tuber. These contain saponin and have been used as a form of detergent for millennia. The most well-known cyclamen is the frost-tender *Cyclamen persicum*, grown as a windowsill plant and florists' flower. Several other species are surprisingly hardy and deserve more attention from discerning gardeners and silver lovers. They are characterized by heart- or ivy-shaped foliage, purplish beneath, often beautifully marked or marbled on the surface with gray, silver, or white in various patterns, topped by nodding flowers with flared back petals in the pink to carmine range as well as white. Although individual blooms are small, from 0.25 to 1 in. (0.5 to 2.5 cm), their effect is showy because of their numbers and color. Cyclamen's common name in Hebrew is Solomon's crown, for the flower's resemblance to a king's crown. Elsewhere, the flowers are compared to those of its close relative—shooting star, *Dodecatheon*.

"The hardy cyclamens," proclaimed Dan Hinkley of Heronswood Nursery, "are amongst the chosen that I wish to have consume my garden." The easiest to grow and most adaptable to southern heat and northern cold is *Cyclamen hederifolium/ C. neopolitanum*, baby cyclamen. Its foliage is preserved in the Latin epithet meaning ivy-leaved. It is certainly similar in outline to the leaves of English ivy, *Hedera helix*, but it can be nearly orbicular to heart-shaped, too. Remarkably true to its Mediterranean origins, even when grown in the temperate American Northeast, the plant breaks dormancy in late summer to early fall and remains in active growth until the spring. First the blooms appear—vivid pink with a V-shaped blotch at the base of each petal—followed by foliage, which varies in length from 2 to 6 in. (5 to 15 cm). In harsh winter areas where snow cover occasionally retreats, the foliage clumps reappear, none the worse for their frigid blanket. Fruits freely self-seed, producing many variant patterns on a silver theme, as if each one had been carefully hand-painted by a master craftsman. In such a variable species, it is not surprising to find some more heavily silvered than others. In *C. hederifolium* 'Silver Leaf', the foliage is nearly all silver with a thin green margin, and it largely self-seeds true to type.

Cyclamen coum has smaller, rounder leaves, 1–2.5 in. (2.5–6.5 cm) long, from shiny and unmarked deep green to silvery patterned types. These emerge in the fall, while the flowers bloom in early spring, often through the snow at their range's limit. Flowers are compact, rather blocky in form, in colors from white and pink to carmine shades, each with a white-rimmed mouth. A selection of silvery variants usually called Pewter Group offers a mix of flower colors from white to magenta paired with heavily pewtered foliage edged in dark green.

Ellen Hornig, proprietor of Seneca Hills Perennials in Zones 5–6, says that snow is a big advantage if you want to grow cyclamen in the cooler climates. Without it, you have to be careful to site plants away from winter wind and sun and mulch them with a loose mulch. Experienced growers everywhere agree that cyclamens prosper in a free-draining, sheltered site. In the American Northeast, that is often under a deciduous tree or shrub in well-drained humusy soil (soggy soils send plants to an early death), where plants are encouraged to emerge from dormancy in response to increased light levels as the tree or shrub sheds its leaves in the fall. In our Connecticut garden, where it is planted on a shaded, rocky slope in damp, but very well-drained conditions, *Cyclamen hederifolium* has prospered in the same ground as pulmonaria because the soil is quick-draining. As a bonus, cyclamen flowers in the fall are very pretty against silvered pulmonaria. Ellen says that if you purchase two- or three-year-old potted cyclamens and plant them 6 to 8 in. (15 to 20 cm) apart, they create a gorgeous drift their first year in the garden. A colony usually attains solidity after three or four years, because by then the original plants have become substantial and seedlings appear everywhere, filling in gaps.

Cardoon (*Cynara cardunculus*).

CYNARA

Common name: artichoke thistle
Family: Asteraceae, aster
Description: downy perennial
Origin: stony slopes, grasslands; Mediterranean
Soil and site: sun; moist, fertile, well-drained
Height and width: 6–8 ft. (1.8–2.4 m) tall; 3–4 ft. (1.0–1.2 m) wide
Hardiness: Zones 6 or 7b–10

Two in this genus of ten species are cultivated as ornamentals for their statuesque proportions. Thick, somewhat succulent stems grow up from deep roots to form dense clumps of giant-sized foliage to 3–4 ft. (1–1.2 m) long at the plant's base, diminishing in size as it ascends upward. Bristly in texture, deeply to shallowly lobed, foliage is gray-green above and whitish and woolly beneath. Sweet-scented flowerheads to 5 in. (13 cm) wide resemble giant, bluish purple thistles. When plants bloom in late summer, bees come in droves to harvest nectar.

Cardoon (*Cynara cardunculus*) and globe artichoke (*C. scolymus*) have been eaten for millennia. Globe artichoke, possibly developed from cardoon, has been known since ancient times for its delicious immature flowerheads. Unlike other silvers, these take heat and humidity, a boon in the southeastern United States. Site plants so they are sheltered from strong winds. Where summers are very hot, give them a little shade. Where they are marginally hardy, mulch plants with a thick layer of straw after a hard freeze. In areas where they are perennial, they have become seriously invasive. Gray mold, root rot, and aphids can be problems, mitigated by keeping clumps free of decayed vegetation. Terms like "bold" and "architectural" are often used to describe these giants. Garden visitors are mesmerized by their imposing, hard-to-ignore forms, whether in foliage or in bloom. Standard advice is to leave at least 3 ft. (1 m) between plants, but we can't imagine wanting to grow more than one, which alone provides a singular vertical accent that always elicits surprise and awe. First-year plants are stunning in containers.

Cardoon, grown as an ornamental more often than globe artichoke, produces its stiff, silvered leaves in arching form, like a giant vase, its basal leaves sometimes reaching 3 to 4 ft. (1 to 1.2 m) in length. In full bloom, plants reach 8 ft. (2.4 m) tall. Cardoon tolerates drier conditions than globe thistle. Reports of hardiness vary, but it appears to winter over in the warmest areas of the American Northeast, probably to Zone 6, depending on the site. In Zones 8 and 9 it grows as a short-lived perennial. Globe artichoke, more compact to about 5 ft. (1.5 m), with smoother, less spiny foliage, needs more moisture but will grow in most clay soils. It is hardy from Zones 6 or 7 to 9.

DIANTHUS

Common name: pink
Family: Caryophyllaceae, pink
Description: waxy perennial
Origin: rocky limestone meadows, mountains; Mediterranean, Europe, Asia
Site and soil: sun; sharply drained
Height and width: 3–12 in. (7.5–30.5 cm) tall; 6–18 in. (15–46 cm) wide
Hardiness: Zones 3–9

Pinks have been cultivated for millennia, loved for their perfumed flowers—sweet and spicy—that were once greatly prized for flavoring, as the old name sops-in-wine suggests. While most attention has been lavished on the blooms (the genus name is derived from the Greek for divine flower), when we evaluate pinks for their foliage we discover that the genus offers rich treasures for the silver collector in plants that look good long after their fabled flowers are spent. Most pinks are evergreen with narrow, lance-shaped leaves, from rich green and blue-green to gray-green and silver-blue, on low-lying mats. The dominant species, longest in cultivation, are *Dianthus caryophyllus* (clove pink) and *D. plumarius* (cottage pink). Summer-blooming clove pink, native to the Mediterranean, is characterized by a branching form to 24 in. (62 cm), with narrow, gray-green leaves attached at swollen intervals along wiry stems from a sprawling mat. Flowers—red, pink, or white—are broad-petaled, serrated at their edges, often double, long lasting, and highly perfumed. Cottage pink, from central and southern Europe to the Caucasus, has silvery green, grasslike leaves that grow in wide mats. In late spring or early summer, innumerable stems to 9 in. (23 cm) bear a profusion of jagged-petaled, feathery flowers; single, semidouble, or double; colored in shades of pink and white, sometimes with a darker eye or band; and, like clove pink, powerfully scented. A wealth of hybrids between these two species includes many with especially silver-gray or blue foliage. Also, important groups such as cheddar pinks, bred from *D. gratianopolitanus*, a species that grows wild in Cheddar Gorge in England, as well as diminutive alpines as low as 3 in. (7.5 cm), form tight, silvery mounds or tufts. All sorts have had a prominent place in the silver/gray/white garden genre.

Consider this a partial selection, hardy from Zones 3 to 8 unless noted; then search nurseries and gardens for more. *Dianthus anatolicus*, an alpine 12 in. (30.5 cm) tall and 18 in. (46 cm) wide, has bright, silver-gray needlelike foliage and pale pink flowers; it is rated hardy from Zones 6 to 9. Other alpines include *D. gratianopolitanus* 'Karlik', a form of cheddar pink, with gray foliage and pink, fringed, fragrant flowers in early summer; *D. haematocalyx*, a diminutive cushion plant, 5 in. (12.5 cm) tall and 6 in. (15 cm) wide, from southeastern Europe, with sharply pointed, gray-green foliage and clusters of long-blooming rose flowers from summer to fall; and *D.* 'LaBourboule', one of the most celebrated silver-foliage pinks, and also one of the smallest, forms a tight mound 3 in. (7.5 cm) tall and 6 in. (15 cm) wide, topped by small, fragrant, pink, fringed flowers (there's also a white-flowered form).

Some pinks with good blue-gray foliage are *Dianthus* 'Blue Boy', *D.* 'Little Boy Blue', and *D.* 'Kinsey Blue', about 6 in. (15 cm) tall and 9 in. (23 cm) wide, and good ground covers. *D.* 'Frost Fire' grows well in the U.S. West. Its blue-gray foliage carries a close crown of fragrant, double-red flowers. It is hardy from Zones 4 to 9.

Several antique pinks are choice for their silvery foliage. *Dianthus* 'Bath's Pink', 12 in. (30. 5 cm) tall and wide, is one of the finest representatives of the cheddar pinks, with single fringed, light pink, fragrant blossoms in late spring over silver-blue foliage. It is a good choice for hot, humid conditions. Two pinks much praised by Mrs. Underwood and still popular are *D.* 'Crimson Treasure', with gray-green foliage beneath crimson flowers in spring, on a compact plant 8 in. (20.5 cm) tall and 12 in. (30.5 cm) wide, ideal for rock work; and 'Desmond', a classic double, red, fragrant carnation for the border, regarded as the best red. Its color is intensified by a 12 in. (30.5 cm) mound of very silvery foliage. We don't know the origin of *D.* 'Mars', but it is a striking plant for its diminutive form, to 4 in. (10 cm), ideal for tucking into rocks. It bears semidouble, crimson-maroon flowers, fragrant and long-blooming, over a tight tuffet of silver-blue foliage.

Other pinks combine tolerance of heat and humidity with silver foliage and fragrant flowers, a bonus for gardeners in the U.S. Southeast. *Dianthus* 'Bewitched', a sport of blue-green–leaved 'Firewitch' with powder-blue foliage and heavily fringed, light pink flowers, is hardy from Zones 3 to 9. *D.* 'Greystone', also hardy from Zones 3 to 9, is descended from *D.* 'Bath's Pink' and has been tested in the Juniper Level Botanic Gardens at Plant Delights Nursery for heat and humidity tolerance. 'Greystone' forms a 4 in. (10 cm) wide, tight mound of steel-gray foliage, which sends up heavily fringed, very fragrant, single white flowers. In cool temperatures, flowers have a hint of pink. A special prize should go to *D.* 'Mountain Mist', a repeat-blooming pink (spring and fall) with extraordinarily glistening silver foliage and ruffled, clear pink, lightly fragrant flowers in spring and early summer. It grows 10 in. (25.5 cm) tall and 15 in. (38.0 cm) wide and is hardy with protection from Zones 5 to 8. Tony Avent of Plant Delights Nursery praises 'Mountain Mist' as the most silvery foliaged pink that can be grown in the U.S. Southeast. It also grows well as far south as central Florida, where flowering is sparse because of the absence of winter chilling. Its foliage, however, is not dimmed.

DICHONDRA ARGENTEA
Common name: silver ponyfoot
Family: Convolvulaceae, morning glory
Description: downy perennial ground cover
Origin: dry habitats; southwestern United States
Site and Soil: sun or partial shade; well-drained
Height and width: 3 in. (7.5 cm) tall; 3–6 ft. (1–1.8 m) wide
Hardiness: Zones 7–10

Silver ponyfoot is a silver-leaved species of *Dichondra*, whose natural range extends from west Texas to southeastern Arizona and Mexico. Most often grown as a ground cover, it is a creeping, trailing plant that roots at its leaf nodes, spreading to 6 ft. (1.8 m) in favorable conditions (sufficient moisture and a long growing season). Foliage to 1 in. (2.5 cm) is leathery, rounded, somewhat kidney-shaped (kidneyweed is another common name), and densely covered with tiny hairs pressed very close to the leaf's surface. In the sun, leaves have a metallic sheen, but they are actually soft to the touch, like silk. The charms of this silver ground cover have spread beyond its home ground to nursery plant centers in the American Northeast as well as the pages of mainstream seed catalogs, where it is promoted as a container and window box plant for its trailing habit. A strain marketed as Silver Falls Dichondra is easy to grow from seed. Where Silver Falls is grown as an annual, stem growth may reach 4 ft. (1.2 m) and does not need pinching to encourage branching. Plants are very tolerant of heat and drought, preferring hot, dry growing conditions, and they perform well in partial shade as well as sun. If watered after wilting in prolonged dry spells, they recover fast.

DICLIPTERA SUBERECTA
Common name: hummingbird plant, king's crown
Family: Acanthaceae, acanthus
Description: downy tender perennial
Origin: Uruguay
Site and soil: sun or partial shade; rich, well-drained
Height and width:18 in. (46 cm) tall; 24 in. (61 cm) wide
Hardiness: Zones 7 or 8–11

Dicliptera suberecta, with marguerite daisies in Monet's garden, Giverny, France.

The only species in the genus that is commonly cultivated, *Dicliptera suberecta* is a compact subshrub with striking foliage and flowers in a combination that is hard to top. Lance-shaped, gray-green leaves have a velvety texture. At their tips, upright and angled stems bear double-lipped flowers from rusty to reddish orange with prominent gray-green bracts, in rounded clusters. From spring through summer, hummingbirds come to sip nectar from deep within each bloom, a characteristic preserved in the plant's common name. This is a fast-growing, warm-climate native that thrives in heat, the hotter the better. In common with many tropical and subtropicals, it needs some protection from direct sun. Intrepid gardeners as far north as Zone 7 are learning that they can overwinter subtropicals if the ground does not freeze deeply and if plants are mulched. Woodlanders plant nursery advises its customers in marginally hardy zones to cut back plants after frost kills the tops, and then mound them with a 10 in. (25 cm) layer of coarse sand over their stubs. Mulch over that with straw. In spring, when the weather is steadily warm—and not until then—remove the covering to let new shoots emerge. Indoors, grow *D. suberecta* in bright light but not overexposed to hot sun. Water freely with a balanced liquid fertilizer once a month. Often grown in Zones 9 and warmer, *D. suberecta* is beginning to make waves in various parts of the United States in the wake of intense interest in colorful subtropicals. We first admired it at Caprilands, then in Monet's garden, paired with the finely cut, blue-green foliage of a marguerite daisy, and closer to home at Logee's Greenhouse. Logee's advises customers to grow it outdoors in summer, where it's a great filler plant in the border, or in a potted container where its velvety texture can be appreciated and touched. This is an easily grown exotic bound to gain in popularity.

ECHEVERIA
Common name: hens and chicks
Family: Crassulaceae, stonecrop
Description: waxy succulent
Origin: semi-desert; Texas to Argentina, Mexico
Soil and site; sun or partial shade; dry, gritty, well-drained
Height and width: 6–12 in. (15.0–30.5 cm) tall; 12–16 in. (30.5–40.5 cm) wide
Hardiness: Zones 8–11

Of the 150 species of echeverias, many are of interest to silver aficionados for their frosted green to powder-blue, fleshy foliage covered with a mealy or starch-like coating to protect them from prolonged drought. Growing close to the ground or from a short stem in spiraling, symmetrical rosettes, leaves are linear, cylindrical, spoon-shaped, or broadly triangular, often sharply tipped and tinged reddish at their edges. Flowers on long stems bloom from late winter through summer depending on the type. Their bright color, complemented by silvery rosettes beneath, is usually in the orange-red range. Closely related *Dudleya*, from coastal cliffs and mountainous areas of California and Mexico and once included in the *Echeveria* genus, is quite similar.

Often confused with the hardier *Sempervivum* (also known as hens and chicks), echeverias are frost-tender succulents often grown as indoor potted plants. The genus was named for the 18th-century botanical artist Atanasio Echeverria Codoy. When in bloom, these succulents benefit from occasional thorough watering, but they are otherwise kept dry. Outdoors, most types lose some of their lower leaves in winter. This is a natural condition and helps to prevent excessive moisture gathering in the foliage. Congested rosettes combined with humidity or wet conditions result in death from rot or fungus disease. For indoor houseplant culture, give the plant at least four hours of direct sunlight a day. Where echeverias grow outside all season, consider mixed plantings of succulents and drought-tolerant grasses, as they grow in nature. The interplay among their forms and often brilliant colors is arresting, especially on a dry hillside. Group pots and tubs in a patio or against a stone or brick wall.

One of the most striking echeverias is *Echeveria runyonii*. Growing in an 8 in. (20 cm) wide stemless rosette of spoon-shaped, powdery gray-blue foliage, about 3 in. (7.5 cm) long, it produces coral-pink flowers from spring to summer. The cultivar 'Topsy Turvy' forms a rosette about 8–12 in. (20–30 cm) wide of powdery, gray-blue foliage curled downward at the edges and tips. The species is rated hardy from Zones 8b to 11. The cultivar is hardy from Zones 9b to 11.

Echeveria elegans, Mexican snowball, grows 6–8 in. (15–20 cm) tall and 12–16 in. (30.5–41.0 cm) wide on short stems. Aptly named, its pale gray-green leaves more than 2.5 in. (6.5 cm) long are heavily coated with white powder. Golden-centered, deep-pink flowers bloom from late winter to early summer. The cultivar *E. elegans* 'Kesselringii' forms a rosette of globular, blue-gray foliage. Painted lady echeveria, *E. derenbergii*, is named for its red-tipped, golden-yellow flowers that bloom from late winter to early summer. Plants form rosettes, 6 in. (15 cm) tall and 8–16 in. (20.5–40.5 cm) wide, of rounded, wedge-shaped foliage, intensely frosted light green with red margins, and very thick. *E. gibbiflora* is distinguished by its powdery, pale, bluish green leaves to 14 in. (35.5 cm) in rosettes, 12 in. (30.5 cm) tall and 6 in. (15 cm) wide, on short stems or branches. Flowers in late summer to winter are pale red, yellow inside; *E. gibbiflora* var. *mettalica* has silver-gray foliage with a metallic sheen. Bristle-tipped peacock echeveria, *E. peacockii*, forms a 12 in. (30.5 cm) tall and wide, stemless or short-stemmed dense rosette of red-tipped, heavily frosted, pale blue-gray foliage. Up to 20 soft orange to pink-red flowers bloom in early summer. These are hardy from Zones 9 to 11.

Some of the most striking echeverias are crimped or frilly leaved. *Echeveria* 'Arlie Wright', rated hardy from Zones 9b to 10, is a classic with gray, crinkled, pink-edged foliage. Plants form a 16 in. (40.5 cm) wide rosette. *E.* 'Kirchneriana' has frilly, 4 in. (10 cm) wide, powdery blue-gray foliage with orange-tipped yellow flowers in the spring. The cultivar *E.* 'Lace' is similar but the foliage is frillier. These are rated hardy from Zones 9 to 11.

ECHINOPS

Common name: globe thistle

Family: Asteraceae, aster

Description: downy perennial

Origin: dry grasslands, gravelly habitats; Europe, western Asia

Site and soil: sun; lean, well-drained

Height and width: 3–4 ft. (1–1.2 m) tall; 2–3 ft. (0.6–1 m) wide

Hardiness: Zones 3–8 or 9

The most widely cultivated plants in this genus of about 100 species are similar in appearance. Stiff, stout, silvery stems grow up from a deep taproot. These carry coarse, spiny, lancelike foliage as long as 14 in. (35.5 cm), larger at the base of the plant and usually green and hairy on their upper sides and very downy, nearly white, on their undersides. Long-blooming flowerheads, the plants' glory, are metallic, golf ball–shaped globes of varying size from 2 to 3 in. (5.0 to 7.5 cm) wide, and from gray-white to deep blue, composed of tightly packed, tiny, star-like florets held by bristly bracts. A lot of activity centers around globe thistles when by midsummer their opened blooms waft a sweet scent throughout the landscape, luring bees during the day and moths in the evening in search of nec-tar. The genus name, from the Greek *echinos* (hedgehog), records the plants' dis-tinctive prickly characteristics. In their native habitat, globe thistles grow and thrive in hot, dry conditions, so they are a good choice for coastal sites, but they have proved to be quite adaptable, which helps to explain their enduring popu-larity. Globe thistles can be bothered by crown rot and aphids, but we have not encountered either of these problems. The nomenclature of this genus is a mud-dle. We advise gardeners to visit nurseries and gardens to get an idea of the types available. Cultivars with larger flowers, globes of varying hues, and plants with a more compact habit are available. If nursery plants are raised from seed, the results will always be variable. Taller types are spectacular rising from the center of an island bed or border surrounded by complementary yellow yarrows and early-blooming phlox, a soft note to globe thistle's rigid, upright form. Globe thistle naturalize well among daylilies, which are also good companions in the garden proper.

Echinops ritro, small globe thistle, is the premier globe thistle, from 3 to 4 ft. (1.0 to 1.2 m) tall with metallic bluish globes. *E. ritro* subsp. *ruthenicus* (perhaps a separate species) is even more compact to 3 ft. (1 m) with showier flowers to 2.5 in. (6 cm) wide on pure silver stems clothed in foliage with a silvery sheen. Plants are ornamental in or out of bloom. The quest for blue-flowered globe

flowers, from intensely blue to metallic silver-blue, has given rise to several popular cultivars whose origin is in doubt. Most are ascribed to *E. bannaticus* or *E. ritro*.
The former is described as very similar to *E. ritro*, except that its leaves are hairier,
its flower stems are usually unbranched, and its leaves are more deeply divided.
E. bannaticus 'Blue Globe', to 3 ft. (1 m), has dark blue flowers. *E. bannaticus*
'Taplow Blue' (also ascribed to *E. ritro*) is distinguished by the prolific production
of large, metallic blue flowers, 3 in. (7.5 cm) wide, on 3–5 ft. (1.0–1.5 m) stalks;
E. bannaticus 'Taplow Purple' bears flowers with a violet-blue tinge. Cultivars generally ascribed to *E. ritro* include 'Blue Cloud' to 3 ft. (1 m) with soft, blue flowers; 'Royal Blue', to 2.5 ft. (0.8 m), with metallic blue globes; and the very
popular dark metallic blue 'Veitch's Blue', from 3.0 to 3.5 ft. (1.0–1.1 m).

ELAEAGNUS

Common name: oleaster
Family: Elaeagnaceae, oleaster
Description: downy shrub, tree
Origin: dry places, thickets; Asia, southern Europe, North America
Site and soil: sun; well-drained
Height and width: 6–20 ft. (1.8–6.1 m) tall; 6–20 ft. (1 8–6.1 m) wide
Hardiness: Zones 2–10

A group of incredibly tough, deciduous or nearly evergreen trees and shrubs, the
oleasters are also beautiful silvers. Foliage is usually narrow and willowlike, often
silvery on both sides in their early growth and then dull green above and silver-
white below—their massed effect is intensely silver. Flowers, often insignificant,
fragrant, and bell or tubular in form, are borne in clusters in leaf axils, followed
by edible fruits (especially prized by birds). They are small and oval, like miniature olives, hence the genus name from the Greek *elaeagnos* (wild olive). In some
cultures, trees are cultivated for their sweet/acid fruits or distilled for beverages.
In the United States, their image has been tarnished by invasive species originally
planted as windbreaks. Their seeds, widely dispersed by birds, have spread
oleaster far beyond where it was wanted, along roadsides, at the edges of woodlands, in any unused space where it can take root, crowding out better native
plants. The culprits are variously described as *Elaeagnus umbellata* (autumn olive)
and *E. angustifolia* (Russian olive), but not all authorities agree. Some, like tree and
shrub guru Michael Dirr, single out only autumn olive, whose fruits are especially
tasty to birds. From our Internet search of the USDA Plants Database web site
(see Bibliography), we discovered that along with *E. umbellata*, *E. angustifolia* is

Elaeagnus angustifolia.

listed as a noxious weed in Colorado, New Mexico, and California, and *E. pungens* is listed on exotic plant pest lists in Florida and the U.S. Southeast. Consult the local agricultural extension service to find out which species are invasive in your area, and then make an appropriate choice.

It's not difficult to see why these trees and shrubs are so valued. They take it all—dry soil, drought, coastal winds, salt, extreme cold, and extreme heat—and they fix atmospheric nitrogen in the soil, to boot. They grow in alkaline soil but may become chlorotic in shallow soil conditions. Suckers offer ready-made plants that can be dug up and replanted in spring or fall. Oleasters make fine protective screens, and they can be trimmed to form sparkling hedges, grown as natural espaliers, or used to control erosion on steep banks. They create very effective contrasts to surrounding greenery in a mixed tree and shrub border. We still look forward every year to seeing a full-grown Russian olive tree, planted in a gap by an old stone wall between green-leaved hardwood trees on either side. Its silver crown, wide and glowing among greenery, dominates the scene.

Russian olive, from southern Europe to Asia, was established in the American Northeast in early colonial times and is the most popular oleaster. It is a fine, small tree that usually reaches 20 ft. (6 m) tall and wide of loose, rounded habit, with silver-backed foliage 1–3 in. (2.5–7.5 cm) long, silver-white to yellowish flowers, and silver-yellow fruit. We wondered if our local specimen was sterile since we have never noticed either flowers or fruit, but they are usually hidden by abundant foliage that holds on into winter. Bark, best seen after leaves fall, is dark brown and shredded. Widely planted in the U.S. Midwest along highways because of its tolerance to salts used for de-icing, Russian olive is reported hardy to -50°F (-45°C). But it has its limits: it does not do well in mild winter climates or where summers are cool or very humid.

Elaeagnus commutata, silverberry, is a deciduous shrub native to the western United States, to 12 ft. (3.7 m), with an open, slender form and red branches that become coated with silvery scales. Its oval leaves are silvery gray on both surfaces; even its oval fruits, favorites of birds, are coated in silver. It is a suckering shrub that forms colonies. *E. commutata* 'Coral Silver' is an improved form with bright-gray foliage and coral-red berries.

Less hardy, to Zone 6, is *Elaeagnus ×ebbingei* (*E. macrophylla* × *E. pungens*), distinguished by its upright form, 10–12 ft. (3.0–3.7 m); leaves 2–4 in. (5–10 cm) long, silver on both sides when young and then dark green above, silver beneath; intensely fragrant, waxy silver flowers; and red fruits reported good for jelly. *E. pungens*, from Japan, is less hardy, to Zone 7. A large evergreen shrub of sprawling habit, 6–15 ft. (1.8–4.6 m) tall and wide, its leaves are long, 1–3 in. (2.5–7.5 cm), and gray with wavy edges and brown dots, with a drab-olive effect. But two cultivars are of interest: *E. pungens* 'Fruitlandii' has rich green leaves above and very silvery below, and the foliage of 'Marginata', silver-edge elaeagnus, has silver-white margins that convey a silvery effect.

Elaeagnus 'Quicksilver' is an exciting development in the oleaster line because it is reported to be a sterile hybrid that can be planted without fear of its spreading out of bounds. It is quick-growing, as its name suggests, with silvery shoots that form an open, pyramidal shape to 12 ft. (3.7 m), a fine border plant for juxtaposing with purple-leaved shrubs. It is a study in silver with tapered silvery leaves to 2 in. (5 cm) and yellowish flowers that form from silvery buds. *E.* 'Silverscape' is as tough as they come. A cross between *E. angustifolia* and *E. commutata*, it also bears sterile fruit, is not as suckering as silverberry, and retains the salt and drought resistance of Russian olive.

ELYMUS

Common name: blue wheat grass
Family: Gramineae, grass
Description: waxy perennial
Origin: high elevations; South America
Site and soil: sun or partial shade; sharply drained
Height: 3 ft. (1 m)
Hardiness: Zones 6–9

Elymus magellanicus/Agropyron magellanicum, blue wheat grass, is a spectacular grass native to high elevations in South America. It establishes clumps of striking, silver-blue foliage that grow to 3 ft. (1 m) or more and makes a fine container plant. As Rick Darke observed, other silver-blue grasses like *Festuca glauca* and *Helictotrichon sempervirens* are dull by comparison. In his own garden, he shows the impact of combining foliage textures and forms among plants of similar hue in the silver spectrum. The fine foliage of blue wheat grass, blue oat grass (*Helictotrichon sempervirens*), and *Miscanthus* 'Purpurascens' are played off broad-leaved *Stachys byzantina* 'Big Ears' and tall, woolly *Verbascum bombiciferum* with arresting results. In summer, blue wheat grass produces narrow, silver-blue flowerheads that turn light beige by fall. It is a cool-season grower that resents heat and humidity. In these conditions, offer it light shade to relieve stress. It does well, though, in cool, breezy coastal areas. Look for the cultivars *E. magellanicus* 'Blue Sword' and 'Blue Tango'. Blue wheat grass is hardy from Zones 6 to 9.

ERICA

Common name: heath
Family: Ericaceae, heath
Description: downy shrub
Origin: boggy areas; western Europe from Arctic Circle to southern Spain
Site and soil: sun; moist
Height and width: 8–12 in. (20.5–30.5 cm) tall; 12–18 in. (30.5–45.5 cm) wide
Hardiness: Zones 3–7

Erica tetralix, cross-leaved heath, so-called because of the way its needlelike leaves grow in whorls to form crosses, is one of 700 species in the genus. It is a dwarf, spreading, evergreen shrub of neat, compact habit, distinguished among other heaths by its gray-green, woolly foliage and hardiness. Pale pink flowers, held in short, green calyces, bloom in pendulous terminal clusters prominently displayed from summer to fall. The mouth of the flower is constricted, as if a seamstress had drawn in the flower's edges with a gently gathered thread. Heaths intermingle with heathers in boggier moors or heaths, and like heather, their sweetly scented flowers contribute to the unique flavor of heather honey. The genus name comes from the Greek *eriko* (I break), a reference to the plant's brittle stems. The culture of cross-leaved heath is similar to that of heathers, except it prefers a more moist and peaty soil, acidic if possible, although alkaline soil is tolerated. Where summers are very hot, give plants partial shade.

The most popular silver heath, *Erica tetralix* 'Alba Mollis', was introduced more than 100 years ago. Its virtues, recognized as an RHS AGM, include silver-green, iridescent foliage; pure white flowers; and an extraordinarily long-blooming season, from early summer through autumn. It is an upright form, 8 in. (20.5 cm) tall and 12 in. (30.5 cm) wide, whose ghostly appearance creates a strong highlight wherever it is needed. *E. tetralix* 'Bartinney', 8–10 in. (20.5–25.5 cm) tall and 12–18 in. (30.5–46.0 cm) wide, has especially silver foliage and is early blooming with white flowers. 'Curled Roundstone' is a unique prostrate form for tubs, window boxes, and hanging baskets. It has gray-green foliage on curling stems and pale pink flowers from summer to late fall. *E. tetralix* 'Darleyensis' (not to be confused with the species *E.* ×*darleyensis*), is a small, springy mat, 8 in. (20.5 cm) tall and 18 in. (45.5 cm) wide, of frosty, dull, gray-green foliage above and white wool beneath, enhanced by waxy, salmon-pink bells all summer. 'Dee' grows 8–10 in. (20.5–25.5 cm) tall and 12–18 in. (30.5–46.0 cm) wide, has silver-gray foliage, and long-blooming, white flowers that fade to pale pink. 'Hookstone Pink', to 12 in. (30.5 cm), has very gray-green to silvery leaves and clear pink flowers, an outstanding combination. 'Pink Glow' forms a neat mat of gray-green foliage, 8 in. (20 cm) tall and 24 in. (61 cm) wide, adorned with bright magenta flowers from early summer through autumn.

ERYNGIUM

Common name: sea holly

Family: Apiaceae, parsley

Description: waxy perennial

Origin: dry and rocky to moist grassland; Europe, Mediterranean, eastern United States, central Asia, Middle East

Site and soil: sun; moderately enriched, well-drained

Height and width: 6 in.–6 ft. (15. cm–1.8 m) tall; 12 in.–2 ft. (30.5 cm–0.6 m) wide

Hardiness: Zones 3–9

Eryngiums resemble ornate silver thistles, cut with flair and imagination as if by a devoted tinsmith. Deep, carrotlike taproots send up stiff stems clothed at their base by a rosette of foliage—smooth, shiny green, or gray; rounded or heart-shaped; sometimes deeply toothed and spiny; often prominently veined in silver-white. The tinsmith's art is most apparent in the production of thistle-shaped flowers surrounded by a ruff of intricate silvery bracts. As the steel blue, violet, or ivory flowerheads mature by midsummer to late summer, their color gains in metallic intensity, giving the entire head a glistening quality. Mature plants glisten and gleam like well-polished ornaments. Better known in the ancient world as *eryngo*, *Eryngium plenum* and *E. maritimum* were once used in preparations as a general restorative and to help break up kidney stones. The genus name is said to be based on the Greek word for thistle; the common name is based on *E. maritimum*, which grows near the sea. Plants grow best in deep soil, from loamy or sandy to clay. Site plants with care since their taproots, while fine for seeking moisture in drought times, are difficult to dig up. Of the 200 species in the genus, only a handful is cultivated. In North America, the best known is *E. giganteum*, a fabulous accent plant often called Miss Willmott's Ghost. This is not a cultivar name but a synonym for the species itself, based on the story that Ellen Willmott, a well-known early 1900s English gardener, was fond of dropping seeds in gardens where she did not see plants already growing. It is an outstanding species, 4–6 ft. (1.2–1.8 m) tall, with 4 in. (10 cm) wide ivory-white heads. Native from the Caucasus to Iran, it may grow as an annual, biennial, or perennial depending on circumstances. Cut back flowers before they set seed to prolong life. Plants die after seeding, but they usually leave progeny behind. It is hardy from Zones 4 to 7.

Eryngium yuccifolium, rattlesnake master, is native to the eastern United States in prairie and woodland-edge habitats. It is gaining attention for its adaptability to growing conditions from dry to moist (it even survives short periods of flood-

Eryngium giganteum, Miss Willmott's Ghost.

ing) and for its unusual form. Grown as much for its striking yuccalike, gray-green foliage as for its bell-shaped clusters of cream-white flowerheads, it does best in well-drained loamy or clay soil. Tolerant of both heat and drought, it is a fine candidate for a prairie planting of native wildflowers and grasses. Plants form a knee-high clump of foliage with flowering stems that may reach 6 ft. (1.8 m) by midsummer. Its common name records its use by American Indians for treating snakebite.

Our favorable experience with *Eryngium amethystinum*, amethyst sea holly, encouraged us to explore other lesser known eryngiums. This European species, hardy from Zones 2 to 8, is very upright to about 2.5 ft. (0.8 m), branching near its top to carry many small, metallic-blue flowers 0.25 in. (0.75 cm) wide. While its basal foliage is smooth and green, the plant in bloom is undeniably silvery. We found this transformation intriguing and began to look for other such gems. Some of the best are *E. alpinum*, alpine sea holly, a European species hardy from Zones 4 to 7, with heart-shaped, green foliage and silver-blue flowers, that grows 1–3 ft. (0.3–1.0 m) tall. Its cultivars include light blue-flowered 'Amethyst' (very metallic); large-flowered, lavender-blue 'Blue Star'; 'Opal', a beautiful silvery-blue; and 'Superbum', a vigorous cultivar with extra-large, dark blue flowers. The species and cultivars bloom in early summer, about a month before other types. Both 'Blue Star' and 'Superbum' come true from seed.

Eryngium bourgatii, Mediterranean sea holly, is native to the Pyrenees. It grows 12 in. (30.5 cm) tall and 12–18 in. (30.5–46.0 cm) wide and is small enough to use effectively in a rock garden. It has coarse, spiny, white-veined, dark green, palmate foliage and metallic purple-blue thistle flowers, 8–10 in. (20–25 cm) tall, surrounded by numerous silver bracts, borne on silvery stems. 'Oxford Blue' has silvery blue flowers. Both are hardy from Zones 5 to 7.

EUCALYPTUS

Common name: gum tree
Family: Myrtaceae, myrtle
Description: waxy tree or shrub
Origin: mountainous regions; Australia, Tasmania
Soil and site: sun; well-drained
Height and width: 6–100 ft. (1.8–30.5 m) tall; 10–40 ft. (3.0–12.2 m) wide
Hardiness: Zones 7–11

Eucalyptus belongs to a large genus of more than 500 vigorous trees and shrubs from the Southern Hemisphere, all but a few of them from Australia. From a sil-ver-fancier's perspective, they offer intriguing variants on a silver theme from white-blue to blue-gray, arresting not only for their foliage, but for their hand-some flaking bark and flowers in showy umbels of cream-white to red, striking pods, and often pendulous habit. Eucalyptus leaves are packed with oils that have a long history of use in perfumery and medicine, while the leaves themselves are sought for fresh and dried bouquets and crafts. Leaf aroma, according to type, smells like peppermint, lemon, honey, or apple, but the characteristic eucalyptus scent, the one we associate with the gum tree, is a combination of all of these with a dash of camphor. Most eucalyptus are giants, soaring as high as 250 ft. (76 m), but since they are amenable to cutting back and pruning, they are often cultivated as shorter trees, standards, bushy shrubs, and even container plants. In many species, as untrimmed silvery trees mature, their round and opposite young foliage is transformed both in appearance and shape to elongated, green, and alternate. To maintain their silvery appearance, trees are coppiced by cutting them back nearly to the ground, or to within two or three buds at their base, causing them to produce numerous shoots bearing juvenile leaves; then they are fed with rotted manure or compost and well mulched. Eucalyptus is also amenable to pollarding, cutting branches to the trunk to encourage small shoot growth and produce a shorter tree with a dense, radiant crown. Standards are raised to a single bare stem, usually no taller than 6 ft. (1.8 m), or to a half-standard, from 3 to 4 ft. (0.9 to 1.2 m) tall.

Although many eucalyptus are frost tender from Zones 8 to 10, some species are remarkably hardy (not surprising considering their provenance in cool, even snowy, mountainous areas). These can be brought through the winter in Zone 7, some even in Zone 6, if planted in a sheltered spot and heavily mulched. Fortunately for the gardener in cooler climates, eucalyptus grows very fast from seed and an increasing number of species are grown as annuals. Beware that when cultivated in encouraging conditions, eucalyptus grow at a phenomenal rate, from 6 to 12 ft. (1.8 to 3.7 m) a season or more, and it quickly become rootbound when grown in pots (roots spiral around and pots tip over). Experienced eucalyptus grower Sean I Iogan advises discarding such plants since they never recover. He advises planting out smaller potted plants that will actually grow faster than larger, potbound plants. For pot culture, root prune when potting up, move to a large tub, and fertilize often since roots take up a lot of nutrients. Untrimmed or pollarded trees are magnificent accents, bushy forms can be incorporated into beds and borders, and container-grown eucalyptus are very handsome.

Commonly grown in the American Northeast as a bushy annual from 3 to 6 ft. (1.0 to 1.8 m) in a single season as a tree, *Eucalyptus cinerea*, or silver dollar gum, has a broad, irregular growth from 20 to 50 ft. (6.2 to 15.2 m). Silver dollar gum is fast growing, and it withstands wind and drought. It will put up with poor soil and hot summers, but it does not like lime or salty soil. Although rated hardy to Zone 9, Mark Weathington at the Norfolk Botanical Garden in Zone 8a says if it makes it through its first winter, it will grow as a perennial. It is one of the hardier eucalyptus, surviving 14°F (-10°C). Where they are marginally hardy, overwinter in containers, first cutting back specimens severely by stooling. The dauntless Adelma Simmons overwintered hers in her Connecticut greenhouse so it could be featured as a tree in her silver Piper's Garden. Silver dollar gum foliage is choice for fresh or dried crafts and is hardy from Zones 7 or 8 to 10.

One of the first eucalyptus to be cultivated for its beautiful foliage, *Eucalyptus cordata*, heart-leaved silver gum, 10–69 ft. (3–21 m), grows naturally near marshy flats or on steep, wet slopes in Tasmania, so it needs moist rather than dry soil conditions. A study in gray, its branches to the ground and rounded, wavy-edged foliage are gray, but in contrast, buds and fruits are quite white. Recommended for pruning, coppicing, and tub culture, it is hardy to Zone 8.

Broadly conical in shape, Tingiringi gum, *Eucalyptus glaucescens*, to 30 ft. (9.1 m), has round, blue-white juvenile leaves that become lance-shaped and blue-gray in maturity. Striking as a mature specimen tree with its dangly leaves against an almost white trunk (it sheds red flakes), it has been described as sensational, quickly growing to 30 ft. (9.1 m) in a season in the American Northwest. Its white flowers bloom in autumn. It is hardy from Zones 8 or 9 to 10.

In maturity, *Eucalyptus globulus*, Tasmanian blue gum, 50–160 ft. (15–50 m) tall and 30–80 ft. (9.3–24.4 m) wide, is a dense, spreading tree, the most commonly grown eucalyptus in California. It has creamy bark that sheds in strips to reveal light green inner bark, and cream-white flowers bloom from spring to summer. In maturity, foliage changes from oval and blue-white to deep green and lance-shaped, so trees can be coppiced to produce a new crop of leaves. Planting in deep soil produces best results. Extracted oils are used for cough drops. It is hardy from Zones 9 to 10.

Long popular in Europe, cider gum, *Eucalyptus gunnii*, is gaining favor in North America as a very ornamental and hardy eucalyptus. Its steel-blue, rounded foliage, half the size of *E. cinerea*, is red-tipped, becoming lance-shaped and a dull blue-gray in maturity when trees reach 100 ft. (30.5 m) tall and 40 ft. (12.2 m) wide. Mrs. Underwood's method for maintaining cider gum as a 3 ft. (1 m) bush was to lop off its top when it reached 5 ft. (1.5 m), then cut back side branches (which she used in floral arrangements) as they grew. It prefers moist soil conditions. A cultivar, 'Silver Drop', has silver-green leaves and is said to grow only to 24 to 36 in. (61 cm to 1 m). Cider gum is hardy from Zones 7 or 8 to 10 or 11. At the limit of its hardiness range, try wrapping the trunk with straw during the winter.

A very wide-spreading silver-gray shrub with smooth, gray bark that sheds to pinkish-red, *Eucalyptus macrocarpa*, mottlecah, grows only 6–12 ft. (1.8–3.7 m) tall and 10–40 ft. (3.0–12.2 m) wide. Its low form is striking for its white buds, deep red flowers with gold tips, and extraordinarily ornamental pods, 2 in. (5 cm) wide and woody, often dried for crafts. Both juvenile and adult foliage is ovate and silvery, so it doesn't need coppicing to produce new foliage, but it does require pruning to contain its sprawl. It is hardy from Zones 10 to 11.

Dense and wide, 40 ft. (12.2 m) tall and wide, with smooth, whitish gray or pale brown bark, *Eucalyptus paucifolia*—cabbage gum, weeping gum, or ghost gum—has gray-green, oval juvenile leaves and narrow, pendant, and lustrous blue-green adult leaves. Creamy flowers are produced in late spring or summer. It tolerates wet to dry soil. It is hardy from Zones 9 to 10. *E. pauciflora* subsp. *niphophila*/*E. niphophila*, alpine snow gum, has been called a gem among trees. It is very desirable for its hardiness, its silver-blue foliage, its twigs covered in a waxy white bloom, and its relatively small stature, a mere 20 ft. (6.1 m), as well as its wind tolerance. It is a good choice for slopes and hardy from Zones 7 to 10.

Eucalyptus pulverulenta, silver-leaved mountain gum or powdered gum, is an exceptional eucalyptus in an all-white ensemble of meal-covered rounded leaves, flower buds, and fruits (a characteristic preserved in its Latin epithet, meaning powdered), and smooth white bark. In temperate climates, it grows to 30 ft. (9.1 m) if left uncoppiced, but it should be cut back to maintain juvenile foliage and to correct its irregular, sprawling form. Its foliage is recommended for using fresh or dried. It is hardy from Zones 9 to 10.

EUPHORBIA

Common name: spurge
Family: Euphorbiaceae, spurge
Description: waxy perennial, shrub
Origin: dry regions; Mediterranean, Europe, Africa, Asia
Site and soil: sun or partial shade; light, well-drained
Height and width: 4 in.–4 ft. (10.2 cm–1.2 m) tall; 12 in.–4 ft. (30.5 cm–1.2 m) wide
Hardiness: Zones 4–10

This large genus of about 2000 species includes succulent, cactuslike types as well as the upright and prostrate perennials and shrubs discussed here. Some of these have closely set, succulent, gray-green foliage and striking, clustered flowering heads that bloom from late winter to early summer in temperate climates. The individual flowers are known as *cyathia*. These are small, often bright yellow or yellow-green, and sport dark purple, even black nectar glands that look like eyes, the whole surrounded by colorful, long-lasting, cupped bracts. Even when not in flower, euphorbias, especially the large and shrubby sort, have a strong presence, enhanced by their grayish foliage and colorful bracts. All euphorbias contain a caustic milky sap, so beware when handling them. Depending on their provenance and type, euphorbias are either quite drought resistant or require moderate watering. Generally, the ones described here get along with little water. Shrubby euphor-

Euphorbia myrsinites.

bias are ideal for combining with Mediterranean flora, such as lavenders and rose-mary, and with native salvias that thrive in warm, dry summer regions.

Euphorbia myrsinites, donkey tail, is a very willing plant. Although considered a pernicious weed in the dry U.S. West, it poses no problems elsewhere. Plants grow from 4 to 10 in. (10 to 25 cm) tall and 20 to 24 in. (51 to 61 cm) wide on sprawling, snakelike, woody stems clothed in fleshy, oval, blue-gray leaves to 4 in. (10 cm) long in whorls. In spring, terminal clusters of bright green cyathia held by electric greenish yellow bracts make a long-lasting, splashy show, while the foliage looks good all season. In our Connecticut garden, we planted it in a wall, where it keeps its color all winter. Although short-lived, it ensures its sur-vival by self-seeding. *E. myrsinites* is rated hardy from Zones 6 to 10 but makes it through our frigid Zone 4 winters. In these conditions, good, light soil and per-fect drainage is vital. Native to dry, rocky areas from Portugal to Syria, *E. rigida/ E. biglandulosa* is a subshrub 12–24 in. (30.5–61.0 cm) tall, similar to an erect ver-sion of donkey spurge. Its upcurving stems, clothed with stiff, fleshy, gray-green leaves, are topped in early summer with bright yellow cyathia in cupped, yellow bracts. It is rated hardy from Zones 7 to 10.

Some of the best shrubby euphorbias with grayish blue foliage are allied to *Euphorbia characius*, a perennial subshrub from the Mediterranean region and southern Europe. In its native habitat it grows 6 ft. (1.8 m) tall and 5 ft. (1.5 m) wide, but some selected forms, based on the species's variable nature, are shorter. The cultivar 'Portuguese Velvet' is a compact plant whose gray leaves are covered with silvery down, very soft to the touch. Cylindrical flowerheads, green spotted black, bloom in mid-spring. Plants grow 24–30 in. (61–76 cm) tall and 24 in. (61 cm) wide and do well in full sun to light shade. *E. characias* subsp. *wulfenii* grows on erect stems thickly covered with narrow, bluish gray leaves. By spring, shrubby plants are embellished with cylindrical yellow flowerheads. They are very tough and drought-resistant but prefer some shade in a hot, dry climate. Plants grow 3–4 ft. (1–1.2 m) tall and 3 ft. (1 m) wide and are hardy to 5°F (15°C). The hybrid *E.* 'Cherokee' was selected by Canyon Creek Nursery, located in the foothills of the Cascade Range and the Sierra Nevada, where shrubby euphor-bias thrive. It is a robust plant to 4 ft. (1.2 m), with gray-green foliage lightly tinted bronze, which are blushed purple by fall. It carries large, yellow-green flowerheads, each flower marked by a dark eye. All of these are reliably hardy from Zones 7 to 10.

EURYOPS

Family: Asteraceae, aster
Description. downy shrub
Origin: stony, rocky mountains; South Africa
Soil and site; sun; moderately fertile, well-drained
Height and width: 12 in.–3 ft. (30.5 cm–1.0 m) tall; 18 in.–3 ft. (45.7 cm–1.0 m)
    wide
Hardiness: Zones 7–10

Of the 100 or so species, 2 are generally in cultivation: the shrublet *Euryops acraeus/E. evansii*, 12–18 in. (30.5–46 cm) tall and 18 in. (46 cm) wide, and the more robust *E. pectinatus*, to 3 ft. (1 m) or larger, tall and wide. They are grown for their narrow, linear, or deeply cut, silvery foliage combined with long-bloom-ing yellow daisy flowers that start to open in the spring. Where the climate is favorable, they are seldom out of bloom. Native to dry, rocky, mountainous areas, they are undemanding and rewarding. The genus name, derived from the Greek *eu* (well) and *ops* (appearance) tells it all. These are handsome silver shrubs.

Native to high-country heathland, *Euryops acraeus* is short-lived in damp cli-mates. It is an ideal alpine for a rockery or rock garden. Its pale blue-gray leaves to 1.25 in. (3 cm) long are toothed at their tip and inrolled at their edges. Its deep yellow daisies bloom from spring through summer in temperate climates,

Euryops pectinatus.

and it is hardy from Zones 7 to 9. Less widely known than *E. pectinatus*, it deserves attention. First collected in 1951, it was grown in England as *E. evansii* even before it was described in the literature in 1961.

Euryops pectinatus, golden daisy bush, is a popular landscaping plant in California, valued for its attractive, very finely cut, silver-gray foliage; long-blooming bright yellow flowers; and low maintenance. In its native habitat, it is found growing in rock crevices and fissures on sandstone formations. Adelma Simmons, always innovative, featured *E. pectinatus* in her silver gardens and over-wintered plants in her greenhouse. Its leaves, she said, were more furry in direct sun. "When a plant of some size is needed," she advised in *The Silver Garden*, "it pays to winter over this eventual giant" and trim it back before it goes into the garden in spring. It is a great background plant, filler shrub, or medium-tall screen, hardy from Zones 8 or 9 to 11.

Festuca glauca.

FESTUCA

Common name: fescue

Family: Poaceae, grass

Description: waxy perennial

Origin: woodlands, rocky slopes, grasslands, open meadows; North America, Europe

Site and soil: sun; well-drained soil, light to heavy, acidic to alkaline

Height and width: 4–18 in. tall; 8–15 in. wide

Hardiness: Zones 4–9 or 10

Festuca glauca, blue fescue, is a warm-season grass that originates in European and North American grasslands and open meadows. As with other grasses, its nomenclature is in a confused state. Plants are sold also as *F. ovina* var. *glauca*, *F. cinerea*, and *F. cinerea* var. *glauca*. Even before the grass revolution, it enjoyed popularity for its stiff, needlelike, silvery blue leaves; easily integrated low form for border or rock work; and adaptability. Mounds grow about 12 in. (30.5 cm) tall and 8 in. (20.5 cm) wide. Flowers in panicles of flattened spikelets bloom from spring through summer and range in color from tannish to steel-blue. It is one of the easiest grasses to grow and thrives in nearly any well-drained soil from light to heavy, acidic to alkaline. It does not do well, however, in high heat combined with humidity or in climates of high summer rainfall. In these conditions, good drainage is essential. Blue fescue retains its best color in cool, dry, intensely sunny weather. Although it is drought-tolerant, it does best with a little moisture. Plants tend to die out in the center after a few years unless divided.

With the introduction of many new cultivars, especially from Europe, the old blue fescue has taken on a new look that is more silvery and blue than the variable seed-grown species. Our favorite is *Festuca glauca* 'Elijah Blue', a heat-resistant cultivar that keeps its powder-blue foliage looking good all summer. Plants form spiky, 10 in. (25.5 cm) mounds and produce gray-green flowers that hover over foliage on strong, thin, blue stems in early summer. European introductions include soft blue 'Blaufink' (blue finch), to 10 in. (25.5 cm). 'Blaufuchs' (blue fox), to 12 in. (30.5 cm), is very blue. 'Blauglut' (blue glow), to 10 in. (25.5 cm), is electric blue—a medium, shimmering blue. 'Blausilber' (blue silver), one of the finest, is 8 in. (20.5 cm) tall and so silvery that no green undertones are present unless you rub the leaf vigorously. 'Fruhlingsblau' (spring blue), the same height, is light blue. 'Solling' is silver-gray. Another noteworthy European native, *Festuca valesiaca* var. *glaucantha*, is the source for 'Silbersee' (silver sea), a dwarf compact cultivar to 4 in. (10 cm), with very fine, silvery blue foliage. It is rated hardy from Zones 4 to 7. All the others are hardy from Zones 4 to 9 or 10.

Among native fescues, one of the most ornamental and long-lived is the western *Festuca idahoensis*, blue bunch grass, 14–18 in. (35.5–46.0 cm) tall and 12–15 in. (30.5–38.0 cm) wide. Numerous tan flower spikes appear in the spring. Native to open woods and rocky slopes from British Columbia to Alberta, and south to central California and Colorado, it resists drought, wind, and deer. Its densely tufted foliage varies from blue-green to silver-blue and is similar to blue fescue, but plants are longer lived and more tolerant of wet winter soils. *F. idahoensis* 'Siskiyou Blue' is an especially silvery blue variant. This is a great plant for dry gardens in the U.S. West or perhaps containers, and it is hardy from Zones 5 to 9.

GAZANIA

Common name: treasure flower
Family: Asteraceae, aster
Description: downy annual, perennial
Origin: garden
Site and soil: sun; light, well-drained
Height and width: 8–10 in. (20.5–25.5 cm) tall and wide
Hardiness: 8–10

Gazanias are sun-loving members of the vast family Asteraceae, native to South Africa and known for their large, exotically colored daisy flowers and (in some types) silvery foliage. The cultivars or seed strains sold today are the result of intensive breeding to improve the original rather lanky, orange-flowered perennial that opened with the sun and closed at night and at the slightest hint of cool or cloudy weather (a survival mechanism to protect the plant's pollen from rain). Their increasing popularity shows that breeders are on the right track. Thick, glossy, dark green leaves, downy beneath or felty silver-gray on both sides, and linear to deeply lobed, form a compact, arching, circular clump (some types are trailing). Long stems hold wide, brilliantly colored, solitary daisies, from 3 to 4 in. (7.5 to 10.0 cm) wide or wider, with large yellow or dark centers, often ringed and striped in contrasting colors. Depending on the climate, flowers open from spring to frost in shades of red—from pink to rust—and orange, bronze, yellow, cream, and white. The genus is named for a monk, Theodore of Gaza, who translated the botanical works of Theophrastus into Latin in the 15th century. Gazanias are tough plants, immune to drought, heat, wind, salt spray, and most pests and diseases except for powdery mildew and crown rot. They thrive in dry climates and high summer temperatures, although the new hybrids are more adaptable to changing conditions, even occasional cool and wet periods. The new wave of gazanias, improved to remain open longer, offer a long season of splashy flower display and all-season silver foliage interest. Grow them in containers, as an edger, massed in borders, in rock gardens, or in dry wall plantings, especially in a dry or seaside garden.

The best silver gazanias are derived from *Gazania rigens/G. splendens*. The recently introduced Talent Series is the most silvery leaved of all gazanias. It combines large, crisp daisies in shades of white, yellow, orange, and rose. Even when the blooms close—and they remain partially open on a cool, rainy day—the foliage remains an attractive silvery clump. A few other strains are worth growing for their combination of silver foliage with exotically colored flowers. The earlier strain, Carnival Hybrids, is similar to the Talent Series but less compact. The Mini-star Hybrids, with darker spots at the petal bases and some zoning, are also dwarf, like the Talent Series. The hybrids are about 4–6 in. (10–15 cm) tall and 20 in. (51 cm) wide. Look for the Chansonette, Daybreak, Mini-star, and Talent Series: G. 'Aztec', shading to purple-brown toward the center; G. 'Cookei', burnt-orange petals shading to taupe toward the center; and G. 'Cream Dream', cream rays, are green at their base. The Sunshine Giant Hybrids are named for their huge daisies—4–5 in. (10.0–12.5 cm) wide, in shades of yellow, cream, orange, rose, and red in single and bicolors.

HELIANTHEMUM

Common name: sun rose
Family: Cistaceae, rock rose
Description: downy shrub
Origin: Mediterranean, Asia Minor
Site and soil: sun; low fertility, sandy, gravelly, neutral to alkaline, sharply drained
Height and width: 6–10 in. (15.2–25.4 cm) tall; 18 in. (45.7 cm) wide
Hardiness: Zones 4 or 5–10

In a genus of 110 species, sun rose is variously described as a shrub, shrublet, or subshrub. It is a woody, low-growing plant with green or gray-green, evergreen linear foliage to 1 in. (2.5 cm) long on a sprawling mound firmly anchored by a deep taproot. Flowers, to 1 in. (2.5 cm) wide, produced in racemes are, as the common name suggests, roselike, composed of five silky petals surrounding bushy, golden stamens. Although fleeting, new flowers open every day over a period of weeks from late spring through midsummer. Interspecific hybrids offer flowers in luscious colors, including clear pink, rose, bright red, apricot, salmon, peach, and white over silvered foliage, an irresistible combination. The genus name comes from the Greek for sun flower, a reference to sun rose's affinity for growing in sunny, exposed conditions. If you have a suitable hot, dry spot, plant sun roses. Winter mulch plants in windy sites and where winters are harsh. Hardiness depends very much on a favorable microclimate, which means superior drainage and sunny conditions, not too exposed to wind. Sun roses are a ideal plants among rocks, in a rock garden or natural rocky outcrop, cascading over a stone wall, established as a ground cover on a sunny bank, or at the front of an herbaceous border.

The hardy silver species is *Helianthemum appennium*, a spreading, loosely mat-forming shrub 16 in. (40.5 cm) tall and 24 in. (61 cm) wide, found naturally in

Helianthemum 'Rhodanthe Carneum'/ H. 'Wisley Pink' with Perovskia atriplicifolia.

mountainous areas of Turkey and southern Europe, with downy stems, light gray to whitish foliage, and sparse white flowers with conspicuous yellow stamens. Also, *H. nummularium* 'Mutabile', from southern Europe, North Africa, and Asia Minor, with gray-green foliage, and loose corymbs of pink or yellow flowers, is reported to be easy to grow from seed and may be overwintered with protection in Zone 3.

Less hardy but more colorful are the hybrids from these species and *Helianthemum croceus*: *H.* 'Cheviot' has peach-colored flowers over pearly gray foliage on plants 10 in. (25.5 cm) tall and 18 in. (46 cm) wide. 'Fire Dragon'/'Mrs. Clay', 8–12 in. (20.3–30.5 cm) tall and 18 in. (46 cm) wide, has vivid, orange-red flowers that complement a spreading gray-green mat. 'Henfield

Brilliant', 10 in. (25.4 cm) tall and 18 in. (46 cm) wide, is similar, with silver-green foliage and orange-red flowers. 'Rose of Leeswood', 8 in. (20.3 cm) tall and 18 in. (46 cm) wide, is distinguished by its soft, double-pink flowers over a mound of gray-green leaves. 'Rhodanthe Carneum'/'Wisley Pink', the most popular cultivar, forms a tight silvery mound, 12 in. (30.5 cm) tall and wide, enhanced by rose-pink flowers. 'Wisley Primrose', 12 in. (30.5 cm) tall and 18 in. (46 cm) wide, forms a soft gray carpet of large-petaled primrose-yellow flowers with deep golden centers.

HELICHRYSUM

Common name: everlasting flower
Family: Asteraceae, aster
Description: downy perennial, subshrub
Origin: rocky, mountainous; Mediterranean regions, Africa, Turkestan
Site and soil: sun or partial shade; dry to moist, neutral to alkaline, well-drained
Height and width: 2–20 in. (5–51 cm) tall; 16 in.–6 ft. (40.5 cm–1.8 m) wide
Hardiness: Zones 5–11

The widely distributed helichrysums are a treasure trove of silvers, since so many of the species are protected from hot, dry conditions by a coat of white wool on their stems and foliage. The majority of these are designed around a common theme that combines plentiful but small silvery foliage with dense clusters of button flowers in the yellow range, from soft cream to bright and brassy. Forms vary from mounding and bushy to trailing. Where they are frost-hardy, their spread can reach 6 ft. (1.8 m) across. Several species have a fragrance reminiscent of Indian curry, but their foliage has a bitter flavor and should never be used in cooking. The genus name from the Greek *helos* (sun) and *chrysos* (everlasting) is a reference to the plants' sun-loving, long-lasting flowers. The silver helichrysums need protection from cold, drying winds and wet or damp conditions at the plants' crowns. Hardy types are more adaptable; tender ones are similar to rosemary in their growing requirements. Depending on type, the silver helichrysums are striking additions to the rock garden, border, container, and window box.

Helichrysum thianschanicum, silver everlasting, from Turkestan is easy to grow in full sun, in soils from dry to moist, and it is hardy from Zones 5 to 11. It grows to about 16 in. (40.5 cm) tall and wide, creeping along the ground until mid-summer to late summer, when it produces small, golden flowers in 3 in. (7.5 cm) clusters. According to the late herb authority Gertrude Foster, old herbals referred to the species as "goldilocks." You may find it described as 'Golden Baby' in catalogs and plant nurseries. *H. thianschanicum* 'Icicles', with long, very slender leaves of bright silver, is 10–16 in. (25–40.5 cm) tall and great in containers as a fine-textured contrast with bolder forms.

The most widely (and easily) grown tender helichrysum is *Helichrysum petiolare/petiolatum*, commonly known as the licorice plant for the aroma produced by rubbing a leaf. A woody-based shrub from South Africa, 20 in. (50.8 cm) tall with a spread of up to 6 ft. (1.8 m), it used to be grown primarily in greenhouses and conservatories until it was marketed as an annual for containers and hanging baskets, where its white, woolly, trailing foliage to 1.5 in. (4 cm) complements bright annuals (its insignificant off-white flowers rarely bloom in the American Northeast). In the garden proper, it is a very effective edger, a bright foil to thread through hot and cool colors. Hardy only from Zones 10 to 11, most gardeners let it die back after several hard frosts, but it is easy to propagate and overwinter indoors from late-summer cuttings. Even in our Zone 4 Adirondack garden, *H. petiolare* benefits from some shade. In warm weather it grows with astonishing vigor and will not be cramped by other plants. It simply overtakes them unless pruned back or given more space. Tom Cooper described to us how Christopher Lloyd turns the vigor of *H. petiolare* to advantage by turning it into a standard form in his Great Dixter garden. He trains one main stem up a bamboo stake about 3 ft. (1 m) tall in the center of the pot. As it grows, Lloyd keeps tying the main stem to the stake. The plant sends whirls of branches that weave out into the air and among the tops of an assortment of plants at its base. In this ingenious treatment, the standard becomes the superstructure, with lower plants at the pot's rim.

A dwarf, small-leaved version often marketed as *Helichrysum petiolare minus*, *H. petiolare* 'Minus', or *H. petiolare* 'Petite Licorice' has been reclassified as *Plecostachys serpyllifolia*. An especially attractive form is sold as *H. petiolare minus* 'Silver Mist'. It is well-branched with lilting stems and round to oval, well-silvered foliage, 0.25 in. (0.5 cm) long. Plants grow 6–8 in. (15.2–20.3 cm) tall and 18 in. (46 cm) wide. Unlike vegetatively propagated plants, this seed-grown strain never needs pinching to look its best. In common with *H. petiolare*, 'Silver Mist' does not take on its most intense silvery coloring until high summer when the sun is brightest. Although we have never experienced disease or insect problems with these helichrysums, they are subject to leaf miners and to rot when butterfly larvae dine on them. When this happens, we cut the plant back and it regrows.

In the hills of Tuscany, the air is redolent with the aroma of *Helichrysum italicum*, which smells like thyme and curry combined. Described in John Gerard's *Herbal* (1597), it is hardy from Zones 7 or 8 to 9. Its nomenclature is difficult to untangle. According to some authorities, synonyms include *H. angustifolium*, *H. microcephalum*, and *H. serotinum*. The RHS Index of Garden Plants lists the latter as *H. italicum* subsp. *serotinum*. For gardeners, it's necessary only to keep in mind that two forms exist, the species and the subspecies, a larger plant and a smaller version. The species *H. italicum*, from dry, sandy grasslands in the Mediterranean region, is a slow-growing, dwarf subshrub, 18–24 in. (45.7–61.0 cm) tall, that can spread to nearly 3 ft. (1 m) under optimum conditions. It has narrow, silver-gray, woolly leaves nearly 2 in. (5 cm) long and virtually stemless, bright yellow flowers in dense clusters by summer. It is very aromatic and will grow in any sunny site in well-drained, light soil, from acidic to alkaline, from dry to moist if it is well-drained. Plants should be regularly pruned to maintain a more compact form. The subspecies, *H. italicum* subsp. *serotinum*, most often offered in North America as *H. italicum microphyllum*, is a smaller plant, under 16 in. (40.5 cm) tall, with a spread of nearly 30 in. (76 cm). Dark yellow flower clusters bloom from summer to fall. It, too, needs full sun but is less tolerant of any but the driest growing conditions and the sharpest draining soil (think of rosemary). Where either of these plants are not hardy, take cuttings in the summer and overwinter indoors. Both types make good houseplants. The species can be trained as topiary. Another form is sometimes offered: dwarf curry plant goes by the name of *H. italicum*/*H. italicum* 'Dwarf'/*H. angustifolium*. It grows 8–10 in. (20.5–25.5 cm) tall with the usual yellow button flowers, but it is described as less fragrant than the others.

Alpine helichrysums are more demanding but choice. *Helichrysum milfordiae*, 2 in. (5 cm) tall and 12 in. (30.5 cm) wide, is a cushion-forming subshrub from South Africa with spatulate leaves heavily covered with down. Deep red to pink buds open white in spring. It is hardy from Zones 7 to 9. *H. sibthorpii*, from Greece, grows into a 4 in. (10 cm) tall and 18 in. (46 cm) wide white cushion, and in summer it bears yellow button flowers held in white bracts. It is hardy from Zones 9 to 10. Among the less hardy helichrysums, *H. splendidum* is a fall to winter–flowering shrub from southern Africa, suited to warmer regions. Its silver-gray foliage forms a compact bush, 4 ft. (1.2 m) tall and wide, topped by small yellow to orange flowers. It is hardy from Zones 8 or 9 to 11.

HELICTOTRICHON SEMPERVIRENS

Common name: blue oat grass

Family: Poaceae, grass

Description: waxy perennial

Origin: rocky slopes, wasteland; Europe

Site and soil: sun or partial shade; poor to moderately enriched soil on the alkaline side

Height: 12 in.–2.5 ft. (30.5 cm–0.8m)

Hardiness: Zones 4–8 or 9

Blue oat grass, *Helictotrichon sempervirens*, a middle-sized, cool-season grower, is loved for its brilliant steely, near-turquoise foliage, in a 2.5 ft. (0.8 m) upright, spiky mound with a mass of straw-colored panicles on stiff stems in early to midsummer. Plants grow best in poor to moderately enriched soil on the alkaline side. Rust can be a problem when blue oat grass is grown in shady conditions. *H. sempervirens* 'Sapphiresprudel' (sapphire fountain) is a more rust-resistant and heat-tolerant German selection, 12–18 in. (30.5–46.0 cm) tall with a wider blade than the species. We grew 'Sapphiresprudel' in our Connecticut garden for several years and loved it for its intensely silver-blue explosion of grass, appearing as sharp as a porcupine. We loved the way it and fine-textured *Festuca glauca* softly echoed yuccas planted throughout the garden. Blue oat grass is hardy from Zones 4 to 8 or 9.

HEUCHERA

Common name: coral bells

Family: Saxifragaceae, saxifrage

Description: variegated perennial

Origin: woodland, rocky sites; North America

Site and soil: sun or partial shade; well-drained

Height and width (foliage mounds): 6–12 in. (15.0–30.5 cm) tall; 6 in.–3 ft. (15 cm–1 m) wide

Hardiness: Zones 4–9

Native to rocky slopes and open woods from New England to California and south to Alabama, heucheras grow from woody rootstock to form clumps of lobed, toothed, sometimes ruffled foliage from just under 1 in. (2.5 cm) to 5 in. (12.5 cm) or longer, hairy or glossy and leathery in texture. In some species, leaves are strongly veined, reddish, and marbled with a darker color. Beginning in late spring and continuing throughout the summer, masses of dainty, tubular or bell-shaped flowers in sprays—reddish, rose, white, or greenish—are borne atop slender stems that rise up from basal mounds, bringing the height of the plant to 24 in. (61 cm) or more when in bloom. For years, "heuchera" meant the well-loved, green-leaved *Heuchera sanguinea*, coral bells, a neat plant, 12–24 in. (30.5–61.0 cm) when in bloom, with small, scalloped-edge foliage, universally valued for its dependability and prolific production of long-lasting, tiny, coral-colored flowers. But recently, heucheras have been dominated by dramatic foliage plants, the result of intense plant collecting and breeding that builds on the plants' natural inclination to hybridize. The results are heucheras we never dreamed of in our humble cottage garden coral bells. The heady mix of genes from variable wild species and seed strains has given us silver-leaved heucheras in designer styles. Leaves are elegantly patterned with contrasting veins that create a silver webbing effect; marbled with contrasting purples, wines, and bronzes; or these characteristics are combined in ever-new, even startling, ways. Although foliage is the main attraction of the new silver heucheras, the prolific flowering we associate with coral bells is achieved in a few types by adding *H. sanguinea* or *H. ×brizoides* (a hybrid group with *H. sanguinea* bloodlines) to the mix, resulting in airy towers of larger flowers that bloom over an extended period. As a bonus, they are attractive to hummingbirds and butterflies, and many are great cut flowers. These silver riches are intoxicating for plant lovers but a headache for taxonomists.

The heuchera revolution was launched more than two decades ago with the discovery in England of a purple-leaved seedling of unconfirmed parentage, named *H.* 'Palace Purple'. In the late 1980s a plant from 'Dales' Strain', seed-grown variants of *Heuchera americana*, self-hybridized at Montrose Nursery, resulting in a natural cross, 'Montrose Ruby', with silver mottling. Breeding has produced a bewildering number of silvery hybrids, probably only a few of which will probably stay the course.

Charles and Martha Oliver of Primrose Path Nursery have introduced many variations of silver heucheras. In *Heuchera* 'Frosted Violet', to 12 in. (30.5 cm), new foliage is pink-violet, silver in spring and summer, and then dark bluish violet in winter where foliage is evergreen. Flowers in complementary pink bring the height of the plant to 30 in. (76 cm). *H.* 'Jade Gloss' is a heavy spring bloomer with large white flowers, pink in bud, on stems to 18 in. (46 cm), over glossy, silvered leaves with bronze veining. The Olivers warn that this hybrid is less tolerant of heat than others, so grow it in partial shade or shady conditions in the southern United States or in other hot and humid climates. The Petite Series, involving crosses between western dwarf alpine species *H. hallii* and *H. pulchella*, with a large-leaved, bronze foliage type, produce compact mounds, 6–8 in. (15.0–20.5 cm) wide, topped by showy flowers on 10–12 in. (25.5–30.5 cm) stems. *H.* 'Petite Lime Sherbet' has small green leaves with silver veining and masses of bright pink flowers on 12 in. (30.5 cm) stems. Other cultivars from this series—'Petite Marbled Burgundy', 'Petite Pearl Fairy', and 'Petite Ruby Frills'—feature bronze leaves with silver markings and pink flowers on stems from 10 to 12 in. (25.5 to 30.5 cm). *H.* 'Quilter's Joy', an early effort and still one of the best (an RHS AGM winner), has neatly scalloped foliage with silver marking against a bronze background, enhanced by white flowers on 18–24 in. (46–61 cm) stems in late spring. Martha Oliver suggests pairing it with *Penstemon digitalis* 'Husker Red'. The most silvery Oliver introductions, which emphasize foliage rather than flowers, are *H.* 'Silver Light', metallic-silver foliage with frilly, light pink flowers on 18 in. (45.7 cm) stems in late spring; *H.* 'Silver Lode', a tall type to 3 ft. (1 m), with white flowers carried over pewtered foliage, burgundy on reverse; and *H.* 'Silver Scrolls', the most silver of all, with rounded, metallic-silver leaves marked with a dark-purple veining, paired in spring with wands of white, pink-tinged flowers. This is a vigorous hybrid to 24 in. (61 cm) in full bloom and is reported to perform well in heat and humidity. A recent introduction, *H.* 'Raspberry Ice', described as a sister of 'Silver Scrolls', looks promising for its silver theme, large flowers, and extraordinary vigor. Foliage is marked with silver and burgundy, and flowers in late spring are pink on 24 in. (61 cm) stems.

Terra Nova Nurseries, a wholesale source in Oregon, breeds heucheras dominated by large foliage types of western U.S. heritage. Flowers are less important and should be cut back in most cases to discourage sprawl. Gardeners in the American Northeast report mixed results with Pacific coast–bred hybrids. Except where noted, most are happiest in partial shade. *Heuchera* 'Can Can' forms a tight mound, 8 in. (20.5 cm) tall and 18 in. (46 cm) wide, of very ruffled, jagged-edged, purple foliage with metallic silver veining. *H.* 'Cascade Dawn', 8 in. (20.5 cm) tall and 17 in. (43 cm) wide, has large, silvered leaves outlined and veined in lavender. *H.* 'Geisha's Fan' is a very showy foliage plant with charcoal veining over jagged, brightly silvered leaves and pretty, light pink flowers in the spring. *H. americana* 'Ring of Fire', for partial shade or shade, has rounded silver leaves suffused with purple veining; with the onset of cool weather in the fall, it develops a bright coral-rimmed edging. *H.* 'Mint Frost' is different for its silver coloration over a mint-green background and mint-green veining. When the leaves turn rosy in the fall, veins change to silver. *H.* 'Montrose Ruby', a parent of all silver- and purple-leaved heucheras, produces a 12 in. (30.5 cm) tall mound of glowing red foliage marked with patches of silver-gray. Popular

H. 'Persian Carpet' features 6 in. (15 cm) mounds of large, dark-purple–edged foliage to 6 in. (15 cm) long, compelling for its change of colors over the season. The overall scheme is rose-burgundy coloring highlighted by silver with dark-purple veining. Greenish white flower spikes in spring bring the height of the plant to 18 in. (46 cm). *H.* 'Pewter Veil', a Terra Nova classic, has 6 in. (15 cm) copper-pink spring foliage, scalloped and rounded in form on a neat mound of foliage 12 in. (30.5 cm) tall and 18 in. (46 cm) wide. As the leaves mature, they turn metallic silver with a purplish undertone, embossed with charcoal-gray veining. Blush white flowers with purple and green tones bloom by midsummer on 24 in. (61 cm) stems. *H.* 'Stormy Seas' is an extremely vigorous plant with a 36 in. (1 m) spread. Foliage is ruffed with an applique of silver, lavender, pewter, and charcoal gray.

Heuchera sanguinea 'Frosty', to 20 in. (51 cm) when in bloom, brings us back to the old-fashioned coral bells but with a very new look. Better for sun, sharp drainage, and a cool climate, it is a dainty plant with small, scalloped, green foliage frosted nearly white. It creates a complementary base for the wealth of slender stems that rise from the clump, topped with numerous sprays of bright, coral-pink flowers over the summer.

×*Heucherella*, foamy bells, is the result of an intergeneric cross between heucheras and species of *Tiarella*, dainty native woodland flowers noted for their masses of tiny star florets in packed spikes over heart-shaped or lobed foliage. The hybrid forms blend the characteristics of both parents. Lower growing than most heucheras, they have larger 0.25 in. (0.5 cm) flowers in denser clusters. Tubular, bell-shaped, or starlike, in pink or white, they bloom and rebloom on branched spikes beginning in mid-spring and continuing through fall. Foliage is strongly veined and sometimes hairy and can be either evergreen like heucheras or deciduous like tiarellas. Some of the best have beautifully silvered leaves in the heuchera tradition. All forms are sterile.

Growers agree that heucherellas vary considerably in their vigor and character. Not all of the introductions make the transition from plant nursery to less-than-ideal garden conditions. One of the best, from the Olivers' Primrose Path Nursery, is prize-winning ×*Heucherella* 'Quicksilver', which does well in dry shade. It features metallic-silver foliage with bronze-maroon veining that turns to dark red in winter. The 18 in. (46 cm), dark stems bear large flowers that turn from pale pink to white as they open atop foliage mounds, 12 in. (30.5 cm) tall and 15 in. (38 cm) wide. In 1997 it won a first prize at the Royal Society for Horticulture in Holland. The good news for gardeners in the southern United States and other hot, humid summer climates is that at the University of Georgia test gardens it bloomed for nine weeks from April to June and received an excellent performance rating. Look for 'Kimono', 'Party Time', 'Silver Streak', and 'Viking Ship'.

HIPPOPHAE RHAMNOIDES

Common name: sea buckthorn
Family: Elaeagnaceae, oleaster
Description: downy shrub, tree
Origin: coastal dunes, riverbanks; Europe, Asia
Site and soil: sun; low fertility, sandy, neutral to alkaline, well-drained
Height and width: 8–30 ft. (2.5–9.0 m) tall; 10–40 ft. (3–12 m) wide
Hardiness: Zones 3–8

Introduced in colonial times, sea buckthorn is an open, mounding, suckering shrub or tree of irregular form. Its silvery willowlike foliage is very similar to Russian olive (*Elaeagnus angustifolia*) in shape and coloring, except that in sea buckthorn leaves grow from spiny or thorny branches. Tiny male and female flowers, yellow in racemes, appear on separate trees. Showy fruits on female trees—bright orange, spherical, and fleshy, to 0.25 in. (0.5 cm)—are borne profusely in the fall. The fruits, high in acid content, are not appealing to birds, which means massed, bright fruit against massed, silvery foliage from fall into winter. Nevertheless, the berries are a source of vitamins A and C and are said to make good sauces, jellies, and marmalade, and decoctions have been used to treat skin irritations. The epithet means "like rhamnus," pointing to the shrub's similarity to buckthorn. Sea buckthorn is one of those incredibly tough silvers that can take it all. It tolerates frigid temperatures, wind, and salt spray. Sea buckthorn is meant to grow near water in a position where the subsoil is evenly moist but well-drained. It will grow in sand and even clay if it is well-drained. In sand it suckers freely and becomes clumpy in form. To ensure that yours will produce fruit, plant one male for every three to six female plants. A clue in sexing trees: flower buds on male trees are large and knobby, while the buds on female trees are small and narrow. The dwarf cultivar, *Hippophae rhamnoides* 'Sea Sprite', is a fruitless male, 5–6 ft. (1.5–1.8 m) tall and 4–5 ft. (1.2–1.5 m) wide, compact and all silver. Sea buckthorn is also a great choice for a windbreak or screen, naturalized planting, or as a single dramatic accent.

JUNCUS

Common name: rush
Family: Juncaceae, rush
Description: waxy perennial
Origin: marshes, cool-temperate regions; worldwide
Site and soil: sun or shade; moist
Height and width: 1–2 ft. (0.3–0.6 m) tall; 2–4 ft. (0.6–1.2 m) wide
Hardiness: Zones 4–9

Of the 400 species in 10 genera, 3 in the *Juncus* genus stand out for their silvery foliage. *J. inflexus* 'Lovesick Blues', a warm-season grower, has steely blue foliage and is smooth and cylindrical, with a strongly weeping form, 12 in. (30.5 cm) tall and 2.5 ft. (0.8 m) wide. It is hardy from Zones 4 to 9. *J. patens*, native to marshes in California and Oregon, is a very stiff-leaved rush, usually gray-green to gray-blue in color. *J. patens* 'Carman's Gray' has spiky, round, leafless stems that are rigid and steely-blue on plants that grow 1–2 ft. (0.3–0.6 m) tall and 2 ft. (0.6 m) wide. It is hardy from Zones 7 to 9. *J. polyanthemos*, Australian silver bush, is a warm-season grower to 4 ft. (1.2 m) that produces long, slender, very silver-blue foliage for a rush. Rust may occur in shade conditions. In water, plant it 4–6 in. (10–15 cm) deep. Its tolerance to heat is a great asset where summers are hot. Rushes look best anywhere near or even in water.

JUNIPERUS

Common name: juniper
Family: Cupressaceae, cypress
Description: waxy tree
Origin: dry forests, hillsides; Northern Hemisphere
Site and Soil: sun; open, dry, well-drained
Height: 12 in.–90 ft. (30.5 cm–27.4 m)
Hardiness: Zones 2–10

The phenomenal ability of junipers to thrive in adverse cultural conditions—such as exposure to wind, prolonged drought, and poor, rocky soil—has endeared them to home gardeners and professional landscapers. But they would not be so popular if they were not also beautiful. Their clearly defined forms vary from tall, upright, and columnar, and medium-height, irregular, and bushy, to low, creeping, and wide-spreading. Foliage is from green-gray to silver-blue. Whatever their coloring, foliage appears in two stages, juvenile and adult.

Younger leaves are usually sharp and needlelike. Mature foliage develops into overlapping scales, either lying flat along shoots or spreading. In some types, foliage turns purplish in winter. Female cones or fruits are round and berrylike, to 0.25 in. (0.5 cm), blue with a silvery or whitish bloom, and are especially showy nestled against green, gray, or bluish foliage. Male fruits are spherical or ovoid and often yellow or brownish. Junipers have high wildlife value for their berries, nesting sites, and winter shelter. Highly variable, junipers are a headache for botanists, so nomenclature is confused and confusing. Most cultivars arise from sports on tree branches. We have confined our selection to junipers with the greatest apparent silver power from among the many that are very blue.

Juniperus ×*pfitzeriana* 'Pfitzeriana Glauca', a sport of *J. chinensis*, or Chinese juniper, is a popular male cultivar that grows naturally in the East (China, Japan, and Mongolia). It grows 5–10 ft. (1.5–3.0 m) tall, with angled, spreading branches, their outer tips pendulous. Foliage varies from silver to gray-blue. Hardy from Zones 3 to 9, it is often used as a foundation shrub and to mass on banks. It is reported to be more deer-resistant than other types.

Native to mountainous regions throughout the world, *Juniperus communis*, common juniper, is extraordinarily varied in shape, growing from low, spreading, ground covers to shrubby or columnar trees 40 ft. (12.2 m) high. *J. communis* varies in color from dark green to silver-blue. Its fruits are essential ingredients in gin and were used, when roasted, as a coffee substitute by early Americans. *J. communis* 'Berkshire' is a tight, miniature bun, 9–12 in. (23.0–30.5 cm) tall and 12–15 in. (30.5–38.0 cm) wide, with steel-blue foliage, good for rock or trough gardens. It is hardy from Zones 6a to 8. 'Saxatilis', dwarf mountain juniper, is a very hardy miniature to Zones 3 to 8 for the rock or trough garden. It is 4 in. (10 cm) tall and 36 in. (1 m) wide, with ropelike branches that hug the ground and twist to display silver-backed needles. With an open form, it makes a striking display as it weaves around neighboring plants. It is hardy from Zones 4 to 8.

Juniperus conferta 'Silver Mist', 1.5 ft. (0.5 m) tall and 6–9 ft. (1.8–2.7 m) wide, has blue-green foliage beautifully overlaid with silver. Although it does lose some sheen in winter, the silvery cones keep their color throughout the year, a positive bonus. As its common name suggests, this cultivar of shore juniper is especially suitable for saline and sandy soils.

Juniperus horizontalis, creeping juniper, native to the American Northeast, is a naturally wide-spreading form, 1–4 ft. (0.3–12.2 m) tall, with soft, plumelike, blue-green needles that turn deep purple in the winter. It is hardy from Zones 3 to 9. 'Grey Forest', 6 in. (15 cm) tall and 8 in. (20.5 cm) wide, is a miniature erect form with fine gray foliage that turns purplish in winter, hardy from Zones

5 to 9. It is ideal for trough or scree plantings. 'Wiltonii', blue rug, 4–6 in. (10–15 cm) tall and 6–8 ft. (1.8–2.4 m) wide, is very popular for its extraordinary hardiness to Zone 3 with no winterkill in the harshest winter climates, for its intense silver-blue coloring, and its prostrate form. It is a fine ground cover, especially when allowed to drape over walls.

Of garden origin, blue-gray *Juniperus chinensis* 'Shimpaku', only 12 in. (30.5 cm) tall and 30 in. (76 cm) wide, with thready, dense, soft foliage, is a miniature form prized for bonsai and for rock gardens. Prune annually to keep it very small. It is hardy from Zones 5 to 10.

A counterpart to *Juniperus virginiana*, eastern red-cedar, *J. scopulorum*, Rocky Mountain juniper or western red-cedar, to 36 ft. (11 m), is a tall, softly pyramidal form, with needles that vary in color from blue-green to gray-green. 'Moonglow', a moderate grower to 20 ft. (6.1 m), is upright, branched, and pyramidal with intensely silver-blue foliage and bright blue berries. 'Tolleson's Weeping', 30–40 ft. (9.1–12.2 m) tall and 3–15 ft. (1.0–4.6 m) wide, is an arresting form with silver-blue foliage that hangs like strings from arching branches, suitable as an accent. It is supposed to be a fine container plant. These junipers are hardy from Zones 3 to 7.

Juniperus squamata, single-seed juniper, is a variable species from Afghanistan, the Himalayas, and China, whose cultivars are the only representatives in cultivation. Silver ones include 'Blue Star', highly regarded for its adaptability. Generally a low, rounded form 12 in. (30.5 cm) tall and 18 in. (46 cm) wide in the American Northeast, where it is a slow grower, it can grow to 3 ft. (1 m) tall and 3–4 ft. (1.0–1.2 m) wide further south, where it is reported to be a fast grower. Its wide, spreading, irregular form shows off in a rock garden or in a mass planting. 'Chinese Silver' is a bright silver-blue tree to 10 ft. (3 m) with a graceful upright, irregular form and weeping branches, most often grown as a specimen. 'Meyerii', fish-tail juniper, set the standard for the group with silvery blue-green, spiky foliage on branches that resemble a fish's tail. It grows 5 ft. (1.5 m) tall and 4 ft. (1.2 m) wide, although it can grow much taller. 'Prostrata' is a flat form that grows along the ground. Its foliage is backed by vivid silvery stomata.

Juniperus virginiana, eastern red-cedar, is very popular for its extreme hardiness, conical shape to 90 ft. (27.4 m), and rich, frosty blue cones against gray-green foliage. 'Burkii' is a dense, upright form, 20 ft. (6.1 m) tall and 3 ft. (1 m) wide, whose blue-gray foliage is purple tinged in winter. 'Glauca', silver red-cedar, has silver-blue foliage (more intense in the spring) and grows 15–20 ft. (4.6–6.1 m). 'Grey Owl', sometimes listed separately as a hybrid, is probably the result of a cross between *J. virginiana* 'Glauca' and *J.* ×*pfitzeriana*. It is a female type with soft foliage and a narrow, pyramidal shape. *J. virginiana* 'Silver Spreader'/'Mona' has silver-blue foliage, grows 6–10 ft. (1.8–3.0 m) tall and 10–12 ft. (3.0–3.7 m) wide, and is a wide, spreading male form with ovoid brown fruits its first year. Eastern red-cedar is hardy from Zones 2 to 9.

LAMIUM

Common name: dead nettle, yellow archangel
Family: Lamiaceae, mint
Description: variegated perennial
Origin: moist woodland, dry scrub; Europe to Asia
Site and soil: partial shade to shade; dry to moist, well-drained
Height and width: 6–24 in. (15–61 cm) tall; 12–18 in. (30.5–46.0 cm) wide
Hardiness: Zones 4–9

These members of the mint family are among 50 species ranging from fast creepers that cover the ground with ease to slower growing, clump-forming types. Dead nettle (the name means "harmless," as opposed to stinging nettle) was once highly regarded for its ability to staunch bleeding and heal wounds and bruises, based on the plant's astringent, tannin-rich properties. Lamiums grow well in virtually any soil but wet. They dislike extended periods of humidity, some more than others. If watering is necessary, water in the morning so the leaves dry quickly; otherwise they could be subject to leaf spot. Lamiums are invaluable for dry woodland gardens, borders, tough open spaces between rocks, and in containers, where they mingle and trail.

Lamium maculatum has small, nearly heart-shaped leaves, 1.5 in. (5 cm) long, spotted white along the midrib. In late spring it bears whorls of 0.75 in. (2 cm) long-lasting flowers—violet-purple, pink, or white—which are showy in their numbers despite their diminutive size. The flower's upper lip arches over the three-lobed lower lip like a hood or a turtle's head. The species has given rise to several desirable cultivars, from 6 to 8 in. (15 to 20 cm), with frosted silver foliage and flowers from white to nearly red. 'Beacon Silver' set the standard for *L. maculatum* types. Shimmering, frosted, silver-green foliage, lightly scalloped, is narrowly edged in jade green. Flowers on stems to 6 in. (15 cm) bear long-lasting whorls of soft rose-colored flowers. This early cultivar, hardy from Zones 3 to 8, is not as tolerant of heat and humidity as the later ones, which can be grown in Zone 9. The foliage pattern of the cultivars is built around the same plan, but flower colors differ. 'Pink Pewter' has shell-pink flowers maturing to clear-pink; 'White Nancy' has pure white flowers; and 'Red Nancy' has bright rose flowers.

L. maculatum 'Chequers', also hardy from Zones 3 to 9, departs from the common theme. Low-growing and heavily marked with silver variegation, it is a dense ground cover that tolerates both sun and dry shade. Its flowers are mauve-pink. 'Orchid Frost' is distinguished from the others by its faster, more vigorous growth. It forms an impressive mat, 6–12 in. (15.0–30.5 cm) tall and 12–24 in. (30.5–61.0 cm) wide, of silver-green foliage edged with blue-green, topped by bright, orchid-pink flowers. Not as tolerant of dry conditions as the others, it prefers steady moisture in sun or shade. In hot climates give it protective shade.

Lamium galeobdolon 'Variegatum', yellow archangel (once classified in its own genus, *Lamiastrum*), is a rampant creeper to 2 in. (5 cm), with smaller, 0.75 in. (2 cm), very narrow and sharply pointed silver-marked leaves and bright yellow flowers in the stem's axils. 'Hermann's Pride' is a vastly improved version, clump-forming and slower growing. Its ever-fresh, jagged, 1.25 in. (3 cm) leaves are laminated with silver and then neatly etched with contrasting green veins. Its flowers are brilliant yellow. Over several seasons it forms a stiff, erect bush, 16 in. (40.5 cm) tall and 18 in. (46 cm) wide. 'Silver Carpet', to 4 in. (10 cm), is also clump-forming with all silver foliage. It is rated hardy from Zones 4 to 7. 'Silver Angel', to 20 in. (51 cm), has a more prostrate form than 'Hermann's Pride'. It is a faster growing spreader with silver-marked leaves. 'Silver Spangled' is a heavily spotted silver. These are hardy from Zones 4 or 5 to 7.

LAVANDULA

Common name: lavender
Family: Lamiaceae, mint
Description: downy shrub, subshrub
Origin: Mediterranean
Site and soil: sun; sharply drained
Height and width: 12 in.–3 ft. (30.5 cm–1.0 m) tall; 20 in.–4 ft. (51 cm–1.2 m) wide
Hardiness: Zones 4–10

Lavender is a classic in every sense, cultivated since ancient times to the present day. It is loved for its bracing and refreshing scent—sharp and sweet, like jasmine or heliotrope with a shot of camphor—and its foliage and flower combination. From a woody-based mound of small, usually linear, leaves, numerous straight, broomlike stems arise in summer. These are topped by slender, conical heads packed with small, two-lipped flowers—in the violet to purple range, occasionally white or light pink—in dense whorls. Flowerheads are enhanced by the beauty of bud and calyx, often flushed in shades of violet-purple. When its scent

Lavenders thrive in rocks.

is released by the sun and suffuses the air, the entire lavender ensemble of foliage, buds, flowers, and aroma is overpowering to the senses, especially when plants are massed. For the silver collector, lavender's appeal is heightened by conspicuously downy foliage, from gray-green and silver-green to woolly white. The genus name is derived from the Latin *lavare* (to wash), from the Greek and Roman tradition of adding lavender scent to bath water. Medicinally, lavender has a long history of use as an antiseptic and for treating headaches, insomnia, and digestion ills. Its greatest practical value has been in the commercial production of essential oil used in perfumes and toiletries, for which special varieties have been developed.

It is not difficult to grow lavender satisfactorily if certain principles are followed. In cooler climates, lavender must develop a woody base before it can survive repeated winter frosts, so for this reason it is best to begin with sizeable purchased plants. Fast-growing *Lavandula angustifolia* 'Lady' is an exception (see below). In the humid U.S. South, lavender must be kept dry with a pebble mulch (light colored to reflect sun is best) at its base. Wherever it is grown, it must have sunny and airy conditions and soil where water never puddles. If these conditions are fulfilled, the hardiest lavender (*L. angustifolia*) can be grown in areas with -30°F (-34°C) winter temperatures. Poorly sited lavender, no matter how hardy, will succumb. Lavenders can be left in place for many years, but with age they usually become a dense mass of woody stems with few blooms and dead patches. It is usually best to propagate them every few years. Fungal diseases, mostly a problem in hot, humid areas, include Fusarium root rot and leaf spot. Note that silveriness is variable depending on the source (the parent plant used for cloning) and that immature foliage is often greener than mature foliage.

Lavandula ×*allardii*, giant lavender, grows 4–5 ft. (1.2–1.5 m) tall and 4 ft. (1.2 m) wide and is a hybrid of *L. dentata*. It has toothed or scallop-edged gray-green to silver-green foliage and bears large, light lavender blooms on long-stemmed spikes throughout the summer and fall. It needs a warm site and is adaptable to hot, humid conditions. It is hardy from Zones 8 to 9.

Lavandula angustifolia, English lavender (also common lavender, hardy lavender, or true lavender), is the lavender of history, the one called to mind when "lavender" is mentioned. It is sometimes called English lavender because of its popularity in English gardens and for its importance in the development of the English perfume industry. The hardiest of lavenders, it is native to the western Mediterranean, probably introduced to northern Europe by the Romans. It is a relatively sweet-scented type with early summer–blooming lavender, purple, or violet flowers over narrow, gray-green to silver-green foliage. Its growth varies according to its habitat. In the most favorable conditions it grows 3 ft. (1 m) tall and 4 ft. (1.2 m) wide, but it may be considerably smaller. Gardeners in the southern United States often grow lavender as an annual. As Madalene Hill has proved in Texas, with special care (raised bed, grit mulch, careful watering to avoid wetting foliage), lavenders can be grown as long-lived perennials.

Several important variants and cultivars have been developed from the species. The hardiest is *Lavandula angustifolia* 'Hidcote' (sometimes described as a strain since it is not the original), a slow-growing, 16 in. (40.5 cm) tall and 12 in. (30.5 cm) wide variety, with narrow, silvery leaves, blackish buds, and deep purple-blue flowers in dense spikes, famous as a low to medium-tall compact edging or hedge; 'Hidcote Pink', pastel pink flowers over a mound of gray foliage (it may not be as hardy); 'Mitcham Grey', faster growing, with purple-pink flowers; and 'Munstead', similar to 'Hidcote', but less compact with light purple flowers. These are reliably hardy from Zones 4 to 10.

Less reliably hardy sorts in the *Lavendula angustifolia* group from Zone 5 include 'Nana', a dwarf version of the species, 12 in. (30.5 cm) tall and wide, with noticeably gray foliage, blue-purple flower spikes, and a late-spring bloom with a heavy scent (try this with *Saponaria ocymoides* in a rock garden or rock wall). The rare white 'Alba', grown in England since the 17th century, is vigorous like the species with long spikes of pure white flowers and soft, silvery gray foliage. 'Nana Alba'/'Baby White'/'Dwarf White', a dwarf version, is 6–12 in. (15.0–30.5 cm) tall and 6–18 in. (5–46 cm) wide, with silver-gray foliage and short, white flowers; it is suitable for low edgings, rock gardens, or containers. 'Grey Lady', to 24 in. (61 cm) tall and 4 ft. (1.2 m) wide, is fast-growing, with larger leaves than the species and blue-lavender flowers. 'Martha Roderick', a neat, semi-dwarf type, is 24 in. (61 cm) tall and wide and carries an astonishing number of stems bearing early-blooming, violet-blue flowers held in light purple calyces. 'Twickel' (sometimes listed under *L.* ×*intermedia*), grows 20–24 in. (51–61 cm) tall and 24–36 in. (61 cm–1 m) wide and blooms in summer with long, fanlike spikes of soft purple flowers above a mound of gray-green leaves. 'Irene Doyle'/'Two Seasons', with lavender flowers, has a similar habit and blooms twice where the growing season is long enough.

Lavandula angustifolia 'Lady', often grown as an annual, is a boon to gardeners in hot, humid regions or wherever lavender is difficult to overwinter. It is a compact, open-pollinated, bushy form; 8–10 in. (20.5–25.5 cm) tall and 12 in. (30.5 cm) wide; looks like *L. angustifolia* 'Munstead'; and comes true from seed. Introduced as an All-American Selection in 1994, it takes from 18 to 20 weeks to grow from seed to bloom. In warm climates, it can be sown outdoors in the fall to bloom the following spring; sown in mid-winter, it will bloom by late spring.

Silver fern-leaf, *Lavandula buchii*, bears light blue flowers. Plants grow 1–3 ft. (0.3–1.0 m) tall and 1–2 ft. (0.3–0.6 m) wide, and once established flower virtually non-stop in the summer and even in the winter on a cool, sunny windowsill. It is hardy from Zones 8 to 10.

Fringed lavender, *Lavandula dentata* var. *candicans*, has white-gray, toothed leaves covered with soft white hairs, which gives the entire plant a fuzzy texture and glowing appearance. It is faster growing than English lavender, reaching 2 ft. (0.6 m) tall and 3 ft. (1 m) wide, and it has larger flowers—powder-blue in whorled clusters—that bloom continuously throughout the summer and fall where it is hardy. In a container, its foliage is a striking contrast among green leaves. As with any woolly plant, it needs extra-sharp drainage and likes dry heat. Madalene Hill reports that it does well in humidity. It is hardy from Zones 8 to 10.

Lavandula 'Goodwin Creek Gray' grows 24 in. (61 cm) tall and 30 in. (76 cm) wide in the ground, but even in a pot it is vigorous and very silvery, with narrow, woolly, notched leaves in up-thrusting thick bunches, topped by deep-purple flowers for most of the summer in mild climates and indoors over the winter. Discovered by Jim and Dotti Becker of Goodwin Creek Gardens, it is a hybrid of *L. dentata* (evident in the foliage) and was nominated for an RHS AGM. The Beckers recommend it for hot, problem areas. It is hardy from Zones 7 to 9.

Lavandin, *Lavandula* ×*intermedia*, is a sterile hybrid, 12–20 in. (30.5–51.0 cm) tall and wide, produced from crossing *L. angustifolia* and *L. latifolia*. It has been grown for centuries in France for the production of oil. It is hardy from Zones 5 to 8. Its cultivars are vigorous, of rounded, compact habit, with spikes longer than either parent. *L.* ×*intermedia* 'Grosso', or fat spike, developed in California for oil production, is 4 ft. (1.2 m) tall and 3 ft. (1 m) wide, with deep-violet flowers on long-waving stems, and it is a champion bloomer with the largest (fattest) flower spikes of any lavender. 'Fred Boutin', 3 ft. (1 m) tall and wide, is one of the most silvery gray lavenders, with violet blooms growing 18 in. (46 cm) above an 18 in. (46 cm) mound of foliage. 'White Spike', 3 ft. (1 m) tall and wide, bears pure white flowers over a bushy, silvery mound of foliage. 'Silver Edge' (also listed under *L. angustifolia*), unusual for its variegated, gray-green to silver-blue leaves edged in creamy white, grows 18–24 in. (46–61 cm), bears soft purple flowers all summer, and is hardy from Zones 6 or 7 to 9. 'Provence', one of the best for fragrance, has slate-gray foliage and lavender-blue flower spikes produced from summer to fall on plants 2 ft. (0.6 m) tall and 3 ft. (1 m) wide; it is hardy from Zones 6 to 9. 'Dutch', 4 ft. (1.2 m) tall and 16 in. (40.5 cm) wide, has narrow, silvery foliage and dark violet flowers that bloom earlier than the others; it is less tolerant of heat and grows best from Zones 5 to 7.

A rare lavender from Spain with a rounded, bushy form, *Lavandula lanata*, woolly lavender, grows 30 in. (76 cm) tall and 36 in. (1 m) wide. Its leaves are covered with distinctive white felt, indicating both its drought-tolerance and need for extra-sharp drainage. In common with other woolly plants, it does not do well in wet, humid areas, but Madalene Hill manages to grow it by adding a thick pea mulch to the planting. In midsummer to late summer, long stalks bear deep-purple flowers, a striking contrast to white, woolly foliage. It is hardy from Zones 8 to 9.

Aptly named for its distinctive foliage, *Lavandula* 'Silver Frost' is regarded as the most silvery lavender of all, and although it may be a slow grower, eventually reaching 16 in. (40.5 cm) tall and 24 in. (61 cm) wide, it is worth the wait to see it in bloom: large flowers—purple to blue—are held in silvery blue calyces on stems with silver-white to powder-white foliage. Extremely heat-tolerant, it is hardy from Zones 6 to 10 and recommended for gardens in the U.S. West.

LEUCOPHYLLUM

Common name: Texas sage, Texas ranger, cenizo
Family: Scrophulariaceae, figwort
Description: downy shrub
Origin: desert; northwestern United States, northern Mexico
Soil and site: sun; gravelly limestone or alkaline, well-drained
Height and width: 3–8 ft. (1.0–2.4 m) tall and wide
Hardiness: Zones 7 or 8–10

Texas sages belong to a group of slow-growing, dense, mostly evergreen bushes that naturally occur on limestone slopes in the Chihuahuan Desert. They begin as compact shrubs of rounded form but sprawl with age. Some have silvery leaves—felted or woolly in texture—to 1 in. (2.5 cm) and slightly curled, designed to take extreme desert heat and drought as well as fierce wind. Two-lipped flowers with spotted throats, like snapdragons or foxgloves, are showy and colorful, pink or purplish, borne singly from leaf axils. Plants bloom sporadically from spring to fall, transformed by summer showers into full bloom, when the magic combination of heat and humidity occurs. *Leucophyllum frutescens* is called "barometer plant" because of this phenomenon. Texas sages are popular throughout the dry southwestern United States and in humid climates like Florida. In the hot, steamy conditions of Southeast Asia, flowering is reported to be magnificent. Texas sage is hardy to 10°F (-12°C)—or even 5°F (-15°C), but expect some leaf drop. Water plants well at first, and then treat as desert types, with no further watering necessary. Gardeners who fall in love with compact Texas sage are often disappointed when theirs assumes an unsightly sprawl. To avoid this, grow in mean, lean soil and tip prune to encourage dense foliage and a compact form. Diseases and pests, encouraged by wet conditions and overwatering, include stem rot, powdery mildew, and scale insects.

Until the 1980s, as far as gardeners were concerned, Texas sage was synonymous with the species *Leucophyllum frutescens*, but important work at Texas A&M University and elsewhere opened up a new world of interesting cultivars and other species. Breeding focused on compactness, increased bloom, and varied flower colors. *L. candidum*, violet silverleaf, grows wild on West Texas hillsides and is very drought-tolerant once established. *L. candidum* 'Silver Cloud' has the same tiny, 0.5 in. (1.5 cm), silver-white leaves characteristic of the species, bears deep-violet flowers, and grows 4.5 ft. (1.4 m) tall and wide. The very popular 'Thunder Cloud' is similar but more generous with its flowers. Note that both are very susceptible to overwatering.

Texas sage
(*Leucophyllum
frutescens*).

The species *Leucophyllum frutescens*, 6–8 ft. (1.8–2.4 m), is an arching shrub with very woolly leaves and purple-pink flowers. 'Compactum'/'Compacta', the oldest cultivar and still one of the best, is a dense grower, 3–4 ft. (1–1.2 m), with lovely, orchid-pink flowers. 'Bertstar Dwarf', usually sold as Silverado Sage, is even more compact and rounded in form than 'Compactum'. It is dense to its base with more evergreen (silvery) foliage throughout the season, complemented by violet flowers. This form is a dramatic contrast to open and irregularly shaped types. 'Convent', 4 ft. (1.2 m) tall and wide, has dark rosy-purple blooms over silvery foliage. 'White Cloud', 6–8 ft. (1.8–2.4 m) tall and wide, has gray foliage and large white flowers, a foil for bright pinks and purples. *L. pruinosum* 'Sierra

Bouquet' is an open, sprawling shrub, 6 ft. (1.8 m) tall and wide, with silver-gray foliage and violet flowers heavily perfumed like grape bubble gum. Site this where you can enjoy its aroma. *L. zygophyllum* 'Cimarron', one of the best for small gardens—and tolerant of irrigation—grows 3 ft. (0.6 m) tall and wide; bears blue flowers; is distinguished by its gray-green, cupped foliage; and is reported to be less susceptible to root rot than *L. candidum* 'Silver Cloud' and 'Thunder Cloud'.

LEUCOPHYTA BROWNII

Common name: cushion bush
Family: Asteraceae, aster
Description: downy, tender shrub
Origin: coast; south Australia
Site and soil: sun; light, fast-draining, slightly alkaline
Height and width: 12 in.–3 ft. (0.6–1.0 m) tall and wide
Hardiness: Zones 9–11

Mrs. Underwood (1971) aptly described cushion bush as "a neat bundle of twigs dipped in a bath of silver paint." One of 18 species in the genus from

Leucophyta brownii/Calocephalus brownii in a container at Wave Hill, with bat-faced cuphea (*Cuphea llavea* 'Georgia Scarlet') and *Agave patonii*.

Australia and Tasmania, cushion bush is similar in appearance to an overgrown lichen. It forms a dense, compact, and intricately branched dome of intensely bright, silver twigs and branches covered with tiny, scalelike leaves, so small and pressed so tightly against their stems that the plant seems leafless. In summer, small, insignificant, creamy-white button flowers emerge from silvery buds in terminal-clustered bunches. Cushion bush is a tough plant, resistant to drought and used to being buffeted by strong winds and salt spray, so it is especially suited to coastal conditions, where it assumes its best form. Where it winters over, it grows 3 ft. (1 m) tall and wide, but it reaches only 12–18 in. (30.5–46.0 cm) tall and wide where it is grown as an annual or tender perennial. Grow it in a sunny site with good air circulation as in its native habitat, and pinch branch tips to maintain a bushy, compact form. Plants are short-lived and do not respond to hard pruning when the center of the bush dies out, so periodically make new plants from tip cuttings, providing bottom heat for best results. Cushion bush succumbs to the slightest hint of frost and is prone to gray mold in damp conditions. We love this intricately twiggy bush, so brightly silver. Its texture is unique, like juniper with kinky hair. Used in borders and rock work, or as a tall, mounding ground cover where it is hardy, cushion bush is gaining favor in colder areas as a knockout container plant.

LEYMUS ARENARIUS
Common name: blue lyme grass
Family: Poacea
Description: waxy perennial
Origin: sand dunes, grasslands; Europe, Eurasia, California
Site and soil: sun to light shade; most soils
Height: 1–3 ft. (0.3–1.0 m)
Hardiness: Zones 4–10

Leymus arenarius/Elymus arenarius, often mistakenly sold as *Elymus glauca*, is better known as blue lyme grass. It is a warm-season grass native to sand dunes, growing from 1 to 3 ft. (0.3–1.0 m) tall on erect stems, but it stoops to 1 to 2 ft. (0.3 to 0.6 m) tall on lax stems, depending on growing conditions. Glinting, metallic blue foliage, 0.75 in. (1.5 cm) wide and 12–18 in. (30.5–46.0 cm) long, grows up from stout, spreading rhizomes. Insignificant flowers from early to late summer are bluish gray fading to wheat. Blue lyme grass is tolerant of salt spray and wind so it is a good seaside plant, but it is an exceptionally aggressive spreader in light, loose soil and should not be used where it can invade native habitats.

Inland, especially in heavier soils, it spreads more slowly, but it should be watched. It looks great in an old-fashioned metal dishpan with holes for drainage drilled in the bottom. Set the dishpan on a flat rock or other support rather than on the ground, where the plant's roots may seek soil. Look for the new cultivar 'Blue Steel' with more silvery foliage; 'Findhorn' is more compact. Blue lyme grass is hardy from Zones 4 to 10.

LYCHNIS

Common name: rose campion
Family: Caryophyllaceae, pink
Description: downy biennial, short-lived perennial
Origin: southeastern Europe
Site and soil: sun; lean, well-drained
Height and width: 16 in.–2.5 ft. (40.5 cm–0.8 m) tall; 20 in.–3 ft. (50.8 cm–1.0 m)
   wide
Hardiness: Zones 3–10

In its first year of growth, rose campion's basal foliage, narrow and spear-shaped, can be mistaken for lamb's ears. The second year, wide-branching, felted, white stems shoot up bearing bright magenta, 1 in. (2.5 cm) flowers. Blossoms have five broad, slightly overlapping petals, similar to phlox in appearance, but unlike phlox they are borne singly rather than in clusters. The combination in a single plant of vividly colored flowers in profusion among a bright silver superstructure of leaves and stems is quite striking. The genus name is derived from the Greek *lychnos* (lamp), a reference to the brilliance of the flowers in this group, but it could just as well refer to the brilliance of the entire plant. *Lychnis coronaria* 'Alba' has pure white flowers on the same silver-leaved silvery stems. Other forms, not as common in North America as they are in Europe, where rose campion has been grown as a garden plant since the mid-14th century, are dark red *L. coronaria* 'Atrosanguinea', the pinkish eyed *L. coronaria* Oculata Group, and *L.* ×*walkeri* 'Abbotswood Rose', a compact plant from 18 to 24 in. (46 to 61 cm). In Europe, long-lasting, sterile, double-magenta and double-white flowered types (like miniature roses) had nearly displaced single-flowered ones by the mid-17th century, but today these are rare. Blooms of Bressingham recently introduced 'Gardener's World', a double magenta.

   Rose campion, also called "dusty miller," appears to have settled into the *Lychnis* genus after being classified under *Agrostemma*. Bear in mind that rose campion is short-lived. If left to its own devices, though, it will self-sow with abandon, so it will always be around. Longevity can be encouraged by cutting back the coarse flowering stalks in late summer or fall to encourage the formation of plantlets at the plant's base. If plants are cut back after their first bloom in early to midsummer, rose campion blooms again (not quite as vigorously) in late summer, well into the fall. The most common cause of death or unhealthy plants is moisture at the root crown and humid conditions.

In the border, plant rose campion in generous drifts among dark pinks, blues, and purples, which help to tone down the uncompromising magenta flowers. Pale yellow achillea flowers also work well, especially those of *Achillea* 'Moonshine'. We appreciate the magenta flowers even more when they rebloom in late summer, just when most other flowers have faded and we are not satiated by an overabundance of color. For fresh brilliance and dramatic contrast in the autumn garden, pair pristine white campion, abloom on straight, silver stems, with annual *Ageratum* 'Blue Horizon', by late summer a nearly prostrate swathe of profuse, tight, blue flower clusters.

MARRUBIUM

Common name: horehound
Family: Lamicaceae, mint
Description: downy, short-lived perennial
Origin: dry waste places; Mediterranean, Eurasia
Site and soil: sun; dry, sharp to well-drained
Height and width: 4–20 in. (10–51 cm) tall; 12–24 in. (30.5–61.0.cm) wide
Hardiness: 3–10

In a genus of more than 30 species, several marrubiums are grown for their silvery foliage, curled, ruffled, or spoon-shaped, from gray-green to silky white, that sprouts from a semi-woody base. Small white to pale-lilac flowers, typical of the mint family to which marrubiums belong, are small and nondescript, growing in axillary whorls along woolly stems. When marrubiums bloom in summer, bees come to harvest their nectar. The whole plant exudes a bitter, camphorous order when crushed, similar to but not as strong as wormwood. At one time, barrels of dark brown horehound cough drops, made from an extract of *Marrubium vulgare*, or common horehound, were commonly sold in drugstores. Marrubiums have been overlooked as significant ornamentals because of the weedy nature of common horehound. If grown in ordinary garden soil and unattended, plants flop unattractively. For best results, grow marrubiums in lean, sandy, even gravelly soil. Site to avoid cold winter winds and excessive moisture, the most common cause

Marrubium rotundifolium.

of early death. Despite its reputation, we think common horehound, an 18 in. (46 cm) tall and wide mound of ruffled, gray-green foliage, is an asset in the low rock flower and herb border that surrounds our Adirondack kitchen garden. At the first sign of its flowering stem, we cut it back to the basal foliage to keep the plant from sprawling.

Silver horehound, *Marrubium incanum/M. candidissimum*, an undervalued perennial native to southern Europe, was introduced to American gardens by Helen Fox. It is a more silvery marrubium, 8–20 in. (20.5–51.0 cm) tall and 24 in. (61 cm) wide, characterized by densely white, hairy shoots, and scalloped, gray-green, down-turning leaves covered with white silky down, white-felted beneath and very soft to the touch. Flowers in early summer, in denser clusters than common horehound, are pale—lilac-white and held in gray, woolly calyces, which helps to give the entire plant a more silvery appearance than common horehound. Rarely grown *M. supinum* from Spain is similar to silver horehound but more compact and has lavender-pink flowers. Keep these well-clipped for dense foliage mounds. Jim Wilson reports that silver horehound is marginally hardy in Zone 6 and advises overwintering it indoors or potting up branch tip cuttings taken in late summer. Both *M. incanum* and *M. supinum* are reliably hardy from Zones 7 to 10.

We fell in love with silver-edged horehound, *Marrubium rotundifolium*, when we admired its tight rosettes glowing by evening in Lauren Springer's dry mountain garden in Colorado. Plants grow in a low, prostrate mound, 4–10 in. (10.0–25.5 cm) tall and 12–18 in. (30.5–46.0 cm) wide, of cupped, spoon-shaped, light gray-green foliage. Woolly white undersides trace a fine silver line around each leaf, creating an incandescent silver outline. A favorite of Lauren's, she considers it a "refined treasure." If you have a dry spot in your landscape where nothing else will grow, consider yourself lucky and cover the ground with silver-edged horehound. Native to high, dry areas in Turkey, silver-edged horehound is hardy from Zones 5 to 9 or 10.

MENTHA

Common name: mint
Family: Lamiaceae, mint
Description: downy perennial
Origin: damp habitats; Eurasia
Site and soil: sun or partial shade; moist
Height and width: 2–4 ft. (0.6–1.2 m) tall; 18 in.–6 ft. (46 cm–1.8 m) wide
Hardiness: Zones 4–9

Garden mints selected for cultivation among hundreds of species are recognized by their square-sided stems and tiny two-lipped flowers, usually growing in terminal spikes. Their scents vary from species to species (even within species) and from cultivar to cultivar, from sweet to sharp, from fruity to spicy. Because they are so variable, plant identification is often difficult but can be determined by the chemistry of their essential oils. Few silvery varieties exist. Those selected here are ones we grew, identified on the basis of the names that came with them. Their slender leaves are especially downy with a silvery cast that complements their lavender and pink to purplish flowering spikes. Mints have a long history of use for flavoring, although not all mints have equal culinary value, and for medicinal purposes. Preparations from their leaves have been used effectively to treat common complaints ranging from indigestion to insomnia. Plants in bloom attract bees and butterflies, and their flowering stalks add distinction to fresh and dried bouquets. As any mint-experienced gardener knows, mints grow from a deep, spreading root system, so they are invasive unless controlled. Wherever you plant them, have a plan for dealing with them. No matter how innocent a single plant appears, never let it go among other plants, especially where growing conditions in rich, evenly moist soil are very favorable for their spread. Mulberry Creek Herb Farm suggests planting mint in a 5-gallon bucket with drainage holes. After it is filled with soil, sink the bucket in the ground, allowing 3 in. (7.5 cm) of bucket above ground to stop mint runners. If you're especially brave, try their method for a mixed mint planting, where silver and green-leaved mints show off well together (keep flowers clipped). Our own strategy is to plant silver mint in an ancient, leaky sap bucket (no extra holes needed), and set it on a wooden platform so its roots can't find soil.

We planted *Mentha buddleia* in our Connecticut garden. It appeared to be identical to *M.* 'Himalayan Silver', which we saw at Shady Acres Nursery. It, too, grows to 2 ft. (0.6 m), its spearmint-scented leaves are silvery gray, and its showy flower spikes are lavender. We were warned that it "spreads." The first couple of years were fine. This plant has lovely silvered willowy leaves and complementary flower spikes, and it combines well with other plants. Then it got established and really started taking over, so we grew it in a pot, where it was very pretty. Somehow a piece landed under our shaded back porch, where it took root. There it remains, seeking sun, spreading minimally, and still looking good, although not as full and silvery as it was on the back slope.

Mentha longifolia 'Silver Mint' came to us from Richters Herbs. We had the pleasure of observing the native wild horsemint in Israel, where it grows along ditches, waterways, and in swamps. Its gray-green leaves are narrow and toothed along their margins. Each branch terminates in spikes of tiny, purplish pink flower spikes. It is a robust, variable plant with a strong, though not unpleasant, mint flavor. We added this silver mint to our container garden, where its silvery presence shows off against nearby purple basil and crimson-colored fringed pinks. Where else but in a container garden could you consider such combinations? We cut stems all summer for bouquets so plants remain compact. Both mints grow to about 2 ft. (0.6 m) tall and 18 in. (46 cm) wide in containers and nearly double that in the most favorable habitat. Since considerable variation exists in the trade and names are uncertain, visit nurseries to pick out a nice silvery mint, whatever its name.

MISCANTHUS SINENSIS

Common name: Japanese silver grass
Family: Poaceae
Description: variegated perennial
Origin: meadows, streamsides, mountainous slopes; Asia to Africa
Site and soil: sun; moist, rich
Height and width: 5–10 ft. (1.5–3.0 m) tall; 5 ft. (1.5 m) wide
Hardiness: Zones 5–9

Cultivars of Japanese silver grass, *Miscanthus sinensis*, are reported to have been grown in Japan for hundreds of years. In nature, they are found in meadows, by moist streamsides, and on mountainous slopes from Japan to Taiwan. A warm-season grass, it grows best in moist, rich soil in full sun. Newer cultivars, bred for earlier bloom, may self-seed unless they are sterile. This is an important consideration in warmer climate areas, where plants, having had time to ripen seeds, have invaded natural areas. The tallest grasses are a very effective distant accent; all look great by water gardens, by poolside, or in shallow water. Japanese silver grass always looks good in the background of a perennial bed or as a screen or hedge. Watch out for a newly introduced mealy bug, a hitch-hiker from Asia. Japanese silver grass is rated hardy from Zones 5 to 9 but we have had no trouble keeping it in Zone 4, even in the harshest winters.

Japanese silver grass attracts attention with its tall, arching, thinly white-lined foliage—shimmering from reflected light—and silver-rose plumes. In its later stages, as foliage turns buff and plumes are transformed to fluffy silver-white, Japanese silver grass is especially translucent when backlit by the sun. One of the best for silver effect and one of the best ornamental grasses is *Miscanthus sinensis* 'Morning Light', slender and graceful with very fine-textured foliage. It is an imposing presence by virtue of its height and girth—5 ft. (1.5 m) tall and wide, to 10 or 11 ft. (3.0–3.4 m) tall in bloom. Edged with white, it has a luminous appearance, especially compelling at a distance. Late-blooming flowers emerge reddish bronze and then turn fluffy cream as they dry. These are reported to be less problematic for self-seeding, as are many older cultivars that require a longer, hotter summer to mature to the flowering and seed stage. An antique cultivar, 'Variegatus', coarser than 'Morning Light' with wider blades, creates the whitest effect because of its white-striped foliage. Red-tinted flowers open in the fall. Young plants are excellent in containers, but mature specimens, to 7 ft. (2.1 m), may need staking. Another older cultivar, 'Silberfeder', or silver feather maiden grass, has white-lined foliage, but its summer-borne feathery plumes are silvery and silky in texture, so the whole ensemble appears quite silvery. It grows from

5 to 6 ft. (1.5 to 1.8 m) tall and just as wide, and when in bloom the plant can reach 9 ft. (2.7 m).

Because of their scale (flowering stems or culms are almost as tall again as the foliage clump) and prolific bloom, the silver-plumed miscanthus are imposing silvers despite their green foliage. *Miscanthus sinensis* 'Kleine Silberspinne', little silver spider, is upright and narrow to 6 ft. (1.8 m). Its silvery plumes open in late summer. 'Malepartus', to 7 ft. (2.1 m), with wide leaves, blooms by early fall. As a bonus, its foliage turns gold, infused with orange and red. Narrow-leaved 'Graziella', to 7 ft. (2.1 m), is a beautiful grass whose graceful, silvery plumes, held well above its foliage, open by late summer or early fall. Foliage turns copper-red or orange by autumn.

NEPETA
Common name: catmint
Family: Lamiaceae, mint
Description: downy perennial
Origin: stony slopes, mountains; temperate Eurasia
Site and soil: sun or partial shade; sandy to loamy, well drained
Height and width: 6 in.–3 ft. (15 cm–1 m) tall; 12 in.–3 ft. (30.5 cm–1.0 m) wide
Hardiness: Zones 3–10

Catmints are aromatic plants whose silvery forms bear gray-green foliage, downy in varying degrees, small and oval or nearly heart-shaped, sometimes scalloped, and borne on square-sided stems characteristic of the mint family. Little tubular, two-lipped flowers, in shades of lavender-mauve and blue to white, are loosely arranged on spikes that bloom from late spring throughout the summer. Plants range in form from wide, billowy classic border types to small, tight alpine mats. Nomenclature in the genus is very muddled, creating identity problems in the trade. Nepetas produce more flowers in evenly moist soil, but excess moisture at the root crown is the death of plants and the cause of fungus disease, especially for the alpines. Leaves and flowering tops are used to make teas that soothe headaches and have a calming effect. While the plants' oils are said to repel insects, especially ants, their nectar-rich blooms attract bees and butterflies. Contrary to accepted wisdom, felines, even wild ones like bobcats, will demolish catmints by rolling on and crushing them as readily as they destroy catnip. To prevent cats from rolling on catmints, we cover the base of the plants with chicken wire. In our experience, silvery, more aromatic catmints are not bothered by deer or voles.

In the landscape, catmints are wonderful to work with since they complement so many types of plants in form and color. Billowing types are marvelous for softening harsh edges. Plant them where they spill over paths, around rocks, and against or over stone walls and interweave with other robust plants. Dwarf and tight alpines are invaluable for their foliage and long-blooming habit in a rock garden, between pavings, or in rock crevices. In the traditional border, pair catmints with pale yellow *Achillea* 'Moonshine', or use it to tone down hot pinks, strident reds, orange, strong purples, and magenta. Combinations are endless and always satisfying.

The most commonly grown catmint is *Nepeta* ×*faassenii*, a sterile hybrid 18 in. (46 cm) tall and wide, and its many cultivars. Of billowy form with mauve-colored flowers (it is sometimes called mauve catmint), it resulted from a cross between the Caucasian *N. racemosa* and the southern European *N. nepetella*. Dwarf catmint, or Persian ground ivy, a form of *N.* ×*faassenii* often offered as *N. mussinii*, grows 12 in. (30.5 cm) tall and wide and often self-seeds. The species and hybrids are hardy from Zones 3 or 4 to 8. Our first experience was with *N.* ×*faassenii* 'Dropmore', a vigorous Canada-bred catmint, 18–24 in. (46–61 cm) tall and 3 ft. (1 m) wide, with gray-toothed foliage and large, showy, lavender-blue flowers. We loved it for its willingness to flourish in less than ideal Cape Breton conditions. 'Dropmore' proved to be a satisfying substitute for more demanding lavender. In Connecticut, *N.* ×*faassenii* 'Six Hills Giant' is one of the best silvers and best plants in our garden. It is also the best one for surviving wet winters in our area. Growing to about 3 ft. (1 m) tall and wide, it is one of the largest cultivated catmints, taller and tougher than the species, producing clouds of lavender-blue flowers. Young, succulent leaves are a fresher green, but they get more silvery gray-green and fuzzy as the summer heats up. In the spring we cut plants back to about 6 in. (15 cm), so they will grow into neater, fuller mounds rather than splitting apart and sprawling. After their first bloom, which lasts more than a month, we cut them back again for repeat bloom in late summer.

Other catmints in this group are shorter, more upright, and compact. 'Blue Wonder', 18–24 in. (46–61 cm) tall, is early blooming, with rich, blue flower spikes; 'White Wonder' is its mirror image in white. 'Snowflake', 12 in. (30.5 cm) tall and 24 in. (61 cm) wide, carries its pure white flowers over silver-blue foliage, a very effective combination. 'Walker's Low', very free-blooming and compact to 10 in. (25.5 cm), has soft lilac-blue flowers. 'Superba' is a gray-green dense carpet to 12 in. (30.5 cm), with lavender-blue flowers. 'Little Tich', one of the best for planting among rocks or between pavings, produces a gray-green mat, 6–8 in. (15.0–20.5 cm) tall and 12 in. (30.5 cm) wide, with rich blue flowers.

Among classic border catmints, a few are outstanding. One of the most striking hybrids is *Nepeta* 'Joanna Reed', named after the late, great plantswoman
whose Pennsylvania garden was an inspiration to us. It is a big, upright plant,
3 ft. (1 m) tall and 2 ft. (0.6 m) wide, with gray-green leaves and very showy
spikes of pink-throated, blue-violet flowers from spring to early fall. *N. grandiflora*
'Pool Bank', to 3 ft. (1 m), is distinguished from the usual catmint by the soft
rose-purple calyces that hang on after their blue flowers have faded. *N. grandiflora*
'Dawn to Dusk' is unusual for its long spikes of rose-pink, almost salmon-pink,
flowers held in dark pink bracts. Leaves, silver-gray and coarsely toothed, grow
on plants 2–3 ft. (0.6–1.0 m) tall and 2 ft. (0.6 cm) wide.

The most silvery catmint we ever grew is *Nepeta amethystina* subsp. *laciniata*, ideal
for a rocky setting. It is a low, slender plant, 18 in. (46 cm) tall and wide, with
silver-gray, lacy foliage and whorls of pale lavender flowers marked inside a
deeper purple. Although it is rated hardy from Zones 5 to 7, we think it would
make it in Zone 4 in protected conditions. *N. phyllochlamys*, with woolly foliage
and pink flowers, native to rocky slopes in Asia Minor, is a tuft plant to 10 in.
(25.5 cm), or less for a rock crevice, where it will be protected from moisture collecting on its leaves and root crown. Although rated hardy only to Zone 8, it is
grown successfully in Denver, Colorado, Zone 5.

ONOPORDUM

Common name: thistle
Family: Asteraceae, aster
Description: downy biennial
Origin: steppes, stony slopes, disturbed ground; Mediterranean Europe, Asia
Site and soil: sun; fertile, slightly alkaline, well-drained
Height and width: 9–10 ft. (2.7–3.0 m) tall; 3 ft. (1 m) wide
Hardiness: Zones 3–9

The 40 or so species in this genus are plants of impressive dimensions with a
spiny character meant to be taken seriously. Two species are grown in gardens:
Onopordum acanthium (Scotch, giant, or silver thistle) and *O. nervosum/arabicum*
(cotton or Arabian thistle). The first year, they spend their time getting well-
established, quite a labor considering their massive proportions. Spiny-edged,
grayish-white leaves, up to 20 in. (51 cm) long and 8 in. (20.5 cm) wide and covered with fine hairs, grow up from a deep taproot to form large rosettes. The second year, hollow stems emerge from the rosettes to carry massive candelabra-like
side branches that in summer bear bristly, thistlelike flowers to 2 in. (5 cm) wide

and attract bees and butterflies. Established plants can take up 3 square feet (1 square meter) of space. By the time seed heads form, the entire plant collapses, but not before it has left behind a new generation of plants by dispersing a multitude of wind-borne seeds. In hot, dry regions, eradication procedures to extirpate these invasive weeds have become necessary. Elsewhere they are highly regarded ornamentals. Botanically, *O. acanthium* and *O. nervosum* are different species, but garden forms may be hybrids of the two. *O. acanthium*, native from western Europe through central Asia, has yellowish stems, leaves that are sparsely hairy above, and light purple or white flowers. *O. nervosum*, native to Spain and Portugal, has yellowish stems, too, but they are densely covered with cottony down (hence its common name). Its leaves, sparsely hairy below, are distinctively veined on the surface with pale cobwebbing, and its flowers are rose-purple. Both reach 9–10 ft. (2.7–3.0 m) tall. In the trade, plants or seeds offered as *O. acanthium*, the one most commonly available, are said to grow from 3 to 6 ft. (1.0 to 1.8 m) tall and have flowers variously described as rose-mauve or pink-purple. It is rated hardy from Zones 3 or 4 to 9. *O. nervosum*, said to grow to 9 ft. (2.7 m), bears purple-red or pink flowers and is less hardy, from Zones 7 to 9. Sow seeds outdoors where you want them to grow (once they develop their taproot they are difficult to move), and wear gloves when handling mature plants. Slugs, snails, and aphids can damage foliage.

Vita Sackville-West used these thistlelike plants to great effect in her famous White Garden, where she grouped them with the grays, whites, and blues of artemisias, blue lyme grass, and sea kale (*Crambe maritima*). The late John Williamson, landscape designer and enthusiastic gardener, extolled the virtues of Scotch thistle. He could not imagine his Connecticut garden complete without it, statuesque at all times, spectral in the twilight or evening garden, a distant accent that takes us into the garden and beyond.

ORIGANUM

Common name: oregano
Family: Lamiaceae, mint
Description: downy perennial, shrub
Origin: open mountain slopes; Mediterranean region, Eurasia
Site and soil: sun; sharply drained
Height and width: 4–12 in. (10.0–30.5 cm) tall; 12–16 in. (30.5–40.5 cm) wide
Hardiness: Zones 7–10

Native to warm, dry soil habitats, the silvery types in this group of 15 to 20 species are mainly spreading shrubby perennials or subshrubs, often woody at their base, with branching stems of rounded to oval leaves covered with a soft down that gives them a silvery appearance. Tubular flowers in whorls grow from colorful bracts. Plants contain oils that infuse them with their characteristic sweet to sharp camphorous aroma. Bees and butterflies are attracted to their summer blooms. Various oreganos have been used as medicinals and for flavoring for millennia. Among the silvers are both culinary and ornamental, mostly frost-tender, types. By their very nature—their hairier foliage—silvery origanums need sharper drainage than others. V. J. Billings of Mountain Valley Nursery calls them "queen of the dry."

Growers often despair of wintering *Origanum dictamnus*, dittany of Crete, one of the most desirable silver oreganos. Native to the mountains of Greece and Crete, it is an evergreen subshrub, 12 in. (30.5 cm) tall and 16 in. (40.5 cm) wide, with a domelike form and arching branches covered with rounded, densely white-felted leaves, mid-green underneath, to 1 in. (2.5 cm) long. By mid- to late summer, it sends out trailing stems to 12 in. (30.5 cm) from established plants. Bright pink flowers with projecting stamens appear in pairs, held at the tip of layered, reddish purple, cone-shaped bracts, similar in structure to the flowers of the hop vine (*Humulus lupulus*), after which characteristic it is also called hop marjoram. Among the showiest origanums, it also has culinary uses. Its thick, woolly leaves have a sweet, pennyroyal-thyme flavor. Dittany of Crete is hardy to from Zones 7 or 8 to 10. The late Madeleine Siegler, a professional herb grower in Maine, grew it outside in a hanging basket, where it flowered by August, and in the winter she grew it on a sunny windowsill. Once a year she replanted it in a professional growing medium called Pro-Mix, and she fertilized it every other month with a liquid plant food. In late winter she made 5 in. (12.5 cm) cuttings by rooting them in water and then planted them in small pots filled with Pro-Mix. Dittany of Crete sets the standard for silver origanums.

Origanum calcaratum/O. tournefortii, 14 in. (35.5 cm) tall and 18 in. (46 cm) wide, also from Crete, is similar in design but has lilac flowers with pink to purple bracts and less woolly foliage, so where it grows as a perennial subshrub from Zones 7 to 10 it is better able to survive winter. In any case, give it gritty soil to keep it dry. Like *O. dictamnus*, *O. microphyllum* is both showy and useful for culinary purposes. A dainty little shrub, 6–10 in. (15.0–25.5 cm) tall and 12 in. (30.5 cm) wide, its leaves are elegant and silver-green, its long-blooming pink to purple flowers appear in whorls among purple bracts. Grow this in a rock garden where it is hardy, from Zones 7 to 9.

PANICUM VIRGATUM

Common name: switch grass
Family: Poaceae, grass
Description: waxy perennial
Origin: grasslands, wooded areas; Europe, North America
Site and soil: sun; sand, heavy clay, or saline
Height: 3–5 ft. (1.0–1.5 m)
Hardiness: Zones 4–9

Panicum virgatum, switch grass, once covered vast areas of tall grass prairie land in North America. It is at home from the Canadian prairies to Florida, and from the Atlantic Ocean west to the Rockies. A warm-season grass, it has long been a staple of German nurseries and is now becoming popular in its native land. It is valued for its upright stems, curled leaves, showy flowers, fall color, and winter silhouette, as well as for its ability to grow in a wide range of soils and climates. Switch grass tolerates extremes of sand, heavy clay, and saline soil, as well as difficult sites, from dry slope or bog to coastal sites, but it is prone to rust. Leaves vary to 0.75 in. (1.5 cm) in width on stiff, sturdy stems and fade to shades of yellow and then beige from fall to winter. Flowers in midsummer emerge pinkish, reddish, or silvery, and then mature to grayish white or brown, persisting into winter, and usually cut back in the spring. *P. virgatum* 'Heavy Metal' is very handsome, with stiff, metallic-blue-gray leaves. Plants form a tight, upright column 3–3.5 ft. (1.0–1.1 m) tall. 'Prairie Sky', bluer than 'Heavy Metal', produces floppier growth in wetter climates. 'Dallas Blues' is getting a lot of attention. Although found in Dallas, Texas, it adapts well to cold climates. It grows upright to 5 ft. (1.5 m), producing pendant, powder-blue foliage topped by striking reddish-purple plumes. These grasses, hardy from Zones 4 to 9, are unfortunately very attractive to voles.

PENSTEMON

Common name: beardtongue

Family: Scrophulariaceae, figwort

Description: waxy perennial shrub, subshrub

Origin: high and low elevations, prairie; mostly western United States, Canada to Mexico

Site and soil: sun or partial shade; sharply drained

Height and width: 2 in.–5 ft. (5 cm–1.5 m) tall; 12–24 in. (30.5–61.0 cm) wide

Hardiness: Zones 4–9

This large genus of native flora contains some of our most showy flowers—inflated tubular florets like overblown snapdragons, often in bright blues, brilliant reds, and pinks. Foliage is frankly a foil for the blooms rather than a centerpiece in itself, but those penstemons with heavily powdered, waxy, often leathery leaves—gray-green, gray, blue-gray, and silver—not only intensify the impact of the flower-laden stalks that in some types tower above them, but they have the advantage of being attractive all season, with or without bloom. The most silvery penstemons range from low and shrubby alpines to 5 ft. (1.5 m) tall border plant perennials. The genus name comes from the Greek *pente* (five) and *stemon* (stamen), a reference to the flower's design. The common name beardtongue refers to the fifth stamen, infertile and usually quite hairy. One of the most popular penstemons, *Penstemon digitalis* 'Husker Red', is a purple-leaved cultivar, an indispensable silver companion. The culture of penstemons is complicated by their diverse origins. Although all the western species will do best in conditions similar to their native habitat, dare to gamble. Plant on a slope away from direct sun, provide the best soil conditions you can, and in a dry year, especially in the American Northeast, some will survive, even thrive, as they do in stone weaver Michael Peden's Zone 4 alpine garden in the Adirondacks. Most of those described here require the sharpest drainage, in loose, gravelly soil, from clay to mineral-rich sand, with some protection from blazing sun. The wild species do well in drought once established. High Country Gardens recommends planting high to avoid burying the root crown. Avoid organic mulches and fertilize sparingly. Most penstemons are short-lived, from three to four years, so it's a good idea to let some plants self seed. High Country counsels that self-sown seedlings are more vigorous and longer lived than the parent plant. The greatest cause of silver penstemon death is overrich soil and overwatering, but do give them a soaking in prolonged drought and heat. Deer do not appear to favor them, but hummingbirds are drawn to their nectar-rich flowers.

Two of the showier and taller penstemons, native to New Mexico and Arizona, love heat. In early summer, *Penstemon palmeri*, pink wild snapdragon, 4–5 ft. (1.2–1.5 m) tall and 24 in. (61 cm) wide, bears towering spikes of large, pink, fragrant flowers (they smell like honey) over a mound of toothed, silvery, ever-green foliage. This wildflower needs especially sandy, gravelly soil and will die in heavy clay. It is not suited to areas receiving more than 15 to 18 in. (38 to 46 cm) of rain annually. It is hardy from Zones 4 to 9. *P. pseudospectabilis*, desert beardtongue, 3 ft. (1 m) tall and 18 in. (46 cm) wide, bears clouds of hot pink to magenta flowers over large, shield-shaped, gray leaves from spring to midsum-mer. It is hardy from Zones 5 to 10. Both species are especially recommended for dry gardens of the U.S. Southwest, as is *P. grandiflorus*, large-flowered penstemon from North Dakota to Wyoming, Texas, and Illinois. Hardy to Zone 3, it is sim-ilar to *P. palmeri*, with extra-large, solid-pink flowers and thick, gray leaves. *P. gran-diflorus* 'Albus' is a white-flowered form. The showiest form of this northern Great Plains penstemon is 'Prairie Jewel', promoted by the Plant Select program. Its large trumpet flowers—from pure white through shades of lavender and rose-pink to deep purple-violet—grow up from silvery rosettes that are ever-silver where conditions are favorable. In common with all of the silvery penstemons, it struggles and eventually dies out in wet soils.

Many of the tiny alpine penstemons are hardy to Zone 4 or 5, some quite rare in cultivation. *Penstemon breviculus*, reported easy to grow in Colorado by Rocky Mountain Rare Plants, produces a dusty gray rosette topped by dark purple flowers on plants 8 in. (20.5 cm) tall and 6 in. (15 cm) wide. *P. caespitosum*, a tiny gray mat, 2 in. (5 cm) tall and 12 in. (30.5 cm) wide, grows on the western slope of the Rocky Mountains in stiff clay loam beneath sagebrush, a nice combina-tion, especially when the penstemon foliage is covered by brilliant blue flowers in spring. *P. californicus*, 3 in. (7.5 cm) tall and 8 in. (20.5 cm) wide, is reported to be particularly tough, and though originating in southern California, it has proved hardy in Denver. Foliage is powdery white, and flowers are deep purple and bloom most of the growing season. *P. petiolatus*, a gray shrublet for trough planting, is 3 in. (7.5 cm) tall and 7 in. (18 cm) wide, with bright-pink trum-pets most of the season. *P. linarioides* is an especially silvery version of the species from Colorado, also for troughs. It produces tiny mats with lavender flowers and grows 7 in. (18 cm) tall and wide. Michael Peden reports success growing *P. rupi-cola*, rock penstemon, a succulent, silver-blue mat of teardrop-shaped foliage (more blue-green under some conditions) and pink to rose blossoms on plants 3 in. (7.5 cm) tall and 12 in. (30.5 cm) wide. Try to protect it from winter sun. *P. rupicola* 'Fiddler Mountain' has especially silver foliage, a prostrate habit, and red flowers, and it grows 6 in. (15 cm) tall and 12 in. (30.5 cm) wide.

The most silvery of all alpine penstemons (and one of the rarest) may be *Penstemon debilis*, or parachute penstemon, a small plant, less than 6 in. (15 cm) tall, whose arched leaves are almost white (the large, tubular, bell-shaped flowers are white, too). As we learned from Panayoti Kelaidis, it grows only on oil shale, of which the world's largest concentration is located on the Book Cliffs (so called because the layers of shale look like pages in a book turned on its side) behind Rifle, Colorado. He says that although it is a rare plant in nature, it now seems to be securely established in cultivation, so collecting it in the wild is no longer necessary. He reports that at the Denver Botanic Gardens it fills a handsome, northeasternmost trough in the Wildflower Treasures Garden, planted in its preferred oil shale. At Michael Peden's garden, we admired a single plant that grows in clay amended with grit and shale (whether oil or not, he doesn't know, but it lives), in a setting of locally collected limestone rocks.

PEROVSKIA

Common name: Russian sage
Family: Lamiaceae, mint
Description: downy perennial
Origin: rocky, open sites; Afghanistan to Tibet
Site and soil: sun; sharp- to well-drained
Height and width: 2–4 ft. (0.6–1.2 m) tall; 1–4 ft. (0.3–1.2 m) wide
Hardiness: Zones 3–8 or 9

From small beginnings, the merest hint of silver sprouting from bare stems in spring, Russian sage grows almost as wide as it is tall by late summer, when the entire plant is covered with small, gray, serrated leaves along its silver stalks, adorned by a multitude of tiny blue or lavender-blue flowers on slender spikes. Russian sage is neither Russian nor a sage. It is named for a Russian general, and it is called "sage" because of its camphorous aroma. Russian sage has a history of use where it is indigenous. Its flowers are eaten fresh and the aromatic leaves are used like tobacco. Immune to drought, heat, humidity, pests, and diseases, growing as well in the southern United States as in the Northeast, Russian sage is a gardener's dream come true, an outstanding plant of aesthetic value that is relatively easy to grow in virtually every region of the country. Avoid overcrowding, any shade, and rich soil, which promotes leggy, weak growth and a demand for staking. Russian sage nicely dominates the scene wherever it grows, whether as a billowy hedge, a swathe of silver within the border, or a single accent. It goes with rocks, a rock wall, or a rocky outcropping as in its native habitat. Its silvery gray foliage and lavender-blue flowers complement and improve every conceivable

Perovskia atriplicifolia.

color from the brightest to the lightest pastels as well as white. Russell Page first saw Russian sage used to soften bright orange and crimson. Helen Fox thought the violet-blue flowers and silvery foliage effective when mingling among bluish foliage and bright yellow flowers. One of the most effective accent plantings we've seen was on a rise between house and driveway, where a single plant, seen from afar, resembled a wide, airy shrub. Up close, white and lilac-blue alyssum (*Lobularia*) planted at its feet echoed the same color above. It is a companion plant for most border stalwarts, improving all of them by its association.

The best of the Russian sages is *Perovskia atriplicifolia* from Pakistan, with soft blue to lavender-blue flowers. *P. abrotanoides* has more violet flowers and noticeably fringed leaves. *P.* 'Hybrida', a cross between these species, has longer flower spikes of lavender-blue and more fringed leaves than *P. atriplicifolia*. The cultivars *P.* 'Blue Spire' and 'Longin', which also have deeply cut foliage and lavender-blue flowers, are more upright. *P.* 'Filigran' has feathery foliage, an erect habit, and long, blue flower spikes. Recently, *P. atriplicifolia* 'Little Spire', a dwarf plant, has introduced a new look. Growing 20 in. (51 cm) tall and 20–24 in. (51–61 cm) wide with the most silvery of all foliage, almost white—a great contrast to its cool, lavender-blue flower spikes—it is easier to fit into a tight border or rock garden.

PICEA PUNGENS var. GLAUCA

Common name: Colorado blue spruce
Family: Pinaceae, pine
Description: waxy tree
Origin: forests; Rocky Mountains, Wyoming to Colorado
Site and soil: sun; moist, well-drained
Height and width: 50 ft. (15.2 m) tall; 15 ft. (4.6 m) wide
Hardiness: Zones 3–8

Colorado blue spruce is a native evergreen conifer, broadly conical in shape and dense in appearance, with long-lasting, four-sided needles that vary in color from bright green to steel-blue. Trees can reach 100 ft. (30.5 m) and are a handsome sight in varied populations of green and sparkling blue. Woody, oval to oblong female cones, green or red when young, purplish brown when mature, are erect at flowering and then become pendent. Male cones (on the same tree), are yellow to reddish purple and ovoid, borne on shoots from the previous growing season. Trees grow in most well-drained soils, preferably neutral to acidic, throughout the American Northeast, the Southwest, Great Lakes, Midwest, and on the Pacific Northwest coast. They can be grown in light, dry soils as long as they are watered frequently their first year when they are establishing their roots.

Selected blue forms, known collectively as *Picea pungens* var. *glauca*, have long been popular subjects for landscaping, especially dwarf types. In the Plains and north-central United States, they are often used as protective barriers or shelters for their resistance to constant wind. In a landscaping situation, they look best when they are integrated into the whole landscape rather than stranded in isolation. It is well to remember that the little nursery tree you planted under the living room window may grow only 1 to 2 ft. (0.3 to 0.6 m) a year at first, but it may eventually reach 75 ft. (22.9 m) or more after many years. Dwarf forms are delightful to work with in borders, rock gardens, or in pockets of soil in natural rocky outcrops. We have selected some of the best for their outstanding silvery appearance, but many more are available. Bear in mind that all forms are variable (especially the cheaper, seed-grown varieties), depending on the intensity of blue coloring in the parent plant.

Among the best blues are *Picea pungens* var. *glauca* 'Fat Albert', a cutting-produced form, loved for its dense, wide habit to 15 ft. (4.6 m) across, and its plump, soft blue–colored needles. 'Foxtail', possibly better for the American Southeast, is narrow and upright with needles that grow longer at the base of each branch and shorter at its tip like a fox's tail. 'Hoopsii' is a popular old cultivar, favored for its deep blue needles. It is an upright pyramid with a more open habit than others and is a faster grower. 'Hunnewelliana' is a very dense, pyramidal form with light blue needles, and it reaches only 15 ft. (4.6 m) tall and 18 ft. (5.5 m) wide after 32 years. 'Pendens', with bluish white needles is a weeping form that can be staked to grow upright. 'Thompsenii', one of the palest of the blue-whites, is similar to 'Hoopsii', but its needles are twice as thick.

Dwarf forms are usually slow growing and can be nestled in borders, naturalized plantings, rock gardens, and rockeries. Some of the best are *Picea pungens* var. *glauca* 'Globosa', very dense, round, and shrublike. It can sometimes be purchased as a standard. The popular 'Montgomery'/'R. H. Montgomery' eventually reaches 5 ft. (1.5 m) tall and 3 ft. (1 m) wide, or more, depending on growing conditions. It has a pleasing, broad, conical habit and silver-gray needles. In landscape architect Joe Hudak's Massachusetts garden it is a 6 ft. (1.8 m) specimen, effectively nestled between *Magnolia stellata* and *Juniperus ×pfitzeriana*. 'Montgomery' can be grown as a standard. 'Pendula' has a weeping, irregular form that can be trained virtually to any shape. 'Procumbens' has an irregular, almost recumbent, form that shows off over boulders or large rocks.

PLECTRANTHUS ARGENTATUS

Family: Lamiaceae, mint
Description: downy tender perennial, shrub
Origin: Australia
Site and soil: sun or light shade; evenly moist, well-drained
Height and width: 24–36 in. (61 cm–1 m) tall; 18 in. (46 cm) wide
Hardiness: Zone 10 (50°F, 10°C)

Until recently an obscure member of the same genus to which the familiar Swedish ivy belongs, *Plectranthus argentatus* is becoming popular throughout America for its ease of culture, rapid growth, and most important for its continuous production of soft, silver-gray leaves in the hot summer months. It is a sprawling, branching shrub to 3 ft. (1 m) or more in its native habitat and where it is planted in the ground. Broad, felted leaves on hairy, sturdy, squared stems are ovate to nearly heart-shaped, 2–4 in. (5–10 cm) long and 4 in. (10 cm) or more wide. Their scallop-edged leaves are so heavily textured they appear quilted. In the morning, foliage sparkles from dew caught on the leaves' fine down. Fresh inner leaves, more frosted than older outer leaves, give the entire plant a very silvery presence. By midsummer, pinkish tips begin to form between leaves, gradually developing into spikes of small, pale blue-white tubular flowers in whorls. As a forerunner of the tropical movement, plectranthus has shown the value of tender perennials for borders and containers in the hot summer climate that extends over much of the United States. According to Dr. Thomasz Anisko, curator of plants at Longwood Gardens, the cultivar 'Longwood Silver' is no different from the species Longwood originally introduced from plants received from New Zealand. 'Green Silver' is a widely distributed clone in England.

For best results, protect plants from afternoon glare. In Zones 9 and 10 in the U.S. West this is imperative. Plants need heat to get going and should never be planted out until well after the last expected frost. Plectranthus is adversely effected by temperatures below 50°F (10°C) and strong wind. Plants or cuttings are easily overwintered indoors.

Following White Flower Farm's suggestion, we combined plectranthus with *Strobilanthes dyerianus*, Persian shield, a fabulous foliage tropical from Asia and Madagascar. Strobilanthes's long, pointed, bronze foliage, heavily overlaid with iridescent pink-purple and veined bronze-green, is an exotic foil for plectranthus's soft, silver-gray foliage. When *Petunia integrifolia integrifolia*, a charming variant of wild petunia with small, vivid, magenta-pink blooms and a vining habit, weaves up through and around plectranthus, the result is eye-catching and only gets better throughout the season. As White Flower Farms observes in its catalog, "Grown alone, it's a curiosity, but combined with almost any other plant, plectranthus becomes a thing of remarkable beauty."

POPULUS ALBA
Common name: white poplar
Family: Salicaceae, willow
Description: downy tree
Origin: Europe, Asia
Site and soil: sun; moist, well-drained
Height and width: 40 ft. (12.2 m) tall; 80 ft. (24.4 m) wide
Hardiness: Zones 3–9

A familiar rural landmark, white poplar is one of 35 tough, deciduous species with coarsely toothed, lobed leaves, lustrous dark green above and tightly packed white hairs beneath, on branches that spread out to create a graceful form. In early spring, male and female flowers appear on separate trees. Their downy buds, ovate to pointed, are reported to have a bitter taste like aspirin, not surprising since the willow family, to which white poplar belongs, is a source of salicylic acid, the chemical basis of aspirin. Males produce pendant red catkins, 3 in. (7.5 cm) long, and females produce greenish flowers to 2 in. (5 cm). Their cottony seeds are dispersed in late spring and early summer. The single, straight trunk is white and smooth, darkening with age as it develops dark splits and ridges. White poplar is known as a "lively" tree, because its leaves are always in motion from the slightest breeze. In folk parlance, it foretells rain when, from shifting winds its foliage turns backward even more than usual, transforming the fluttering leaves to bright, flashing silver. Few authorities have a kind word for white poplar. Its wood is brittle and sometimes breaks in storms; its leaves, pale yellow in fall, begin to drop in summer; its roots crowd out other plants, heave pavement, and clog sewers and drainage lines. So why plant it? Garden writer David Wheeler (2001), who planted a whole avenue of them, states the case well: "To lounge beneath them on a summer afternoon and watch their white dusted undersides quivering against a sapphire sky is one of gardening's sublime rewards." It is also a graceful shade tree, a quick-growing screen, and a nurse tree (temporarily planted in front of young trees to protect them in their early growth), and it is remarkably hardy.

Observing the tree's singular beauty in nature, most apparent from a distance, gives us a clue to its landscape use. It must be a large canvas, where white poplar has space enough to create its own world without harm to others. If it fits your needs for an ironclad hardy tree with a large, bright-silver presence, plant white poplar. Look for the upright version, 'Pyramidalis' (Bolleana poplar), for screening, hedging, or windbreak, to which all the same cautionary advice applies. Its leaves are very woolly when young, and the tree retains its narrow columnar form even as it ages. It is supposed to be adaptable to damp and swampy places. In Finland, we admired a shimmering, fastigiate tree that is widely used to line streets. It was identified for us as *Populus alba columnifera* 'Nivea'. According to botanist Arno Kasvi, the cultivar came from Russia and is one of the few columnar trees that can withstand Finnish winters.

PULMONARIA

Common name: lungwort
Family: Boraginaceae, borage
Description: variegated perennial
Origin: mountainous woodland; south and central Europe
Site and soil: partial shade or shade; moist and humusy, well-drained
Height and width: 6–16 in. (15.0–40.5 cm) tall; 24 in. (61 cm) wide
Hardiness: Zones 4–8

Pulmonarias grow beneath the protective canopy of deciduous trees, whose growth cycle perfectly matches the needs of the plants growing at their base. In early spring, bare branches let in the light that pulmonarias need to initiate new growth. As the trees' leaves develop, they shield plants from summer sun. Then as autumn leaves fall, they form an incomparable mulch that gives roots the cooling moisture they need to survive and prosper. This mulch adds its nutrients to the soil as it decomposes. Pulmonarias are low and spreading to more upright and arching in form. All species grow by creeping roots that form mats of foliage. Flower buds, nestled in the decay of last season's foliage, begin to emerge early even through light snow. Tiny clustered trumpets—0.25 to 0.75 in. (0.5–1.5 cm) wide—are pink in bud and then quickly turn blue as they open, a characteristic of the borage family. The two-color phenomenon has given rise to many affectionate folk names such as Jack and Jill, William and Mary, and soldiers and sailors. Barely discernible in the budding plants, small, bristly, pointed leaves on alternate sides of the stem are light to mid-green, often splattered with little silvery moon shapes. As flowers fade, the leaves grow in size and distinction until late spring, when they assume their mature form. Foliage varies in size from 4 to 24 in. (10 to 61 cm) and in shape from very narrow and pointed to nearly heart- or lung-shaped.

Pulmonaria officinalis, the archetypal lungwort, was a cottage garden favorite, cherished for its early flowers (an important source of nectar for returning hummingbirds), ease of culture ("hundreds and thousands" aptly describes its phenomenal ability to multiply), and all-season decorative leaves. It forms clumps of bright green leaves up to 8 in. (20 cm) long, spotted with pale gray to white moons of varying size. Its flowers pass through pink and blue to shades of amethyst to mauve, finally turning white as they wither, so clusters are always multi-colored. Based on 17th-century thinking that a plant's appearance suggests its curative powers, *P. officinalis* earned a reputation for healing bronchial and lung problems because of its spotted (as if diseased) and roughly lung-shaped leaves. Both the genus and common name preserve its association with healing lung ailments.

Of the approximately 18 species, 4 others, besides common lungwort, have been cultivated for more than 200 years. *Pulmonaria angustifolia* has bright blue-violet flowers and narrow, unspotted, dark-green leaves. *P. longifolia* has more narrow leaves, but its flowers are dark blue and its leaves are well spotted with silvery white. *P. rubra* (sometimes listed under *P. montana*) is an especially vigorous, early-blooming type with coral-red flowers and large, unspotted, bright-green foliage. *P. saccharata* carries pink and blue flowers over oval, profusely spotted, silver-white leaves. For many decades, virtually all cultivars were chance seedlings or natural hybrids of these species, originating in Europe around the turn of the 20th century.

We are in the grip of a pulmonaria revolution dominated by silver-leaved types bred from these familiar species and a few others. Some are extravagantly spotted, others lavishly painted over with a metallic sheen, while still others combine a silver overlay with splattered moons, on leaves of varying lengths and widths—some waved, all sporting flower clusters in designer shades from ice blue to coral-raspberry and from 0.75 to 1.0 in. (0.5 to 1.2 cm) wide. From the humble medicinal lungwort to high fashion, pulmonaria has shot up almost overnight to become a garden star, with silver varieties earning the highest accolades. New silver cultivars in bewildering variety and numbers expand the role for silver plants, lighting up the darkest garden corners. They are brilliant partners for each other—moon-spattered green leaves against solid platinum, silver dust against silver streak—their brightness made more brilliant by a surrounding carpet of earth, one of the most enduring and effective foils for all plants. In our experience, Terra Nova pulmonarias, bred in the Pacific Northwest for beauty as well as mildew resistance, more than make the grade in the mixed conditions of the American Northeast. Among these are *P.* 'Apple Frost', 'Berries and Cream', 'Excalibur', 'Polar Splash', 'Baby Blue', 'Victorian Brooch', 'High Contrast', and 'Trevi Fountain'.

Pulmonarias love dappled or full shade and deep, moist, humusy soil, which means they need protection from the sun and a cool root run. The silvered areas on foliage cover air pockets that prevent lower layers of cells from overheating and reflect, rather than absorb, the sun's rays. This survival strategy, developed to give plants protection from unfavorable conditions in the wild, is an asset for gardeners who cope with less-than-ideal conditions in the garden. Pulmonarias with more solid silvering are more heat- and drought-resistant, as are those of the *Pulmonaria longifolia* type with narrow leaves. The foliage of all silver types becomes more silvered in heat, when plants need extra protection, but you may still experience pulmonaria meltdown if soil is inadequate or if strong sun hits them at noon. Slugs and snails are fond of their leaves, especially the thinner, less silvery ones.

Pulmonaria 'Apple Frost' resembles old-fashioned lungwort, but its spreading apple-green foliage, slightly ruffled, is showier. Leaves are heart-shaped and entirely splattered and blotched with silver that merges toward tiny moons on its green edges. Its flower clusters, similar to those of the common lungwort, bear pink buds that open to light blue, very pretty against freshly spotted foliage. This tough cultivar was one of the least affected by the adverse growing conditions of our first season trial in the Adirondacks (early heat, cold, earthquake).

Pulmonaria 'Baby Blue' is floriferous with pink to sky blue flowers above refined leaves with markings like splattered paint.

Pulmonaria 'Berries and Cream', a hybrid of 'Excalibur' × *P. rubra* 'Red Start', has undulating, splotched silver leaves, spotted toward a ruffled edge. Flower clusters are quite distinctive, starting raspberry-pink in bud and then opening to large, 1 in. (2.5 cm) wide flowers, raspberry-pink at first, maturing to purple-blue. Foliage is attractive to slugs.

According to experts, true *P.* 'British Sterling', an English introduction, no longer exists. We got ours from a friend's garden and have grown to admire it very much for its arching form and oversized foliage, entirely to irregularly heavily splotched sterling silver, with green, moon-splattered margins. Smallish flowers are magenta in bud, aging to blue.

Pulmonaria 'Cotton Cool', an English introduction, grows close to the ground with upright, spotted foliage merging into a metallic overlay. Long-blooming blue flowers, similar to those of *P. longifolia*, are quietly dazzling in the spring against fresh, cool, green-silver leaves. Its *P. longifolia* heritage also recommends it for sites with morning sun. It is attractive to slugs.

Pulmonaria 'Excalibur' is the star of our Connecticut woodland garden and a true silver classic. It starts out in late winter looking like other spotted pulmonarias, blooming blue from pink buds before the snow melts. As days get longer and warmer, its leaves grow larger and tougher and turn shiny silver with green-silver–speckled margins, as if they had been gilded with silver. It is slug and snail resistant.

Pulmonaria 'Milky Way', of 'Margery Fish' heritage, has beautifully drawn lance-shaped leaves, heavily marked with spots that catch the sun. An abundance of deep black-raspberry–colored buds open to pink-wine, the flowers changing to deep azure blue. Recommended for the U.S. South.

Pulmonaria 'Moonshine' is compact, and its large, rounded leaves are painted with platinum silver. The inner rosette, a cool lime-green, is a pleasing contrast to the outer edge of the leaf, dark green and spotted. Small flowers are blue-white and long lasting. It is mildew resistant.

Traditionally described as an offspring of *Pulmonaria saccharata* (there is some doubt now), 'Mrs. Moon' is a late 19th-century cultivar, still a favorite for its heavily spotted foliage and handsome flower clusters, pink in bud and then blue, carried on rather tall stems to 12 in. (30.5 cm). The name 'Mrs. Moon' refers to the wife of illustrator H. G. Moon and not, as one would think, the plant's moon-splashed foliage.

Pulmonaria 'Polar Splash' is like an oversized, old-fashioned lungwort, very arching in form, but its large leaves are brilliantly spotted. Its bears the typical pink-in-bud and blue flowers. A very tough plant, it was least affected by adversity in our trials, and we were able to divide it at the end of the season. Terra Nova correctly notes that it is more tolerant of sun than most other pulmonarias.

Pulmonaria 'Raspberry Ice', a variegated type, is so unlike any other pulmonaria we have ever grown or seen that it could be regarded as belonging to another group altogether. Terra Nova reports that it takes full sun in the American Northwest. Its narrow, arching leaves—over 8 in. (20.5 cm) long—taper to a sharp point. The color is frosted mint, trimmed in cream, giving the plant a very light appearance. Although foliage looks like smooth suede or velvet, it is bristly to touch, like all others, except in early spring. Adversely affected by poor growing conditions (leaf burn, slug holes) their first season in the Adirondacks, plants bounced back the following spring to bear full, long-lasting clusters of reddish pink, narrow flowers, as striking in bud as in bloom, over fresh, silver foliage. The buds and flowers make a vivid contrast against light foliage. This cultivar offers scope for landscaping and plant combinations beyond the usual. Try it in a container.

The most vigorous and least affected by adversity, *Pulmonaria* 'Raspberry Splash' has well-spotted, long and narrow leaves, 8 in. (20.5 cm) long and 1.5 in. (4 cm) wide, typical of the *P. longifolia* type. Burgundy buds in large clusters open to narrow flowers, salmon to raspberry-pink. The most immune to dry spells in our trials (although planted in a more exposed site than the others), it is a hybrid of *P. longifolia* and *P. rubra* and shows endurance and vigor from both parents.

The large, 7 in. (17 cm) long foliage of *Pulmonaria* 'Silver Shimmers' on a low-spreading clump is painted with platinum. Contrasting spotted bands on dark green along ruffled edges gives the plant distinction, as do its large, 0.75 in. (2 cm) spring flowers. These are blue, trumpet-like in form, long lasting, and very striking against platinum foliage. Mildew resistant.

Pulmonaria 'Silver Streamers' claims *P.* 'Excalibur' in its bloodlines. It has long, light green foliage with spots that merge into a metallic overlay. Ruffled edges are narrowly banded with tiny spots over a medium-green background. Large-flowered clusters, rose-pink and blue, are long lasting, and the plant is mildew resistant.

Pulmonaria 'Sissinghurst White', traditionally listed as an offspring of *P. officinalis*, is now thought to be a hybrid. A classic introduced via the Sissinghurst Castle gardens before 1960, its leaves are dark green with bright silver spots. It is a vigorous type and unusual for its pure white flowers.

New hybrids that we'd like to try in the future, all bred for mildew resistance, include *Pulmonaria* 'Dark Vader', named for its dark green, silver-spotted foliage, vigor, and dark blue flowers (it has been tested for dry, arid conditions), and *P.* 'Victorian Brooch', for its long, silver-spotted foliage and outfacing magenta-coral flowers with ruby-red calyces. *P.* 'High Contrast', regarded by Terra Nova as having the best performance in the U.S. Midwest and South, has wavy, spear-shaped, dark green leaves infused with silver, and large pink flowers that fade to blue. *P.* 'Trevi Fountain', an arching or fountainlike form with bright silver-spotted foliage, bears profuse clusters of large, cobalt-blue flowers, the best true dark blue. With *P. longifolia* in its heritage, it takes morning sun and is recommended for southern U.S. climates.

   P. saccharata 'Mrs. Moon' and *P.* 'Sissinghurst White' received the highest (four-star) rating in the 2001 Chicago Botanic Garden's pulmonaria trials for the U.S. Midwest. *P.* 'Excalibur' received a three-star rating, while *P.* 'British Sterling' did not make the grade at all.

PYRUS SALICIFOLIA
Common name: silver pear
Family: Rosaceae, rose
Description: downy tree
Origin: rocky hillsides; Europe, Asia
Site and soil: sun or light shade; well-drained
Height and width: 20 ft. (6.1 m) tall and wide
Hardiness: Zones 4–8

Silver pear was discovered by botanist-explorer P. S. Pallas and introduced to Britain in 1780. It is a slender, upright to pendulous, deciduous tree. Silver pear is distinguished among others in the genus by its silvery, willowlike foliage, very woolly in early spring growth, turning silver-green by summer. Cream-white flowers, like small wild roses, emerge from pink-tipped buds to grow in dense clusters by early spring. The fruits that follow are small, green, and insignificant. The form most often offered is 'Pendula', weeping silver pear, whose branches are significantly more pendent than in the species, and it is generally smaller, 15 ft. (4.6 m) tall and wide. The cultivars 'Silver Frost' and 'Silver Cascade' are considered to be the same as 'Pendula'. Growing best in cool climates, silver pear is adapted to a range of soils, including moderately moist, so long as it is well-drained. Some growers report frustration with maintaining the tree's weeping habit. This may be a problem inherent in the form or due to variability of seed-raised stock. The species can be grown from seed, although it will be variable in its tendency toward weeping. The cultivar must be vegetatively reproduced. To maintain a cascading effect, prune out any branches that don't follow the pattern. Silver pear, unfortunately, is very susceptible to fire blight.

   In Vita Sackville-West's famous White Garden, the silver pear has a place of honor as the focal point at the end of a walk that separates beds of silver foliage and white-flowered plants. The tree and lead statue of the virgin highlight the garden's aura of ethereal beauty. Not everyone celebrated silver pear's virtues. In 1987, when it blew down in the garden during a big storm, critics, who considered it "dumpy," suggested it be replaced with something different. It was eventually replaced with another silver pear. In the intervening years, Sackville-West's original judgement has prevailed, and silver pear is now regarded as "a tree of ultimate chic and desirability," according to English garden writer David Wheeler (2001). Grown at its best, with its crown of silvery, pendulous branches weeping over a straight trunk, it is anything but dumpy. Dan Hinkley grows pink-flowered *Clematis montana* 'Freda' through its branches for a spectacular late-spring show. Silver pear grown as a hedge, and underplanted with low mounds of bright yellow, silver-leaved *Brachyglottis* 'Sunshine' is a very satisfying combination of color and form.

RUTA

Common name: rue
Family: Rutaceae, rue
Description: waxy shrub
Origin: limestone slopes; Europe, Mediterranean regions
Site and soil: sun; sharp to well-drained
Height and width: 2–3 ft. (0.6–1.0 m) tall; 24–30 in. (61–76 cm) wide
Hardiness: Zones 4–9

Common rue, *Ruta graveolens*, one of eight species in the genus, is a low, wide plant with lacy foliage segmented into oval lobes that grows from a woody base on stems to 3 ft. (1 m). In the literature, rue's foliage is described as blue-green, but we regard it as a borderline silver because in our experience, its blue-green leaves are frosted with sufficient waxy bloom to give the impression of silvery highlights. From midsummer until fall, the top of the plant is covered with small, bright yellow flowers in clusters that are very attractive to butterflies. Each incurving flower surrounds a prominent greenish center, and when the petals fall, the knoblike green pods are left behind, giving the whole plant a decorative air over a long season. The flowerheads are regularly dried for bouquets. From its association with church services, where it was used as a brush to sprinkle holy water, rue earned the name herb-of-grace. Its reputation throughout the different cultures of Europe as a charm or repellent against evil spirits has its origin in rue's strong, pungent odor and from the acrid juice in its stem. Under certain conditions, the action of sunlight on the oils in the plant's leaves can cause skin irritation to anyone handling them. The intensity of the oil increases in older plants, so those with sensitive skin should wear gloves and long sleeves. Rue is said to repel cats in the garden but, in our experience, not deer. Rue grows well in a hot, dry site, but in extreme conditions it will be stunted and very blue, as well as very beautiful. In harsh winter areas, rue may die back almost to the ground, but it rebounds as the season warms unless it is killed by excessive winter moisture. Once confined to the knot or herb garden, rue is now moving to the forefront of the flower border. It is appreciated as a handsome, undemanding shrub with lovely foliage and a desirable mounding shape, suggesting striking combinations with plants of contrasting foliage, color, and form.

Ruta graveolens 'Jackman's Blue' is more compact than the species, to 2 ft. (0.6 m), with strikingly blue, more silvery, foliage. *R. graveolens* 'Blue Mound' is a dwarf form from 12 to 24 in. (30.5 to 62 cm), superior for edging. Mulberry Creek Herb Farm suggests growing it in groups to counterpoint roses or combining it with yellow conifers for winter color where it is evergreen. *R. chalapensis*, fringed rue, a more robust plant than common rue, bears narrow, teardrop foliage that looks fringed and large yellow flowers. In its native habitat it grows on hillsides with very tall wild fennel, and in early spring plants are crowned with flocks of swallowtail butterflies. Hardy to Zone 8, fringed rue can be grown even in the American Northeast, where flowering has been reported from late June through late July and sporadically all summer from plants overwintered indoors. *R. chalapensis* 'Dimension Two' is a prostrate form to grow among rocks or on walls.

SACCHARUM RAVENNAE

Common name: ravenna grass
Family: Gramineae, grass
Description: waxy perennial
Origin: riversides, valleys, tropical regions; North America, southern Europe
Site and soil: full to partial sun; moist to dry, well-drained
Height: 4–12 ft. (1.2–3.7 m)
Hardiness: Zones 6–10

Saccharum ravennae/Erianthus ravennae is among the largest of the cold-hardy grasses. An upright clump-former, it grows from 4 to 5 ft. (1.2 to 1.5 m). Its silvery plumes, tinged with pink in their early stage, rise 8 to 12 ft. (2.4 to 3.7 m) or more above the gray-green leaves, a massive production. Self-sowing will be a problem in warmer regions. Grow ravenna grass as an arresting accent wherever you have room. It is hardy from Zones 6 to 10.

SALIX

Common name: willow

Family: Salicaceae, willow

Description: downy tree, shrub

Origin: riverbanks, meadows, mountain screes; northern temperate regions, worldwide

Site and soil: sun; dry, moist

Height and width: 1.5–75 ft. (0.5–23.0 m) tall; 3–60 ft. (1.0–18.5 m) wide

Hardiness: Zones 2–8

This genus is a large one comprising approximately 300 species of shallow-rooted, fast-growing, and weak-wooded deciduous trees and shrubs. The most well known is weeping willow, *Salix babylonica*, but many others, more silvery, are worth growing. Willows have typically narrow and pointed foliage, green above and woolly beneath, and they range in size from dwarf shrubs to trees more than 60 ft. (18.3 m) tall. Male and female catkins—erect, fluffy, and yellowish or yellow-green—appear on separate trees before or as they leaf out. Willows, in their great numbers, are difficult to identify, and since they readily hybridize taxonomic confusion ensues. Their uses, however, are well known and have been reported since antiquity, when preparations were used to alleviate headache, fever, and pain. Their bark, a rich source of salicin, was the inspiration for synthesizing salicylic acid, the active ingredient in aspirin. Willow branches and stems are famous as a source for making rustic furniture and baskets, plants exude a natural rooting hormone, and the trees themselves are often planted to control erosion. Willows grow best in cool climates and almost any soil except shallow alkaline. A steady source of moisture for most Eurasian types ensures success, while natives prefer drier conditions and are more drought-tolerant. In common with poplars, moisture-seeking roots should be kept away from sewer and water lines, which they will find and clog. This varied group of underused trees and shrubs offers spring catkins, often colored shoots and twigs, and beautifully silvered foliage that stands out in any landscape—the tougher the site, the better. Grow willows as hedges, screens, or windbreaks; as large or small accents in a formal or informal setting, especially by a pond; or naturalize them on banks. Dwarf shrubs highlight borders, rock gardens, and trough gardens and can be trained as topiary.

Among Eurasian willows are good silvers. *Salix alba* var. *sericea*, a fine-textured silvery tree, 60–75 ft. (18.5–23.0 m) tall and 50–60 ft. (15.0–18.5 m) wide, has a rounded crown and long, pendulous branches that need space to be shown to advantage. *S. elaeagnos*, rosemary willow, rated hardy to Zone 5, grows to 10 ft.

(3 m), with dark, glossy green leaves, felted white below, and it resembles an overgrown rosemary from a distance. It is a beautiful distant accent on the grounds at the Well-Sweep Herb Farm, where it lights up in the summer heat. *S. arenaria*, rated hardy to Zone 6, is a creeping shrub to 3 ft. (1 m), with bright golden male catkins, followed by silky, silvery foliage. *S. lanata*, woolly willow, one of the most handsome and silvery of the dwarf willows, is ideal for lighting up a mixed border. A compact, rounded shrub, 4 ft. (1.2 m) tall and wide, with rounded, wavy-edged, woolly leaves, it is hardy to Zone 3. *S. purpurea* is a shrub to 18 ft. (5.5 m), with blue-green foliage and purplish stems. Growers who have discovered it love arctic willow, *S. purpurea* 'Nana', for it for its ability to grow cheerfully in heavy, wet clay and for the way it responds to trimming. In sandy soil it may develop leaf spot. Vermont nursery owner Jo Ann Darling grows it as a single bushy specimen, as a windbreak hedge, and as topiary, which takes two seasons to grow from a cutting (plunked right in the ground) into the desired shape. Plants grow 3–5 ft. (1.0–1.5 m) tall and wide and are covered with pale green leaves, bluish on their undersides, giving a silvery blue effect. In whatever form she grows arctic willow, she says visitors always ask, "What's that?" Twomby Nursery advises cutting it back 8–10 in. (20.5–25.5 cm) every other year to maintain its dark red stems, a source of winter interest. *S. purpurea* 'Canyon Blue' is a rounded shrub with steely blue-gray foliage on purplish twigs. It grows quickly to 4 ft. (1.2 m) tall and wide and is amenable to pruning back to form a lovely low hedge. *S. repens* var. *nitida*, silver creeping willow, has silver-gray foliage that grows into a uniform mound 2–4 ft. (0.6–1.2 m) tall and is reported to be well behaved. These dwarf willows are hardy from Zones 3 to 6 or 7.

The western natives include *Salix geyeriana*, silver willow, a 6–10 ft. (1.8–3.0 m) rounded shrub, hardy to Zone 4, whose twigs are silvery when young and black when older, a stunning contrast behind silvery foliage. *S. exigua*, coyote willow, to 6 ft. (1.8 m), is a clump-forming native shrub hardy to Zone 5, with pinkish twigs covered in silvery foliage. The most drought-tolerant of the silver willows is the tiny dwarf shrub *S. tristis*, or sage willow, native to dry places from Maine to Minnesota and south to Florida. It has long, narrow leaves, woolly beneath, grows only to 1.5–3 ft. (0.5–1.0 m), and is hardy to Zone 2. Dwarf willow is very happy in poor soil on a bank or in a dry rock garden.

SALVIA

Common name: sage, salvia

Family: Lamiaceae, mint

Description: downy annual, short-lived perennial, subshrub

Origin: dry meadows, rocky slopes, scrubland, light woodland, moist grasslands in temperate and subtropical regions

Sun and site: sun or partial shade; dry-moist, well-drained

Height and width: 6 in.–5 ft. (15.0 cm-1.5 m) tall; 12 in.–5 ft. (30.5 cm–1.5 m) wide

Hardiness: Zones 4–10

"The vast number of species and variants of salvia," observed salvia authority Betsy Clebsch in *Herb Companion*, "offer enough diversity to fill an entire garden with interest." Salvias belong to a large genus of about 900 species distributed around the world (more than half of them from the Americas), in varied habitats from dry and rocky to moist and grassy. Plants grow up on square stems that may become rounded in maturity, from rhizomatous or tuberous roots, and are found among very hardy to frost-tender types that must be overwintered indoors as mature plants or cuttings. In mild climates, some are evergreen. Nectar-rich tubular or hooded flowers are attractive to hummingbirds, bees, and butterflies. They bloom sparsely to prolifically on candelabras, spikes, or panicles, enhanced by the colorful calyces that hold them. Flowers in the reddish purple range, as well as cream-white, create attractive combinations with generally hairy, sometimes pebbly, and textured foliage. In some species, like *Salvia argentea*, leaves are quite woolly—from small and lance-shaped to huge and rounded (nearly heart-shaped), from silvery-white to gray-green. Often flowers, foliage, or the entire plant is strongly aromatic, perhaps a defense strategy against browsing animals. Aromas may be quite pronounced, from fruity and musky to camphorous (similar to cooking sage). The genus name is based on the Latin *salvage* (to heal or save), and *salveus* (uninjured) refers to salvias' role as an ancient healing herb as well as food. Many sages, even those regarded as "ornamental," have a history of use in their native habitats. Native salvias, for instance, have been used for centuries by American Indians. Silver sages are workhorses of the herbaceous border, for formal or informal plantings among rocks.

Often grown as a biennial, silver sage, *Salvia argentea*, from southern Europe is a short-lived perennial that in its first year produces rosettes of wrinkled, larger-than-life, easily broken foliage in a mound—each enormous, puckered leaf heavily covered with silvery white, silky down. The next year, a multitude of candelabra stalks bear near-white flowers on plants 1–2 ft. (0.3–0.6 m) tall and

3 ft. (1 m) wide with grayish foliage. It is said to be rather fussy: it must have sharply drained soil and full sun, and the flowering stalks must be cut back right after the plant booms or even beforehand to ensure its survival, which in any case is short-lived. In our experience, silver sage is accommodating to soil conditions (unless wet) and, contrary to expectations, we liked the white candelabra of bloom to lighten the edge of a lightly shaded border. When cut back after bloom, the rosette recovered for another season. We let a few plants set seed to assure a constant supply of seedlings. It is drought-tolerant, but slugs are the bane of its life. Be vigilant in checking under foliage, where they find the dark, moist conditions there conducive to raising large families. A Plant Select for 1997, silver sage is hardy from Zones 4 or 5 to 9.

A drought-tolerant native subshrub of high, dry altitudes in the Sierra Madre, germander sage, *Salvia chamaedryoides*, is a favorite with everyone who can grow it. It is loved for its dainty, mounding habit and profusion of repeat-blooming, sky-blue flowers over quilted, silvery foliage. In hotter regions, flowering occurs in the cool spring and fall. Grow it in full sun, in loamy, quick-draining soil, where it should grow to 24–30 in. (61–76 cm) tall and 20 in. (51 cm) wide.

Plants should be sheared back as needed to maintain foliage and then watered only until they show signs of regrowth. No fertilizer is needed. In the American Northeast, germander sage makes a lovely container plant or hanging basket that can be overwintered indoors. Propagation is by seed, cuttings, and division. It is aptly named after germander, with which it shares running roots. It is hardy from Zones 8 to 10.

Salvia clevelandii, blue or Cleveland sage, is one of the most ornamental of wild salvias and is very popular as a cultivated plant in California. It should be grown elsewhere, too, for it has much to recommend it: large whorls of royal blue, bergamot-like flowers are widely spaced along stems clothed in ash-gray foliage with a penetrating, camphorous, or balsamic aroma and an attractiveness to hummingbirds. It has a history of use among North American Indians for flavoring and medicinal purposes, similar to common or cooking sage (*S. officinalis*). Give it full sun and sharply drained soil for best growth, in which conditions it is 3–5 ft. (1.0–1.5 m) tall and wide. It does not do well in hot, humid climates, and Panayoti Kelaidis reports that neither this sage nor most others that originate in lowland California do well in Colorado. *S. clevelandii* 'Celestial Blue', a hybrid of *S. clevelandii* × *S. pachyphylla* bred by Las Pilitas Nursery, is a knockout, tolerant of gravel soil, extreme heat, and part sun. Its large flowers glow in showy whorls of purplish blue. Both it and Cleveland sage are hardy from Zones 7 to 10.

Salvia daghestanica, dwarf silver-leaf sage, from the Caucasus, is similar to lavender in its cultural needs. It is a gem for a hot, dry site. Plants grow 12–14 in. (30.5–35.5 cm) tall and 12 in. (30.5 cm) wide from a tight rosette of textured, nearly white foliage that is enhanced by tall, showy spikes of large, clear-blue flowers in late spring. Adventurous gardeners in other parts of the country, even in the cool, moist American Northwest, are growing dwarf silver-leaf sage in containers where soil and site can be adjusted. It is hardy from Zones 5 to 8.

A collector's item from Peru, *Salvia discolor*, Andean sage, is a study in contrast: the whole plant appears light, from hairs on the backs of leaves and from the pale green calyces that extend nearly to the tip of black (dark purple) flowers on wiry, white stems. Reaching 3 ft. (1 m), it is grown in sun (partial shade where summers are very hot) and friable soil. It needs staking, whether grown in the ground or in a container. Andean sage flowers during warm and hot spells, doesn't mind humidity, and should be watered during dry spells. It is hardy in Zone 10.

Gardeners in the southern United States, where summers are brutally hot and humid, have long decried their inability to overwinter most salvias, including common sage. In 1991, Madalene Hill and Gwen Barclay purchased some fresh herbs labeled "oregano" in a Houston grocery story. When they looked more closely, they realized they were more like sage. Madalene scraped the silvery wool from the stems and rooted all the cuttings, gave some away to other growers and a plant to Dr. Arthur O. Tucker of Delaware State College, who, with the help of the agricultural research organization *Neveh Ya'ar* in Israel, confirmed that it was one of their hybrids. While awaiting identification, the mystery plant became known as silver sage or silver-leaf sage, a working name based on its silvery sheen and large leaves. *Salvia* 'Neveh Ya'ar' (*Salvia officinalis* × *S. fruticosa*) has proved a boon to gardeners in the U.S. South because it takes heat and humidity in stride and can be grown as a perennial. Not only is it used to replace common sage in cooking (it has less of the sharp camphor content that some find disagreeable), but it is beautiful. Its leaves, Madalene reports, are incredibly soft; its stems are woolly; and its flowering spike is blue-lavender. Most years it does not bloom until April, although plants begin to show some color by mid-March. Repeat bloom, adaptability to humidity and soil, and a long life distinguishes this hybrid from *S. officinalis*. It is hardy from Zones 8 to 10.

The single word "sage" refers to *Salvia officinalis*, a gray-green, short-lived, shrubby perennial that is a popular culinary herb most widely associated with seasoning poultry and pork dishes. Originating in the Mediterranean, it has also been highly regarded as a medicinal from ancient times to the present. Preparations from its leaves have been used to treat many ailments, from indigestion and sore throat to rheumatism, and it is from its curative powers that the genus name is derived. The plant's aroma is strongly camphorous and pungent. Sage leaves are oval in shape, pebbly-velvet textured, of a soft apple green when young, turning silvery in maturity. Many gardeners who grow sage only as a culinary herb harvested in its first year miss the show the second year when stems become woody and send up flowering stalks packed with small, two-lipped blue, purplish, or white flowers in whorls. Plants need full sun and well-drained soil, and in maturity they will reach 3 ft. (1 m) tall and wide. Young plants should be well-watered, but mature plants withstand drought. As they mature and become woodier and less productive of foliage and flowers, new plants can be propagated by seed, cuttings, division, or layering in early summer. In the United States, from Zone 7 south, common sage is usually grown as an annual because it is subject to nematode attack.

Garden sage has given rise to many choice cultivars with aromatic, gray-green foliage, none as dependably hardy as the species. *Salvia officinalis* 'Albiflora' is a white-flowering form; *S. officinalis* 'Berggarten' (mountain garden) was introduced from Germany and has become very popular for its beautiful, wide, rounded leaves and compact form to 2 ft. (0.6 m), and although it bears fewer or no flowers, it is longer lived than the species. Its pungent scent is refreshing to release by rubbing, and we use its leaves just like common sage. *S. officinalis* 'Compacta'/ 'Nana' is a more compact form with slim, silvery leaves, smaller than the species; 'Minimus' is a dwarf form, 15 in. (38 cm) tall and 18 in. (46 cm) wide, reported to be more tolerant of clay; 'Rosea' is the same as the species with bright pink flowers; and 'Tricolor', probably the least hardy, has gray-green leaves beautifully colored with cream-yellow and pink areas. Trial plants of 'Purpurascens'—gray foliage flushed with purple—confirmed its status for use as a silver plant. Tucked into a low rock border, both 'Tricolor' and 'Purpurascens' make handsome rosettes of foliage, their colors playing off each other and the surrounding green and gray flora. These are rated hardy from Zones 6 to 8 but may be hardier depending on site and soil.

A tough and hardy beauty introduced in 2001 by High Country Gardens from seed collected in the California lowlands, *Salvia pachyphylla*, rose sage or giant flowered purple sage, is extraordinarily adaptable and one of the few native California sages able to take modest summer rains in the U.S. Southwest. Panayoti Kelaidis praises its performance in Colorado. It has pink to light purple tubular blooms emerging from very showy, large (almost as large as the flowers), rosy bracts, arranged in dense clusters around upright stems that grow up from ever-silver foliage. Rose sage grows best in the hottest sites in well-drained, sandy or clay loam, where it reaches 3 ft. (1 m) tall and 30 in. (76 cm) wide. As a bonus its pungent aroma keeps deer away. It is hardy from Zones 5 to 9.

Of unknown origin, *Salvia sonomensis* subsp. *clevelandii* 'Gracias', creeping sage, is a drought- and heat-tolerant hybrid perennial regarded as a gray-lover's dream for its early blue flowers over gray foliage; its low-creeping, spreading habit to 6 in. (15 cm); and its ability to spill over and around rocks in a garden or naturalized planting or from a wall. It is hardy from Zones 7 to 10.

SANTOLINA

Common name: lavender cotton
Family: Asteraceae, aster
Description: downy, short-lived shrub
Origin: rocky ground; Mediterranean region
Site and soil: sun; dry, low fertility, sharp- to well-drained
Height and width: 6 in.–2 ft. (15.0 cm–0.6 m) tall; 20 in.–4 ft. (51.0 cm–1.2 m) wide
Hardiness: 6 or 7 (possibly colder) to 9

Santolinas belong to a group of 18 evergreen shrubs that grow from a woody base to form thick bushes. Silver-leaved types are distinguished by their narrow, white or woolly foliage to 1.5 in. (4 cm), serrated like a comb or feather, growing from brittle, woody branches. Rayless button-shaped flowers blooming from early to midsummer on long, leafless stems are shades of yellow, from bright and brassy to mellow primrose. Fragrance varies with the type but is overwhelmingly camphorous. Since ancient times, santolinas have been used as moth repellent and as a vermifuge to expel worms, especially in children. Modern research suggests their antiseptic and antibiotic properties, and their extracted oils are used in perfumes. These low-growing shrubs do best in poor soil that is sandy or gravelly. Enriched soil produces loose, sprawling growth. They do not usually overwinter where moisture is excessive. The key to maintaining compact bushes is pruning, but authorities do not agree on the technique. Some advise hard pruning in spring, but Mrs. Underwood, a careful observer of all the silvers under her care, warned against cutting too far back to hardwood in the spring because plants may be slow to recover. She suggests gentle pruning every spring, and when deadheading later in the summer, shortening foliage. Some gardeners remove flowering stems so the plant's energy is directed into maintaining a well-rounded form. If you want to experience the massed blooms of santolinas, cut back stems just before flowers are spent. Once established, santolinas are very tolerant of drought. In Phoenix, Arizona, where conditions are very hot and dry, santolinas

*Santolina
chamaecyparissus.*

survive well if watered every couple of weeks. Hardiness is variable, largely depending on a favorable growing site. Gardeners in harsh winter regions report that they keep santolinas for years by heaping them with sand before the ground freezes in the fall. Plants can also be protected with evergreen boughs. To establish a santolina hedge or edger, plant 18 in. (46 cm) apart; plant 3 ft. (1 m) apart for a ground-cover effect.

Since they were introduced into England from France in the 17th century, santolinas have been considered indispensable for hedging. What would the knot or herb garden be, asked Adelma Simmons, without this little shrub, so willing to be trimmed and maintained in a stiff, upright form in knots, parterres, clover leaves, and diamond-shaped beds? There is, though, life for santolina beyond the low formal hedge. Santolinas are impressive at the front of a border, island bed, or rock garden, where they create low mounds of beautiful foliage all summer and, if you want them, clouds of plentiful flowers for at least a month. Silver santolinas share cultural requirements with and complement the colors, forms, and fragrance of salvias, nepetas, lavenders, and green santolina (*Santolina rosmarinifolia*). Naturalize them on a sunny bank, rockery, or near a rock wall, where they can attain their greatest height and width; use them to outline a broad stairway or path; or group them together near entrances or to create a low, loose hedge around a sunny patio or deck.

Gray santolina (*Santolina chamaecyparissus*/*S. incana*) may spread 3–4 ft. (1.0–1.2 m) over time. Its leaves are beautifully silvered and so intricately serrated that they look like upright white coral. From early summer through midsummer, the mound of foliage is crowned by golden buttons that rise 6 in. (15 cm) above the plant in such abundance that they seem to be borne in clusters, yet only one golden button, 0.75 in. (2 cm) wide, is borne on each stem. Two forms are especially free-flowering: the dwarf compact *S. chamaecyparissus* 'Nana', 6–8 in. (1–20 cm), and 'Pretty Carroll', a compact hybrid between 'Nana' and the species from the Maryland nursery Carroll Gardens. It grows 10–20 in. (25.5–51.0 cm) tall, with pale yellow flowers. In our experience, the smaller form performs much better than the species. It doesn't sprawl or split open, and we like its small, yellow button flowers. Ours grows where it gets afternoon shade but seems happy. Lauren Springer reports that the dwarf form is superior to the species in Colorado, too. *S. pinnata* subsp. *neopolitana*, Neopolitan santolina, with very white, woolly, feathery foliage, grows 2 ft. (0.6 m) tall and wide and bears sulphur-yellow flowers. 'Edward Bowles' is a gray-green version with primrose-yellow flowers.

SAXIFRAGA

Common name: rock breaker
Family: Saxifragaceae, saxifrage
Description: waxy perennial
Origin: mountains; temperate regions, especially Europe
Site and soil: sun or partial shade; sharp- to well-drained
Height and width: 2–8 in. (5.0–20.5 cm) tall; 5–12 in. (12.5–30.5 cm) wide
Hardiness: Zones 4–9

Saxifrages, or saxes as the devoted call them, belong to the royalty of alpine flora. "No rock garden, raised bed, or alpine-house," observed H. Lincoln Foster

(1968), "would be complete without representatives of this world-wide genus." More than 440 species vary in habit, foliage, and flower. Rosettes of leathery leaves form tiny mounds, cushions, or spreading mats. Delicate flowers—star- or cup-shaped—bloom above foliage from spring to early summer. The genus name is based on the Latin *saxum* (a rock) and *frango* (to break), a reference to saxifrages' ability to grow between rock crevices that appear to break open. For the silver-lover, the choice is narrowed to two of the six groups or sections into which saxifrages are divided by their main characteristics.

Encrusted silvers of Section Ligulatae grow into hard cushion or matted mounds of closely packed rosettes that at first glance resemble sempervivums. Unlike these, however, the saxifrage's foliage is edged with silver beading composed of calcareous or lime encrustations. Starry flowers—red, pink, or white— bloom in open sprays from late spring to early summer. Section Porphyrion, which now combines the Engleria or Kabshia subsections, are classics that come to mind when we hear the term "alpine." These form tight cushions of foliage, sometimes overlapping, with short-stemmed flowers from early to mid-spring that nearly or entirely cover the plant itself. Rugged and hardy, they prefer to grow in light shade or on a northern slope. Like the encrusted silvers, they are ideal for rock gardens, rock crevices, or troughs. All of these are rated hardy from Zones 5 or 6 to 8 or 9, but gardeners in Zone 4 grow many of them successfully, so it's well worth a try in these areas. Lincoln Foster grew such alpine gems to perfection by matching their specific needs to site and soil. In these conditions, rosettes multiplied and flowed along rock crevice joints or between rocks in a natural-seeming landscape. Cultivation varies according to whether the type needs moist moraine or semi-shaded scree conditions. If saxifrages can be grown in either, the semi-shaded face of a raised bed with alpine soil will suffice. Silver beading is strengthened on encrusted silvers by adding lime to the soil, but it isn't necessary for good growth. Wherever they are grown, saxifrages need protection from intense summer heat to prevent leaf scorching. In hot regions, grow them in partial shade. Too much shade or too much moisture results in looser cushions and may lead to the plant's eventual deterioration and demise. Foster observed that detached rosettes often formed roots on their own without any help from the gardener.

Hundreds of species and cultivars are worthy of selection. Regard the following as merely an introduction to the fascinating world of saxifrages.

Partial shaded scree conditions. The following are among the best of the encrusted silvers. *Saxifraga* ×*burnatii*, hardy from Zones 5 to 9, forms a dense tuft of diminutive rosettes with small, narrow, bluish leaves, edged in silver. White flowers are carried on 6 in. (15 cm) spikes. *S. crustata*, from the Eastern Alps and mountains of the northern and central Balkan Peninsula, forms a tight bun 6 in. (15 cm) tall and 10 in. (25.5 cm) wide, with panicles of yellowish white flowers in late spring. The cultivar 'Vochinensis' bears tiny white flowers, sometimes marked with purple at their base. They are hardy from Zones 6 to 9, as is *S. hostii* from the Eastern Alps, a vigorous spreader that forms a 12 in. (30.5 cm) mat of strap-shaped, silvery rosettes. White flowers blooming in late spring are sometimes spotted purple. Foster observed that *S. hostii* is usually seen only in a hybrid form. *S. paniculata/S. aizoon*, variable and very hardy (Zones 2–9) from Norway and Central and Southern Europe, has gray-green foliage that grows into a 6 in. (15 cm) tall and 10 in. (25.5 cm) wide cushion. In *S. paniculata* 'Cock's Comb', a congested 2 in. (5 cm) tall and 5 in. (12.5 cm) wide cushion of thick, silver leaves have a crested ridge down the middle. Both bear white flowers on 6 in. (15 cm) stems. The hybrid *S.* 'Tumbling Waters', 4 in. (10 cm) tall and 12 in. (30.5 cm) wide, is very desirable for its slow growth, silver-green foliage, and 6 in. (15 cm) large, clustered rosettes. Small, open-cup, white flowers bloom in spring after several years. It is reported hardy from Zones 6 to 7.

Moraine, partial shaded scree, or raised bed. These are rated hardy from Zones 5 or 6 to 9. *Saxifraga cochlearis* is an 8 in. (20.5 cm) tall and wide, hard, silvery dome of 1 in. (2.5 cm) wide rosettes. Its white flowers bloom in neat, airy clusters. 'Minor' forms a smaller dome with 2–3 in. (5.0–7.5 cm) tall and 0.75 in. (1.5 cm) wide rosettes, its white flowers carried on 6 in. (15 cm) stems. 'Major' forms densely packed domes of 2 in. (5 cm) wide silvery rosettes. In *S. cotyledon*, native to Iceland, Scandinavia, and the Alps, pale green rosettes are 3 in. (7.5 cm) long with lime-encrusted margins. Flowers in pyramidal clusters are cup-shaped, white, and often marked red. The cultivar 'Caterhamensis' bears strap-shaped, metallic gray leaves to 6 in. (15 cm) long. Heavily red-spotted flowers are borne on 12 in. (30.5 cm) stems.

These saxifrages from Section Porphyrion need scree conditions to thrive. They are rated hardy from Zones 5 or 6 (possibly colder) to 9, unless otherwise noted. *Saxifraga ×borisii* 'Vincent van Gogh' is an open cushion, 6 in. (15 cm) tall and 8 in. (20.5 cm) wide, with lime-encrusted foliage and primrose-yellow flowers. *S. ×boydii* 'Cherry Trees' is reported to be an easy grower. It forms a dense cushion, 3 in. (7.5 cm) tall and 6 in. (15 cm) wide, of pale gray-green rosettes and bears yellow flowers. *S. burseriana* 'Princess', a Foster selection, 4 in. (10 cm) tall and 10 in. (25.5 cm) wide, forms a spiny gray mat topped by long-flowering white blooms. Two worthy Foster hybrids include *S. ×elisabethae* 'Icicle' and *S.* 'Opalescent'. The former, very sun and cold-tolerant, forms a tight, 4 in.

(10 cm) tall and 8 in. (20.5 cm) wide, gray-green mat with long-lasting white flowers. *S.* 'Opalescent', 2 in. (5 cm) tall and 12 in. (30.5 cm) wide, has gray-green foliage topped by soft yellow flowers. Also in the section, look for *S. frederici-augusti* var. *grisebachii*, 6 in. (15 cm) tall and wide. This forms very attractive, symmetrical, silver-leaved rosettes that send up hairy stems bearing clusters of crimson-purple flowers. *S.* ×*irvengii* 'Mother of Pearl', 2 in. (5 cm) tall and 6 in. (15 cm) wide, forms hard pads of silvery rosettes embellished by large, rounded, silver-pink flowers—a beautiful combination. Lastly, *S. stribrnyi* from the Balkan Peninsula, with knifelike silvery leaves, is an exceptionally striking saxifrage of close, irregular clusters that give rise to 10 to 30 purple-pink flowers on each reddish stem. It is reported hardy from Zones 6 to 7.

SCHIZACHYRIUM SCOPARIUM

Common name: little blue stem
Family: Poaceae, grass
Description: waxy perennial
Origin: eastern United States
Site and soil: sun; lean, dry
Height: 12–18 in. (30.5–46.0 cm)
Hardiness: Zones 3–9

Little blue stem, *Schizachyrium scoparium*, is adaptable as well as variable in its blue coloring. It grows in virtually any soil but boggy and wet but retains its upright form best (even through winter snows) in lean soil. It is a warm-season grass and one of the most prevalent native grasses in the eastern United States. The cultivar 'The Blues' has 0.75 in. (1.5 cm) wide foliage to 12–18 in. (30.5–46.0 cm) in length, a beautiful powder-blue. Flower plumes by midsummer become fluffy seed heads that catch the light by fall. The foliage gradually turns bronze and then russet-red, holding its color well over the winter. It is hardy from Zones 3 to 9.

SEDUM

Common name: stonecrop
Family: Crassulaceae, orpine
Description: waxy perennial, succulent
Origin: rocky, mostly mountainous; Asia, Europe, North America
Site and soil: sun; well-drained
Height and width: 2–30 in. (5–76 cm) tall; 8–24 in. (20.5–61.0 cm) wide
Hardiness: Zones 3–9

Sedums belong to a large family of more than 400 species from varied habitats—moist to dry—throughout the Northern Hemisphere, from the coldest reaches of Siberia to tropical mountains, from coastal areas to rocky limestone outcrops and dry cliffs, where they survive by virtue of their thick, moisture-storing stems and foliage. In silver types, normally smooth, green foliage has a silvery blue or gray cast, sometimes heavily dusted with meal or wax. In different seasons it may be tinged purple or pink or edged with red. Round, clustered flowerheads—tight or loosely arranged—are composed of many tiny, five-petaled stars, white, yellow, or in the pink range. When they bloom from spring through fall, they are very attractive to bees and butterflies in search of nectar. In some, the spent flowers are ornamental throughout the winter from the dark red to rust carpels (the combined stigma, style, and ovary) that remain on the heads. The vast majority of silvery sedums are low alpines that grow as ground-hugging mats, cushions, or tufts. The more upright sort, among them some important hybrids, are neat, bushy border plants. Their common name, stonecrop, aptly describes sedums' affinity for rocks. Adding to the problems of nomenclature in this genus, some are now classified under the genus *Hylotelephium*, but most gardeners and plant nurseries still refer to these as sedums, as we do here. Hard-to-find sedeverias (×*Sedeveria*) are similar in culture to sedums. These hybrids between sedums and echeverias bear succulent heads, some of them silver, in cabbagelike rosettes.

With few exceptions, silver sedums need dry, even poor, soil, neutral to slightly alkaline, and gritty for tiny alpines. Border sedums grow well in most soils. Once established, they manage with no further watering except in the hottest climates, where they should be given light shade and an occasional drink. The main causes of failure are very wet conditions and poorly-drained soil. Overrich soil produces rangy plants, overburdened with excess growth. When matched to their preferred growing conditions, they are vigorous, in some cases to a fault. Sedums are not especially splashy, so remember that smaller ones gain

Sedum 'Vera Jameson'.

impact when grown as a mass rather than confined to a single specimen. In small, mixed containers, some types will need curbing or else they should be grown alone. No longer regarded as "utility plants," silver sedums are rising stars in the perennial repertoire for their beautiful coloring and ease of culture.

Sedum 'Matrona' is a self-hybridized seedling (*S.* 'Atropurpureum' × *S.* 'Autumn Joy') introduced from Germany. Its cultivar name, which means matron, describes a robust plant, full and upright, 24–30 in. (61–76 cm) tall and 15–18 in. (38–46 cm) wide, with gray foliage flushed burgundy on shiny burgundy stems, topped by late summer with light pink, clustered, red-centered stars alive with bees. With the onset of rainy fall weather, its leathery foliage, in our experience, turns light green. Among its many virtues, 'Matrona' is accommodating to clay or sand and is hardy from Zones 3 to 9.

Sedum 'Vera Jameson', hailed as one of the great foliage plants of all time, lives up to expectations. Growing 9 in. (23 cm) tall and 12 in. (30.5 cm) wide, it shows off its rounded, gray, plum-blushed foliage to advantage nestled against the rocks of our Adirondack kitchen garden border, where it spills over to consort with an edging of light gray lamb's ears. In late summer, this pairing is enhanced by the sedum's vivid, rose-pink flowers that bloom profusely for several weeks. For a less sprawling habit, trim plants in spring. It is hardy from Zones 3 to 9. Two other low growers, *S. sieboldii/Hylotelephium sieboldii* (October plant, from Japan) and *S. cauticola* 'Lidakense' (developed from the Japanese species) display the versatility of this group. *S. sieboldii*, 4–6 in. (10–15 cm) tall and 24 in. (61 cm) wide, is a spreader with rounded, silvery whorls of green-gray leaves arranged in threes around a radiating stem that bends under the weight of medium-pink flower clusters in fall. Try tucking a plant near the edge of a rock wall, where it will spill over and soften the wall's edge, or grow it in a hanging basket. It is hardy from Zones 3 to 9 and prefers partial shade. *S. cauticola* 'Likadense' is one of the most beautiful low sedums we have ever seen, especially tucked into a crevice. Growing 4 in. (10 cm) tall and 8 in. (20.5 cm) wide, it forms a cushion of purple-edged, light blue-gray, succulent foliage, embellished by late summer with pink stars, dark in bud, and very pretty against the light backdrop. It is rated hardy from Zones 5 to 9 but is probably hardier.

In Michael Peden's garden we saw some less commonly grown alpine sedums, all of which have proved hardy to Zone 4. *Sedum dasyphyllum*, from North Africa, begins as a tight cushion or mound and then spreads into a mat of densely packed, overlapping, powdery gray-blue foliage decorated by pink-streaked small, white star flowers with purple anthers in summer. Take care to watch its spread. *S. dasyphyllum* 'Rifense' is more silvery, with pink flowers. *S. pluricale*, from eastern Siberia, forms a low, gray hummock topped by clusters of purplish flowers, also in summer. *S. reflexum*, rock stonecrop, a European species, grows into a 12 in. (30.5 cm) high mat of linear gray foliage crowned with bright yellow flowers in summer. The cultivar 'Robustum'/'Ruby Glow', also 12 in. (30.5 cm), bears crimson-rose flowers over purple-flushed, gray foliage. Give these sedums dry, gritty conditions.

Several other alpines for a rock garden or trough range from easy to fussy. The easiest, and one adapted to conditions in the southeastern United States, is *Sedum bithynicum*, Turkish sedum, which grows in sun or partial shade and forms a 1 in. (2.5 cm) high mat of rubbery, gray-blue foliage that can spread to 2 ft. (0.6 m) over several seasons. Tiny, white star flowers in late summer are carried on russet-brown stems. In winter, the foliage takes on russet tones. It may be hardy from Zones 6 to 8. The Himalayan *S. ewersii/Hylotelephium ewersii*, is a loose, trailing form with 4–12 in. (10–30.5 cm) twiggy stems clothed with broad, blue-gray, lightly toothed leaves. In summer through fall, it produces clusters of red or pink flowers and is hardy from Zones 3 to 9. In summer, West Coast native *S. spathulifolium* covers rocky slopes and outcrops from British Columbia to central California with sheets of bright yellow stars over spoon-shaped foliage, variable in color from light green to purple. Hardy selections from higher elevations include a silver form from Oregon, *S. spathulifolium* 'Cape Blanco', which produces tightly packed, silvery-gray rosettes—its innermost leaves are heavily powdered with meal or wax—in a spreading mat 4 in. (10 cm) tall and 10 in. (25.5 cm) wide; 'Purpureum', 2 in. (5 cm) tall and 12 in. (30.5 cm) wide, is a silver-flushed purple that turns bright red in winter. Grow these in dry conditions (excess moisture causes the decay of its root system) and with some protection in exposed conditions, especially over the winter. These West Coast sedums are hardy from Zones 5 to 9. *S. pachyclados*, from Pakistan, 2 in. (5 cm) tall and 8 in. (20.5 cm) wide, produces bright, powder-blue, silvery leaves, toothed at their edges and arranged into a small, neat cushion. It bears flesh-colored star flowers in summer and is reported to be one of the easier to grow alpines, accommodating to moist soils. It is hardy from Zones 5 to 8.

SENECIO

Common name: dusty miller

Family: Asteraceae, aster

Description: downy, waxy tender perennial, subshrub

Origin: mountainous, scrubland; Alps, Mediterranean region, South America

Site and soil: sun, sharply drained

Height and width: 8–24 in. (20.5–61.0 cm) tall; 12–18 in. (30.5–46.0 cm) wide

Hardiness: Zones 5–11

Senecio viravira.

In this large genus of more than 1200 species are many silvers, but few are widely cultivated, perhaps because many are similar in appearance. Most are shrubby perennials of varying degrees of frost tenderness with gray to nearly white, deeply cut to lobed foliage and corymbs of small, daisy-like, off-white or yellow flowers. Some worthy types, like *Senecio laxifolius*, have been reclassified as *Brachyglottis laxifolius*. *S. leucostachys*, favored by Mrs. Underwood, is now *S. viravira*, rarely offered but worth looking for. While it may be known as dusty miller, the most familiar one is *S. cineraria*, sold by the millions as a bedding plant in the spring. Its sturdy, feltlike, broad, silver-white foliage (perhaps the whitest of all silver plants), crisply and precisely cut into intricate segments as with tiny scissors, is its main attraction. Small flowers, yellowish in daisylike corymbs, bloom on mature, woody-based plants in late summer and are insignificant. Previous names, other than *Cineraria maritima*, include *S. bicolor*, *S. candicans*, and *Centaurea maritima* 'Diamond'. To add to the confusion, the common name dusty miller is used to describe several other plants with whitish foliage as if dusted with flour, among them *Artemisia stelleriana*, *Lychnis coronaria*, and *Tanacetum ptarmiciflorum* 'Silver Feather'. The genus name, from the Latin *senex* (old man), refers either to the flowerhead's naked receptacle, which looks like a bald head, or to the plant's gray and woolly seeds; the Latin *cineraria* (ash) refers to the color of the plant's foliage. No less a discerning gardener than Gertrude Jekyll amply illustrated the principle that the most common plant is transformed in the hands of an inspired gardener. The same ubiquitous plant of rigid annual planting schemes, *Senecio cineraria* or *S. viravira* becomes an elegant highlight in the perennial border. Jekyll showed the way, using *S. cineraria* for carpeting and edging in beds of blue delphinium and white lavender, along a path backed by purple-blue–blooming catmint and elsewhere for fronting blue-flowered perennial asters. Explore the uses of these singular silver plants for borders, rock plantings, and containers with colorful tropicals.

Natural variations in leaf appearance—from finely to shallowly cut—and in habit—from dwarf to medium tall—has given rise to various *Senecio cineraria* cultivars. 'Cirrus' is a compact form from 6 to 8 in. (15.0 to 20.5 cm) tall, with rounded foliage that when dried looks great in wreaths with wine amaranthus. 'Diamond', especially white, is also compact and grows to 10 in. (25.5 cm). 'New Look', from 9 to 12 in. (23.0 to 30.5 cm), is a very white, oak-leaf type recommended by Alan Armitage for its resistance both to heat and frost (it survives over the winter in the southeastern United States). Very popular for its low, bushy mound of finely cut, ferny foliage, 'Silverdust', to 8 in. (20.5 cm), also winters over in the U.S. South.

Native to Patagonia and hardy to Zone 7, *Senecio viravira* is sometimes offered as *S*. 'Vira Vira'. "It is," Mrs. Underwood observed (1971), "probably the loveliest of all the small silver shrubs." Growing to 24 in. (61 cm) tall and 18 in. (46 cm) wide, its delicately cut foliage is white as well as very brittle, so handle the plant with care. Its ivory to cream flowers can be left on the plant as long as they don't cause the foliage to deteriorate.

Senecio serpens.

These dusty millers need full sun and well-drained, even sandy soil, but in sand they will need regular watering. Like many silvers, they are drought-tolerant once established, but like most very downy plants, they cannot tolerate prolonged wet and humid conditions (foliage turns a sickly green and plants eventually die). In the American Northeast, the dusty millers are grown as summer annuals or tender perennials, but some cultivars of *Senecio cineraria* are hardier than others and may winter over to Zone 5 if well mulched. In our Zone 4 garden, *S. cineraria* 'Cirrus' survived a winter of prolonged frigid temperatures under a natural oak-leaf mulch, but the plant succumbed to the cold, wet conditions of spring and early summer. In subtropical climates such as Florida and the Gulf Coast, *S. cineraria* is grown as a winter annual. In a dry Mediterranean climate, as in most of California, both *S. cineraria* and *S. viravira* can be grown as perennial subshrubs. Some growers pinch back young plants to encourage bushiness, while others let them develop a naturally looser form. Mrs. Underwood noted that when its roots are confined in a 6 in. (15 cm) pot, *S. viravira* maintains the best, most compact form and its foliage remains white all through the season. The biggest problem is aphids and root and stem rot in hot, humid conditions.

Somewhat different, *Senecio incanus* is an exquisite alpine with silver-gray, finely cut foliage growing from a woody rootstock. It is beautiful even without its canopy of yellow daisy flowers in summer. Plants grow 4 in. (10 cm) tall and 8 in. (20.5 cm) wide and are hardy from Zones 5 to 8. *S. serpens*, blue chalkstick, is different, too, because unlike the other senecios we have described, it is waxy, rather than downy. Originating in South Africa, it is a spreading shrub, 12 in. (30.5 cm) tall and 24 in. (61 cm) wide, with narrow, glaucous foliage covered with powdery bloom that gives it a very white appearance. Blue chalkstick is hardy from Zones 9 to 11.

SERENOA REPENS

Common name: saw palmetto
Family: Palmae, palm
Description: waxy shrub or tree
Origin: open forest, coastal dunes; southeastern United States
Site and soil: sun or partial shade; dry to moist, well-drained
Height and width: 10 ft. (3 m) tall; 15 ft. (4.6 m) wide
Hardiness: Zones 7b–10

The only species in the genus, saw palmetto is a hardy palm that forms dense, weedy thickets in coastal plains and in dry-to-moist open forests from South

Carolina to Florida, especially in areas disturbed by fire or clear-cutting. It is slow-growing and extraordinarily tough, able to take saline conditions and most soils, except wet. Plants grow from a short trunk, either subterranean or running along the soil surface, rooting and branching as it spreads. Bark is rough and covered with the reddish brown scars of old leaf bases. Colonies are crowned by whorls of stiff, palmate leaves in fans, 2–3 ft. (0.6–1.0 m) wide, either greenish yellow, blue, or silver-blue. The most silvery leaved types, almost white, are said to occur along the Atlantic coast in Florida. These are sometimes referred to as platinum palmetto or silver palmetto. David Price, director of horticulture at Bok Tower Gardens, reports that the most silvery saw palmettos have a coating of wax on the top and bottom of their leaves as well as their petioles. The common name comes from the 2 ft. (0.6 m) long, saw-toothed spines along the leaf's petiole or stem. Small, white flowers on large, branched clusters in early summer are followed by round, black fruits, about 1 in. (2.5 cm) in diameter, extracts from which are used in the treatment of benign prostate enlargement and as a diuretic. Medicines derived from saw palmetto may help prevent prostate cancer. Saw palmetto's diverse natural range recommends it for various habitats. Fertilize regularly, and where soil is acidic give plants an occasional dose of lime. Such care will result in an elegant specimen, far different in appearance from the weedy, wild types. It is best to establish saw palmettos from nursery-grown stock, since wild plants are difficult to transplant and digging disturbs their habitat. Seed-grown silvery saw palmettos, the only kind available, are extremely variable in coloration, from blue to nearly white. Cultivar names such as 'Cinera' are invalid.

Hardiness has been closely observed by palm enthusiasts who want to grow saw palmetto at the limit of its official hardiness range. Hardiness depends on a favorable microclimate, whether the seed was collected in a warmer or colder part of its range, specific soil conditions, the duration of the plant's exposure to cold, and its age and health (older plants have a better chance of surviving cold winter temperatures). Although rated hardy from the warmer parts of Zone 7, David Francko, botanist and author of *Palms Won't Grow Here and Other Myths* (2003), reports that saw palmetto has survived in Zones 6a and 7a in southwestern Ohio, although leaves are severely burned when temperatures drop below 10°F (-12°C), and plants will be completely defoliated around 3° to 5°F (-15° to -16°C). The good news is that because growing buds are underground, plants may regrow from their base the following season. Winter protection is an option, depending on your passion for growing palms in a cold winter climate and your tolerance of their winter-long unattractive appearance. Measures include heavy mulching, spraying with an antidesiccant, wrapping smaller plants with fabric, and wrapping the trunk and leaf bases with heating cables—but since leaves are stiff, they are usually damaged by such treatment. The author suggests protecting saw palmetto with a leaf pile enclosed by a burlap windscreen to retain maximum plant foliage at temperatures below 0°F (-18°C). He also suggests surrounding young plants with a chicken wire cage to protect them from deer and rabbits who nip off, but don't eat, leaf stems, thus destroying a season's growth in a few seconds' work.

This hardy palm grows well at the shore, near a driveway or sidewalk salted in the winter, or where a sharp, impenetrable barrier is needed. Such uses shouldn't obscure saw palmetto's potential in the ornamental landscape, where its bold, silvery foliage and tropical looks are great assets. Grow it as an intermediate layer in front of larger palms, as massed clumps in a mixed border, or as a striking low silver hedge.

SHEPHERDIA ARGENTEA

Common name: silverberry, buffaloberry
Family: Elaeagnaceae, oleaster
Description: downy shrub
Origin: prairie; North America
Site and soil: sun; dry, alkaline
Height and width: 15 ft. (4.6 m) tall; 12 ft. (3.7 m) wide
Hardiness: Zones 2–7

A deciduous shrub native to the northern latitudes of North America in open, sunny areas on poor soil, silverberry is upright and bushy. It is distinguished from green-leaved buffaloberries by its oval leaves to 2 in. (5 cm), covered on both sides by dense scales that give them a very silvery appearance. These grow on spine-tipped branchlets, silvery when young. Inconspicuous yellow flowers, male and female on different plants, bloom in spring. By fall, bright scarlet berries (sour, but very appealing to birds and used for making preserves) develop from fertilized female flowers. The genus is named for J. Shepherd, curator of the Liverpool Botanic Garden. The common name buffaloberry ties the three shrubs in this genus to their prairie habitat. As a shrub that takes any amount of cold, wind, and alkaline soil, silverberry is popular for exposed sites, especially in coastal regions or wherever the soil is poor and dry. It is a contrast to green in a shrubbery or striking as a single accent. If clipped, it makes an attractive formal silver hedge, and if untrimmed, it makes a colorful splash in fall when its bright berries show off against densely silvered foliage.

SORGHASTRUM NUTANS

Common name: Indian grass

Family: Poacea

Description: waxy perennial

Origin: prairies, dry slopes, open woods; Africa, North America, Mexico, South
  America

Site and soil: sun; moist loam

Height: 6–7 ft. (1.8–2.1 m)

Hardiness: Zones 4–10

Sorghastrum nutans, Indian grass, is one of the most beautiful of all native grasses. A tall prairie grass, its native range is extensive, from prairies and dry slopes and open woods in Quebec and Maine to Manitoba and North Dakota, south to Florida, Arizona, and into Mexico. A warm-season grower, it is tall—to 7 ft. (2.1 m)—and upright with fairly broad leaves to 0.75 in. (1.5 cm), green or glaucous in color. Flowers, by late summer, are showy by grass standards, copper-colored and marked by bright yellow pollen sacs. By fall, flowers turn chestnut brown and remain attractive for a long time in winter. Rick Darke's blue Indian grass selection, 'Sioux Blue', was chosen for its powder-blue foliage, which is transformed to yellow in fall. Plants grow to 6 ft. (1.8 m) in flower, are heat tolerant, and are impervious to rust. This is a good choice for the U.S. Southeast. It is hardy from Zones 4 to 10.

STACHYS

Common name: woundwort

Family: Lamiaceae, mint

Description: downy perennial

Origin: mountainous; Turkey, Asia

Site and soil: sun; light, dry, sharp- to well-drained

Height and width: 6 in.–3 ft. (15 cm–1 m) tall; 18 in.–3 ft. (46 cm–1 m) wide

Hardiness: Zones 4–9

All woundworts have hairy foliage to some degree, but of the approximately 300 species, those of major interest to silver buffs have thick, woolly basal foliage from 4 to 9 in. (10 to 23 cm) long, tapered or rounded, from white to silver or gray-green. Square-stemmed flowering stalks, usually covered in wool, carry small, tubular flowers typical of the mint family. Woundwort flowers attract bees in search of nectar. Some species have a distinct astringent aroma, not exactly pleasant but fortunately not very strong. The woolly types, both astringent and absorbent, have been used as a primitive bandage to clot blood on light wounds. The woolly woundworts are easy (too easy) to grow in the right conditions. In high heat, give them a little shade. Their mortal enemies are wet winter conditions, as moisture collects at the plant's base, and high heat combined with humidity. Rich soil leads to congested basal rosettes that become excellent feeding grounds for slugs. In spring, clean out dead foliage by running your fingers through the clump or by raking briskly. The woolly woundworts are both deer- and drought-resistant.

The most popular is *Stachys byzantina/S. lanata*, native from the Caucasus to Iran. Known popularly as lamb's ears for the shape and soft texture of its leaves, it is a classic of the silver genre, used primarily as an edger and ground cover in light, perfectly drained soil. Its peculiarly vanilla-scented leaves, irresistible to touch, are 3–6 in. (7.5–15.0 cm) long and covered with dense wool that gives them a whitish cast. Plants spread in flat mats, 8–10 in. (20.5–25.5 cm) tall, persisting into winter until covered by a blanket of snow. In early summer they send up numerous stems to 12–18 in. (30.5–46.0 cm), topped by whitish, thick, and woolly heads, their small, tubular, mauve flowers nearly buried in down. Not showy in themselves, they are effective in a mass, like a stand of sturdy fairy wands. Smaller, brighter, with more densely velvety leaves and less susceptible to rotting than the showier *S. byzantina* 'Big Ears', described below, *S. byzantina* takes more shade. It and its variants are ideal for edging, covering ground, tucking around rocks, as an underplanting for shrubs and roses, and for combining with other silvers of differing textures and more upright forms, even in containers. From mid-spring red tulips to colorful late salvias, lamb's ears adds invaluable silver highlights and contrasts to flower borders. As a ground cover, it effectively smothers weeds. The unimproved species is preferred over all cultivars where conditions are less than ideal, since it's more adaptable to thin and dry or heavy soil, partial shade, and humidity. The only problems to watch out for are basal rot and slugs, both avoided by growing in lean soil and keeping foliage clean and uncongested. The most important variant is 'Silver Carpet'. Mrs. Underwood reports that it originated as a sterile sport in a nursery customer's garden. When the gardener complained that her plants never flowered, a new cultivar was born. The foliage of 'Silver Carpet' is a little longer than the species, and since it never tries to flower, its leaves stay fresh all season. We have grown it in partial shade with good results, except that, as you would expect, its foliage is greener than it would be in sun. 'Cotton Boll' is peculiar for its woolly clustered "blooms" in the stem's axils. The foliage of 'Primrose Heron' emerges chartreuse and primrose yellow in spring before summer heat turns it silver. By fall, it reverts to yellow coloring.

A lot of confusion surrounds *Stachys byzantina* 'Big Ears' and 'Helene von Stein'. Some authorities claim that they are one and the same. Gardeners who have visited our gardens and seen the plant we call 'Big Ears' tell us that they bought their smaller leaf version as 'Helene von Stein'. The cultivar 'Big Ears' is so different from either the species or other cultivars that it seems like a different plant altogether. Its erect foliage is huge—8 in. (20.5 cm) long to nearly 4 in. (10 cm) wide. Plants grow as substantial, wide-spreading, rounded mounds nearly 3 ft. (1 m) tall and wide, and upright rather than flat-to-the-ground spreading mats. We grow two plants at the entrance to our rock-edged Adirondack kitchen garden, where they act as sculptured flanking guards, backed by roses and edged in front with wild thyme and Roman wormwood (*Artemisia pontica*). This stachys must be watched, though, for 'Big Ears' can get out of control. As ever more leaves are produced, overspreading their bounds, plants become congested and the inner foliage may suffer. Reduce mounds at the beginning of every season and pull out extra growth any time. *S. byzantina* 'Helene von Stein' looks like something designed with a very refined eye. In form it is between *S. byzantina* and 'Big Ears', more upright than the species, with narrow, tapered leaves, slightly cupped upward from the midrib and arched backward on strong, upright stems, 4–6 in. (10–15 cm) tall. Less downy than the species, the foliage is like gray-green velvet rather than white wool, but coloring depends how you approach the plant. Viewed straight-on, leaves appear gray-green, but viewed from an angle that allows downy surfaces to reflect sunlight, their silver nature is revealed. Gray-green undersides are puckered with a network of heavy veins that are covered, as are stems, with a dense fabric of white hairs, while leaf edges are neatly pinked to reveal a silvery edge on the leaf's topside. As with anything that survives in our Connecticut gardens long enough to become a favorite, deer don't touch it.

Lesser known woundworts, mostly rare, include several alpines for rock crevices. *Stachys citrina*, from Asia Minor, is a tufted subshrub to 14 in. (35 cm), with woolly white leaves and lemon-yellow flowers in erect spikes. *S. iva*, native to Macedonia and also woody-based, is another tufted plant, from 6 to 14 in. (15.0 to 35.5 cm) tall, with a compact spike of yellow flowers in summer. *S. saxicola* is a tender perennial hardy to Zone 10, for warm and dry habitats. It grows 8–10 in. (20.5–25.5 cm) tall with heart-shaped leaves covered with white down. Flowers in terminal spikes are white with purple stamens. *S. inflata*, to 18 in. (46 cm), from the dry, sandy grasslands of Asia Minor, is woody-based with densely covered woolly leaves—and something different for a lamb's ear type, the flowers are pink in showy spikes. *S. albotomentosa* 'Hidalgo', 16 in. (40.5 cm) tall or taller and 2.5 ft. (0.8 m) wide, is fast growing in warmer climates and sprawling, with textured, gray-green foliage, woolly underneath. Long-blooming, small, tubular peach flowers from early summer through early autumn on woolly stems pair well with blue-flowered *Salvia chamaedryoides*. It is hardy from Zones 8 to 10 but is successfully grown in the northern United States as an annual. Gardeners in the U.S. West should check out the hardy (to Zone 5) look-alike lamb's ears with yellow flowers from the little-known genus *Sideritis* from the Canary Islands. Less hardy ones (to Zone 8) have wintered over in Portland, Oregon.

TANACETUM

Common name: tansy
Family: Asteraceae, aster
Description: downy perennial
Origin: mountainous slopes; Eurasia
Soil and site: sun; sharp- to well-drained
Height and width: 10–18 in. (25.5–46.0 cm) tall; 18–30 in. (46–76 cm) wide
Hardiness: Zones 4–9

Silver tansys are one of the best kept secrets in the gardening world. If your only acquaintance with tansy is the tall, rampant *Tanacetum vulgare*, or common tansy, you may be surprised to learn that several others in the genus are worth growing for their silvered, filigreed foliage, prolific bloom, and drought-tolerance. Densely hairy, gray-white to gray, finely cut leaves grow up to form mounds or mats, sometimes from a woody base. Flowers from late spring to fall bloom in clusters—from tight to loose—composed of small, white, yellow-centered daisies or bright yellow rayless buttons. Like common tansy, most have aromatic foliage, somewhat sharp and bracing. Except for the low alpines, they tolerate a range of well-drained soils from moist to dry, but they perish where soil is both heavy and wet. The alpines are best planted in dry scree conditions. Most are short-lived, so watch for deterioration and make softwood cuttings in early summer or grow new plants from seed.

Two perennials are of special interest for their silvered beauty. *Tanacetum niveum*, silver tansy, is an undervalued landscaping plant. It is a vigorous perennial adapted to a wide range of soils, including clay, and is moderately drought-tolerant once established. Finely cut, silvery foliage, similar in appearance to old-fashioned feverfew (*T. parthenium*), forms a mound 12 in. (30.5 cm) tall and wide, transformed by late spring or early summer into a 3 ft. (1 m) tall and wide mass of small, white daisies. Its other common names, white bouquet tansy and snow daisy, are descriptive. Although short-lived, silver tansy is easy to propagate. The first year plants produce their lovely foliage; then they flower their second season.

Tanacetum ptarmiciflorum 'Silver Feather'.

Hardy from Zones 4 to 9, it goes with everything. Its foliage or flowering mound looks good with blue-flowering nepetas or blue-spiked veronica. *T. densum* subsp. *amani*, commonly known as partridge feather, is a 6 in. (15 cm) tall and 15 in. (38 cm) wide ground cover. It forms a dense carpet of soft, upright "feathers," described by its common name. By early summer it is topped by tight clusters of long-lasting, bright yellow buttons, in striking contrast to silver-white leaves. This tansy loves to bake in full sun and the driest conditions. It is not recommended for high humidity. Reclassified at least three times, silver-lace tansy, *T. ptarmicifolium* 'Silver Feather', looks like an exceedingly elegant, finely cut dusty miller senecio. It is a frost-tender, shrubby perennial, 24 in. (61 cm) tall and 16 in.

(40.5 cm) wide, usually grown as an annual in areas colder than Zone 8 or 9. Its larger upright "feathers" grow up from a woody base, and its daisylike flower-heads bloom in dense clusters in late summer.

The tiny alpines are in a group by themselves—tight, bright silver clumps for scree or rock garden. Lace-leaved *Tanacetum marshalliana*, 6 in. (15 cm) tall and 8 in. (20.5 cm) wide, looks like a small silver doily. In summer it is crowned with bright yellow daisies. *T. praeteritium* forms a 12 in. (30.5 cm) clump of powdery, white filigreed foliage covered with white daisies in early summer.

TEUCRIUM

Common name: germander
Family: Lamiaceae, mint
Description: downy shrub, subshrub
Origin: rocky, mountainous areas; Mediterranean region
Site and soil: sun; dry, sharp- to well-drained
Height and width: 2 in.–8 ft. (5.0 cm–2.5 m) tall; 6 in.–12 ft. (15 cm–3.7 m) wide
Hardiness: Zones 7–10

Teucriums belong to a genus of more than 300 species worldwide. Those of interest to the silver collector are mainly confined to the Mediterranean region, where they are found in rocky, dry habitats. They are distinguished by their ovate to lance-shaped downy foliage, white underneath or all woolly, sometimes on woolly stems, on plants that are upright and bushy or trailing. Flowers are like open mouths with a lobed lower lip but no upper, and with protruding, tongue-like stamens. Pink to purple in color, they bloom in whorled clusters from spring through summer. The plant's foliage is aromatic, characteristically resinous, sug-gesting its medicinal uses. Since antiquity, preparations have been used to allevi-ate fevers, sore throats, and headaches. The genus name may come from Teucer, the legendary Greek archer who first put it to use, or from a medical botanist named Dr. Teucer. Silvered teucriums must have perfect drainage in neutral to alkaline soil. It is important that they not be overwatered. They retain their com-pact forms best when grown in gritty, unenriched ground in an exposed, hot, dry site. All types associate naturally with rocks in rock gardens, in rocky outcrops, at the base of a stone wall, tucked into dry rock crevices, or planted in trough gardens with dwarf conifers. Among rocks, teucriums are perfect companions for other Mediterranean flora (lavenders, salvias, rosemary, and santolinas). In cold regions, grow tender teurcriums in containers for wintering over indoors. Try trailers in a hanging basket.

Teucrium fruticans.

The largest of the group is *Teucrium fruticans*, tree germander, a handsome, aromatic, and bushy shrub, 6–8 ft. (1.8–2.4 m) tall and 12 ft. (3.7 m) wide, with long sprays of ascending branches clothed with gray-green foliage, white-woolly beneath. Pale, Wedgwood-blue flowers to 1 in. (2.5 cm) with prominent stamens bloom all summer in terminal racemes to 4 in. (10 cm). We've admired it at the Norfolk Botanical Garden, where it grew in a pyramid; in Austin, where we saw it used as a parterre and clipped into globes; and in Italy, where large, tall clumps repeated throughout gave a silver impression to the whole garden at Venzano. At Quailcrest Farm in Ohio we admired it as a handsome potted shrub overwintered indoors. Whether grown in the ground or a tub, site tree lavender near a stone or brick wall where it can soak up heat. *T. fruticans* 'Azureum' is smaller, 3–4 ft. (1.0–1.2 m) tall and 6 ft. (1.8 m) wide, with similar flowers of a deeper blue.

Teucriums for the rockery or trough are short, even tiny, shrubs or shrublets, upright or low and spreading. The most familiar is *Teucrium marum*, cat thyme, 8 in. (20.5 cm) tall and 12 in. (30.5 cm) wide, with slender, gray, thymelike foliage, a foil for dark pink hooded flowers. Both stem and leaf undersides are covered with white hairs. The entire plant—leaves and branches—exude a sharply pungent aroma that is very appealing to cats. Cat thyme has a long history of use for head disorders and snuff. It is hardy from Zones 8 to 9. Two other exquisite teucriums for rockeries and dry rock crevices are *T. aroanium*, 2 in. (5 cm) tall and 6 in. (15 cm) wide, a compact shrublet from Greece with silver leaves crowned by delicate purple-veined flowers in midsummer, and hardy from Zones 5 to 9; and *T. ackermanii*, 6 in. (15 cm) tall and 18 in. (46 cm) wide, with gray, lavenderlike foliage and rosy-purple flowers in late spring or early summer, hardy from Zones 8 to 9. *T. subspinosum* forms a spiny, gray mat, 8 in. (20.5 cm) tall and wide, profusely covered with crimson flowers. Rated hardy from Zones 7 to 9, it can survive winters in Zone 5 in a sheltered position, according to Rocky Mountain Rare Plants in Colorado. *T. polium*, felty germander, is a variable type, a headache for taxonomists and anyone trying to label nursery plants accurately. The species is a woolly subshrub, 12 in. (30.5 cm) tall and wide, with twisted, branching, white-woolly stems and gray-green foliage often densely white-woolly beneath, that blooms in summer with white or reddish flowers in dense heads. It is found naturally in stony pastures and dry scrubland on limestone soil. *T. polium* is rated hardy from Zones 7 to 9. Several tiny, very tomentose forms 4 in. (10 cm) tall and 12 in. (30.5 cm) wide are rated hardy from Zones 6 to 9. These include *T. polium roseum*, with pink flowers; *T. polium* var. *aureum*, with yellow spikelets (these add little to the plant's overall appearance and could be cut off before blooming); and the similar *T. polium* 'Mrs. Milstead', with bright yellow flowers held in chartreuse bracts. *T. polium majoricum*, usually found under *T. majoricum*, is 8 in. (20.5 cm) tall and 2 ft. (0.6 m) wide and has lavender to rose blossoms all year. It is rated hardy from Zones 8b to 10. *T. polium* subsp. *cossonii*, usually found under *T. cossonii*, forms a mound of narrow, silver-gray foliage, 8 in. (20.5 cm) tall and 18 in. (46 cm) wide, and bears intense violet-purple flowers in summer. *T. polium* subsp. *pulverulentum*, sometimes listed as a synonym under *T. cossonii*, is a woollier variant. These are hardy from Zones 7 to 9.

THYMUS

Common name: thyme
Family: Lamiaceae, mint
Description: downy, variegated perennial, subshrub
Origin: dry, rocky habitats; Mediterranean Europe
Soil and site: sun; sharply drained
Height and width: 1–8 in. (2.5 20.5 cm) tall; 12–24 in. (30.5–61.0 cm) wide
Hardiness: Zones 3–9

Of the 400 or so species of thyme, two basic models prevail: low creepers and small, upright shrubs, both of which are a source of silver. Some hybrids—semi-upright, spreading, and mounding—fall between these two forms. Thyme nomenclature is very confusing for the ordinary gardener and the specialist alike. The genus name is derived either from the Greek *thumos* (courage) or *thymon* (fumigate). Both explanations are probable enough given thyme's many traditional uses as a fortifying and bracing herb to treat coughs and respiratory illnesses, earaches, migraines, and digestive problems. Thymol is a proven disinfectant against bacteria and fungi.

Creepers, as the name suggests, form spreading mats that lie close to the ground. The most well-known silver creeper is woolly thyme, *Thymus pseudolanuginosus*/*T. lanuginosus*. It forms a low carpet about 1 in. (2.5 cm) tall and 24 in. (61 cm) wide, woody at its base. Its tiny, pointed leaves and stems are densely covered with hairs, giving the entire plant a fuzzy appearance. Small, pale pink, two-lipped flowers in early summer are sparse. Unlike other thymes, it is not aromatic in any degree and has no culinary or medicinal application. Although its origins are unknown, it luxuriates in a rocky environment, softening all hard edges in its wake. It can completely cover a large rock. In our Connecticut garden, we planted it at the top of a south- and east-facing stone wall, over which it hangs, sometimes reaching the soil between the stepping stones below. In dry years, it layers itself there and starts new plants. In spells of humidity, it rots, and leaves turn black and fall off. When this happens, we cut back plants or just comb out the dead foliage. As soon as the humidity lowers, leaves recover. If you pine for this little creeper but have no luck keeping it, give woolly thyme a very sunny, dry site in sharply drained, gritty soil, neutral to alkaline, in a rocky environment. This will go a long way toward giving it the habitat it needs to survive bouts of humidity. Natural variations on a woolly thyme theme have different attributes. *T. pseudolanuginosus* 'Hall's Woolly'/'Hall's Variety' is faster growing and more generous with its pale pink to white flowers. *T.* 'Longwood' is also a fast grower with lilac flowers and a lemon thyme flavor. *T.* 'Woolly-Stemmed Sweet' forms large spreading mounds, its leaves are sweetly scented, and it produces a profusion of lavender-colored flowers. It is rated hardy from Zones 6 to 8. The others are rated hardy from Zones 5 to 7, but in our experience they make it through a Zone 4 winter in a favorable site. A less well-known silver creeper, *T. cherlerioides* 'Silver Needles', forms a slow-growing carpet of aromatic, silver-gray, needlelike leaves, similar to a tiny juniper bush. It is rated hardy from Zones 6 to 9.

The silvery bush thymes are derived from *Thymus vulgaris*, cooking thyme. Descended from a wild Mediterranean species and improved over centuries of cultivation, it grows no more than 12 in. (30.5 cm) tall, spreading as wide with age, forming a woody base from which grow many erect, twiggy branches covered with needlelike, shiny, dark green leaves. From early summer to midsummer the diminutive shrub is covered with light pink or white, two-lipped flowers tucked into leaf axils at the top of the plant and borne in profusion. At flowering time—also the time of the greatest concentration of thymol, the essential oil that gives cooking thyme its familiar, peppery mint flavor and scent—bees come in great numbers to harvest nectar. The original silvery bush thyme is *T. vulgaris* 'Argenteus', silver thyme or silver posie thyme. Like other bush thymes, it resembles a little upright shrub, 8–10 in. (20.5–25.5 cm) tall, and in summer it bears a profusion of pale blue flowers. The entire plant is aromatic, with a sharp to sweet, lightly camphorous scent. It appears silvery by virtue of its mass of gray and cream leaf variegation, tinged with pink in cold weather. Hi-ho silver thyme, *T. vulgaris* 'Hi-Ho Silver', is more compact with brighter variegation than silver thyme and is reported to have superior flavor. *T.* ×*citriodorus* 'Argenteus Variegatus', 6–12 in. (15–31 cm) tall, has small, rounded, pewter-gray leaves with white edging. Plants grow in sun or light shade, a nice foil for larger plants. Silver thymes are rated hardy from Zones 6 to 9 but may be hardier.

Two miniature alpine subshrubs, both aromatic, broaden the silver thyme repertoire. *Thymus caespititius* 'Tuffet' is 2 in. (5 cm) tall and 12 in. (30.5 cm) wide, a tight hummock of gray-green foliage topped by rose-pink flowers in summer.

It is hardy from Zones 4 to 9. *T. cilicicus* grows 3 in. (7.5 cm) tall and 9 in. (23 cm) wide and is distinguished by a furry mound of tight, gray-green foliage that is entirely hidden by elongated, lilac-pink flower clusters in summer. It is hardy from Zones 5 to 9.

Words of advice from Mulberry Creek Herb Farm: "Most thymes are hardy for us year after year. The secret is threefold: We always add compost and an organic fertilizer at planting. Secondly, we'll water thymes in really sandy soil or during a drought. We think these two measures reduce the dead wood or even a 'premature departure.' Finally, our thymes thrive in a raised bed supported with a wall of red bricks that add heat and height."

TILLANDSIA

Common name: air plant
Family: Bromeliaceae, bromeliad
Description: downy epiphyte
Origin: scrub, woodland; southern United States, Mexico, West Indies, Central and
    South America
Site: partial shade
Height and width: 2–20 in. (5–51 cm) tall; 3–20 in. (7.5–51.0 cm) wide
Hardiness: Zones 8–11

Silver tillandsias are airborne silver wisps that grow by living on but not feeding from the branches of trees. In a large genus of more than 500 species, they are distinguished by their fine, grayish white, spiky leaves in compact rosettes. By attaching clinging rootlets to their host, they are able to absorb moisture and nutrients from the atmosphere and from decayed vegetation. Their leaves—wiry, nearly tubular, arching, or waved and curly—often grow from a sheath and are covered with tiny, scalelike hairs that protect plants from drying out in difficult, often dryish habitats. As plants mature and get ready to flower—it may take as long as eight years for this to happen—they sometimes announce their imminent bloom by changing in color from gray to shades of purplish red. Tubular flowers—bluish, pink, white, or yellow—held in silver-gray or colored bracts, may be scented and bloom in globular or pyramidal heads in spring or fall. After flowers open, mature, and set feathery parachute-like seeds, the mother plant dies but leaves behind offsets nourished by the decaying parent. The genus is named after 17th-century Swedish botanist Elis Til-Landz.

Given their basic needs—moisture and nourishment—silver tillandsias are amazingly adaptable and low-maintenance plants, either outdoors in all regions

Tillandsia tectorum.

during the summer or indoors in the winter where they are not hardy. The basic procedure is to mimic their natural growth by mounting plants on a tree limb, branch, stick, piece of bark, or container. Wrap roots in damp sphagnum moss, affix the plant to its support, cover its base with a sheet of cork or bark so the moss doesn't dry out, and then lash the "planting" together tightly with fishing line. That's the official version. Actually, enthusiasts often "grow" tillandsias by nailing them to slabs of bark, wood, or limbs and letting them fend for themselves by absorbing surrounding moisture. Outdoors, site tillandsias in partial shade protected from extremes of heat, sun, and rain. Give them a light misting in very hot summer climates. Indoors, silver tillandsias grow best in bright light. Their protective fur allows them to cope with the dry conditions of modern central heating. More favorable microhabitats exist indoors wherever the moisture level is higher—in the kitchen by the dishwasher, the laundry room, or the bathroom. Depending on their moisture needs—some, like Spanish moss, *Tillandsia usneoides*, love humidity—they may need misting every day or a good soaking once or twice a week. Most authorities recommend using rainwater or soft water, but ordinary well or tap water seems fine. Once a month soak plants in a half-strength solution of balanced, water-soluble fertilizer. Other growers mist with an orchid foliar fertilizer at a quarter strength every four to five weeks. Although they vary in their needs, they will shrivel and die if left completely dry.

Tillandsia tectorum is a fairly large type, 20 in. (51 cm) tall and wide, with narrow gray leaves covered with long gray wool. Native to a dry habitat in Ecuador and northern Peru, it is a good candidate for indoor growing because it is so well adapted to a dry environment. In fact, like other woolly plants, it dislikes wet conditions. Plants grow in an open rosette, producing blue-petaled flowers banded white. It is rated hardy from Zones 10 to 11, but it may be hardier. In Florida, tillandsias are a common sight in gardens and in public displays. Among those recommended by Nancy Edmonson (director of horticulture at Selby Botanical Gardens in Sarasota) for growing outdoors in Zone 10 southwest Florida gardens are *T. usneoides* (Spanish moss) and *T. fasciculata*. Spanish moss, native to the southern United States, Central and South America, and the West Indies, is a familiar sight in the southern landscape, where it hangs down in great silvery strands from well-branched trees, especially oaks. A high-humidity tillandsia, its gray, scaly foliage twists and twines on wiry stems to as long as 25 ft. (7.6 m). It is hardy from Zones 9 to 11. *T. fasciculata*, native to Mexico, Central America, and the West Indies, produces rigid, gray-green foliage in an open pineapple-like rosette. We saw its spectacular purple and red flowers clustered on sword-shaped spikes growing in cypress trees in the Florida Everglades. This tillandsia is hardy to 45°F (7°C). Perhaps unappreciated in its normal habitat, where it can be a nuisance by its ubiquitous presence, we were charmed by the native ball moss (*T. recurvata*) that we took home on a juniper twig from Texas several years ago. It summers outside in our Connecticut garden, nailed to the wall of the back porch, and in winter it resides in a greenhouse window over the kitchen sink. Its downward-curving, narrow leaves, almost tubular and furred, are well protected against drying out, so it's very low maintenance indoors, requiring only occasional dunking. Growing 4–8 in. (10.0–20.5 cm) tall and wide, it is reported hardy to Zone 8 if kept dry in winter outdoors. Ball moss's range includes Arizona and Texas to Central and South America.

When we read the account of Tom Christopher's adventures with tillandsia, including our ball moss, in *The 20–Minute Gardener* by Chistopher and Marty Asher (Random House, 1997), we were inspired to try more that could be grown easily outdoors and overwintered indoors where they are not hardy. These include *Tillandsia argentea*—to 10 in. (25.5 cm) tall and wide, with dense rosettes of silvery white, pale-green leaves—and those recommended by Barbara Holladay, whose Holladay Jungle nursery in Fresno, California, specializes in tillandsias. These are adaptable to growing in dryish indoor conditions. Bright light and a watering/fertilizing regime will keep them fresh and silvery. *T. caput-medusae* from Mexico and Central America is medusalike, an outer space–style tillandsia that forms stemless, awl-shaped rosettes of narrow, tapered, and curvy pale-green leaves covered with coarse, silver-gray hairs. It grows 6–16 in. (15.0–40.5 cm) tall and 10 in. (25.5 cm) wide, produces blue flowers in red bracts, and is hardy to 45°F (7°C). *T. brachycaulos*, from a similar native range, also produces stemless rosettes. Its slender, arching foliage is silver-gray, threadlike at its tips, and grows from a prominent sheath that turns bright red as clustered violet flowers from red bracts come into bloom. Plants grow 10 in. (25.5 cm) tall and wide and are hardy to 45°F (7°C). *T. ionantha*, native to Mexico and Central America, is a tough little fur ball, 2 in. (5 cm) tall and 3 in. (7.5 cm) wide, and we think it would grow well indoors, too. Rated hardy from Zones 10 to 11, it is known as blushing bride after its habit of turning red as it flowers (violet in color, they are hidden inside the plant).

We are excited by the possibilities for landscaping or decorating with these odd, yet appealing, silvers. The opportunities for using them even in cold winter climates is as varied as your imagination. Indoors, Tom Christopher suspends his from nearly invisible fishing line hung beneath skylights. Barbara Holladay passed along decor tips from her customers for outdoor or indoor embellishment: place the moss-wrapped base onto a piece of driftwood or into a large shell, or affix it to a handsome rock of darker hue. Even when not in bloom, their charming, wispy form and varied textures add an exciting and unexplored dimension (at least in the northeastern United States) to the landscape.

VERBASCUM

Common name: mullein
Family: Scrophulariaceae, foxglove
Description: downy biennial, perennial
Origin: dry, stony hillsides, waste places; Eurasia, North Africa
Site and soil: sun; dry, sharply drained
Height and width: 3–6 ft. (1.0–1.8 m) tall; 12–24 in. (30.5–61.0 cm) wide
Hardiness: Zones 3–9

Common mullein, *Verbascum thapsus*, typical of the silvers in this genus, is a familiar sight along roadsides, in ditches, in gravelly soil, in old pastures, and growing on dry, steep banks. Rosettes of large, soft, densely hairy leaves, 14–20 in. (35.5–51.0 cm) long, grow up from a deep, moisture-seeking taproot, which allows it and other species to survive in drought conditions. Five-petaled, out-

Verbascum bombyciferum.

ward-facing, saucer-shaped flowers, to 1 in. (2.5 cm) or more, are packed onto densely woolly spikes on tall, erect stems. Flowers are short-lived, but since there are many, they open over a long period from early to late summer. The genus name is derived from the Latin *barbascum* (bearded), a reference to the prominent stamens of some species. Common mullein has an ancient history of herbal and household uses. Based on its mucilaginous properties, it soothed sore throats and healed wounds. Its woolly stems were effective tapers.

Wild or species verbascums are especially suited to dry, lean, alkaline soil. Rich soil produces lax, unattractive growth. They grow best where they are the star of the show, unshaded by nearby plants. Note how verbascums grow to perfection in the wild, unhindered by nearby vegetation. Hybrids, however, are more adapted to garden situations. Hybrids with heavily flowering stems may need staking in windy exposures. Beware of covering the felty rosettes with mulch, which can lead to rot over the winter or during humid spells. Cut down spent flowering stems to prolong the life of the plant, but allow a plant or two to go to seed if you want to collect seed or if you want the plants to self-sow. These perennials, in any case, are short-lived. Hybrids are usually sterile and should be propagated by division or from cuttings. As with other silvers, such as *Salvia argentea*, plants lose their silveryness when sending up bloom stalks. Verbascums may suffer from powdery mildew, fungal leaf spot, or the mullein moth, which causes defoliation. Hand-picking caterpillars is said to be effective.

Verbascums are the archetypal bold accent, an architectural giant that stands out in the landscape. Think of them as a silver statue for galvanizing any mixed border or bed, and keep in mind that the hotter and sunnier the site, the more silvery their foliage. When contemplating a "wild garden," observe wild plants in their natural habitat and try to provide similar conditions—in this case, lean, gravelly soil and a site with sparse vegetation. *Verbascum thapsus* grows to perfection in the wilder parts of our back-slope Connecticut garden, where it self-sows and rosettes stay silver all winter, and the flower stalks stand out at a distance.

An RHS AGM winner, Turkish mullein, *Verbascum bombyciferum*, is the woolliest verbascum. The hotter it bakes, the more silvery it gets. As Adelma Simmons noted in *The Silver Garden*, "The stalk looks as though it had just put on a furry coat." Its rosettes are huge and silvery, and its downy spires of sulphur-yellow saucer flowers are borne on white, fuzzy stems that reach 6 ft. (1.8 m). It grows readily from seed and is the source of several important hybrids. *V. bombyciferum* 'Polarsommer' (arctic summer), growing to 5 ft. (1.5 m), has heavily felted, silver-white foliage and yellow flowers. 'Silverkandelaber' (silver candelabra) grows 5–7 ft. (1.5–2.1 m) tall and bears candlelike spikes of yellow saucers in mid- to late summer. 'Silver Lining', often cultivated as an annual, has very silky foliage and produces its yellow flowers on fleecy stems to a towering 6.5 ft. (2 m). *V. olympicum* is similar with large, silver-white basal rosettes and deeper yellow, wide-open flowers.

Verbascums readily hybridize. The Cotswold hybrids are known for their beautifully shaded flowers and shorter stature, easier to integrate into a bed or border. The first was *V.* 'Cotswold Queen', introduced in England in 1925 and still a favorite for its vivid yellow flowers with deep maroon centers on stems that reach 4 ft. (1.2 m); 'Cotswold Beauty' has buff to apricot flowers with showy purple-pink stamens; 'Gainsborough', also to 4 ft. (1.2 m), is an RHS AGM winner with creamy yellow flowers and felted gray foliage; 'Helen Johnson', a chance seedling at Kew in the late 1980s, is a neat plant to 3 ft. (1 m), with furry gray leaves and dusky apricot to pink flowers; 'Jackie' is a semi-dwarf hybrid to 2 ft. (0.6 m), with branched spikes of dusky pink flowers above gray, furry foliage; 'Jackie in Pink', ideal for containers, is even more compact, to 16 in. (40 cm); 'Mont Blanc', to 3 ft. (1 m), combines felted gray foliage with pure-white flowers. All the mulleins are rated hardy from Zones 5 to 9, except for common mullein, which is hardy from Zones 3 to 9.

VERONICA

Common name: speedwell
Family: Scrophulariaceae, figwort
Description: downy perennial
Origin: dry, rocky steppes; Russia, Eurasia, Middle East
Site and soil: sun; sharp- to well-drained
Height and width: 3–12 in. (7.5–30.5 cm) tall; 6–8 in. (15.0–20.5 cm) wide
Hardiness: Zones 2–9

Among the 250 or so species that belong to this genus, a few are outstanding for their spreading mats of woolly, white foliage combined with blue flowers. In late spring, woolly stems send up spikes of bloom, distinguished by their graceful shape that swells out at its base and then gently tapers to a point. Each spike, no matter how small and slender, whether densely or loosely packed, looks full, almost fluffy, from the long stamens that protrude from the center of every tiny bloom. The common name is based on the Anglo-Saxon word *speed*, as it was said upon leave-taking, a wish for good health and happiness. This may be a reference to the plant's medicinal history, or it may describe the way the tiny flowers readily fall from the spike in farewell. The genus is named for Saint Veronica. Although native to dry, rocky habitats, the silvery speedwells adapt to a variety of habitats, from moderately dry to moist but well-drained soils in a raised bed. The fussier alpines need scree conditions.

The most well-known of the type is the Russian native, *Veronica spicata* subsp. *incana*/*V. incana*, silver speedwell, which does well in most well-drained soils. It forms a slowly spreading mat, 12 in. (30.5 cm) tall and wide, of woolly, white foliage that carries purple-blue or pink flower spikes beginning in spring. The cultivar 'Silver Slippers' has brighter silver-gray foliage on a flatter mat that doesn't produce flowers, and 'Wendy', to 18 in. (46 cm), forms a looser gray mat and throws up bright blue flowers. One of the best silver speedwells for both foliage and flowers is *V.* 'Minuet', to 15 in. (38 cm). It bears clear-pink flower spikes above silvery foliage mats and blooms all summer. The creepers make striking ground covers or border edgers and always look at home in a rockery.

The fussier alpines are less well-known, but choice. *Veronica bombycina* from Lebanon forms mats 2 in. (5 cm) tall and 6 in. (15 cm) wide of tiny, round, silver leaves and china-blue flowers in short spikes. It needs extra protection from overhead water and should be cut back hard after bloom to maintain a neat clump. It is rated hardy from Zones 5 to 8 with winter cover. *V. caespitosa* from Turkey forms a tight, gray cushion, 3 in. (7.5 cm) tall and 6 in. (15 cm) wide, embellished by blue flower spikes in spring, and it shows off in a trough. It is hardy from Zones 5 to 8. Confusion in the trade exists regarding *V. cinerea* and *V. thymoides* subsp. *pseudocinerea*, also sold as *V. pseudocinerea*, all rated hardy from Zones 5 to 9, with the exception noted below. Some nurseries offer *V. cinerea*, from the mountains of Turkey, as a prostrate, wiry form, 4 in. (10cm) tall and 18 in. (46 cm) wide, with sky-blue flowers; while *V. thymoides* subsp. *pseudocinerea*, said to originate in Asia Minor, is described as similar to *V. cinerea*, but slightly taller and much greener with narrow, thymelike foliage and pale-blue, white-eyed flowers. Others describe *V. cinerea* as having an upright form, with narrow, linear, needlelike foliage and pale-blue flowers, while *V. thymoides* subsp. *pseudocinerea* is described as having a prostrate form, ovate leaves, and dark blue flowers. A prostrate form with light blue flowers, hardy from Zones 3 to 8, is also offered. Lauren Springer reports that her prostrate form of *V. thymoides* subsp. *pseudocinerea* is much easier to grow than *V. cinerea*. If you want a silver alpine that will cascade over a wall, better check with the nursery before ordering. *V. orientalis*, woody oriental speedwell, is an Asian species that has bloomed reliably in High Country Gardens nursery for several years, surviving summer heat and drought. It forms woody-based mounds of gray-green, needlelike foliage, nearly covered with deep blue flowers in early to mid-spring. It is hardy from Zones 4 to 9.

VIOLA KOREANA

Common name: Korean violet
Family: Violaceae, violet
Description: variegated perennial
Origin: mountains; Asia
Site and soil: sun or partial shade; moist, well-drained
Height and width: 2–6 in. (5–15 cm) tall; 12 in. (30.5 cm) wide
Hardiness: Zones 4a–8a

In a genus of about 500 species, the Korean violet is an alpine species unique for its silver-patterned foliage. A miniature of exquisite beauty only 3 in. (7.5 cm) tall, each cyclamen-like leaf is overlaid with silver and then broadly veined and edged in an elaborate symmetrical green design, and as a final touch, flushed purple underneath. Small, blue-violet flowers appear in cool weather from mid-spring to early summer—perhaps sporadically all summer—but are cleisotamous (they do not open). This does not prevent them, however, from self-sowing prolifically, especially if they are grown in a protected, shady spot. The cultivar 'Sylettas', to 2 in. (5 cm), which shows better coloration of leaf pattern and earlier flowering, is an original selection from Thompson and Morgan Seed Company. The cultivar is more likely to produce a multitude of flowers that bloom in the conventional way. These are mauve-pink and held well above the foliage. Depending on climate, Korean violets do well in sun or partial shade. In the U.S. South, partial shade is definitely recommended. For best results, the soil should not be allowed to dry out, but kept evenly moist without overwatering. Seeds of the cultivar are reported to come true. They need to be prechilled for three weeks before sowing (indoors in most climates). If seeds are sown in late winter, plants are reported to produce flowers their first summer. Korean violets are said to be fine houseplants if kept cool. We saw Korean violets for the first time at Well-Sweep Herb Farm, where they were planted with other violas in a partial shade planting. It was mid-May and a few flowers lingered on 'Sylettas'. Foliage, as claimed, has an astonishingly beautiful silver pattern.

YUCCA

Common names: soapweed, Adam's needle, Eve's darning needle,
   Spanish bayonet, Spanish dagger, woody lily
Family: Agavaceae, agave
Description: waxy perennial, shrub, tree
Origin: deserts, plains, sand dunes; Americas, West Indies
Site and soil: sun to partial shade; sandy to clay, well-drained
Height: 20 in.–6 ft. (50.8–1.8 m)
Hardiness: Zones 5–10

These tough plants are spread across the American Southwest to the Southeast, and even to the eastern United States. While most are adapted to hot, dry conditions, some come from wetter areas. These traits, combined with remarkable hardiness, recommend their use in a variety of habitats. Clump-forming yuccas grow from rosettes of stiff, erect, lance-shaped leaves, often with fibrous edges and very sharp tips (characteristics that are preserved in many folk names). Tree yuccas with short to long trunks, sometimes shaggy, bear heads of widely radiating, narrow, stiff foliage. Those yuccas with the most powerful silver wattage are steel- to powder-blue in coloring. In the wild, yuccas are especially conspicuous in a spare landscape, when their structural form is enhanced by masses of waxy, cream to ivory bells on tall, branching stems to 10 ft. (3 m). For millennia, yucca leaves have provided food and fiber, while their roots yield saponin to make soap. As garden plants, yuccas survive low winter temperatures best if they are protected from wind and provided with perfect drainage. At the limit of their hardiness range, it is advisable to wrap trunks of tree yuccas with burlap. Mulching with gravel or grit keeps roots cool in the summer, protects them from moisture in the winter, and helps to control weeds. They should not be planted in lawns, where creeping grass roots create a problem. We admired them along roadsides in the Texas Hill Country, naturalized with little blue stem grass and *Guara lindheimeri*. Woody, flowering stems should be cut back after blooming. Young plants can be divided. Roots for cuttings can be taken from older plants by slicing off 4–6 in. (10–15 cm) long pieces. Seeds, which are long-lived, germinate in one to four weeks (stragglers may take two or three years). Follow Nancy Webber's advice regarding self-protection when in the vicinity of or handling sharp yuccas, as mentioned in the introduction to this chapter. Smaller specimens can be grown indoors over the winter and watered sparingly. Pests and diseases include cane borers, scale insects, desert beetles, and fungal leaf spot.

Along with agaves, yuccas are part of a new gardening wave of dramatic, tropical-looking plants grown for their dramatic form. Often naturalized in the U.S.

Southwest in dry gardens with cacti, agaves, grasses, and other drought-tolerant plants, they are suited to other roles that should not be overlooked. Gertrude Jekyll used taller and shorter clump types together in her gray border as strong, spiky background accents. In the northern United States, both clump and tree types look good in containers, where they are dwarfed. Tree forms are sensational alone for their dramatic silhouettes, and they bring a tropical look when combined with palms, bamboos, and other exotics. When silver-toned yuccas are paired with their green and green-gray cousins, they appear more intensely silver. The large, fearsomely tipped yuccas are very effective security barriers. The ones listed here may vary in their color according to their source.

Yucca glauca, native to the U.S. Southeast, is one of the most popular and hardy yuccas. Gray-green, pointed leaves, with thin, fibrous threads and narrowly edged in white, form neat clumps 3–4 ft. (1.0–1.2 m) wide. White flowers on 4–5 ft. (1.2–1.5 m) stems bloom in summer. *Y. glauca* is hardy to Zone 3.

Yucca pallida, blue or paleleaf yucca, is native to north-central Texas, where it grows on limestone rocks. Its powder-blue, finely serrated leaves—not dangerously sharp—give the appearance of being slightly twisted. A valuable garden plant for its low form, 20 in. (51 cm) tall and 30 in. (76 cm) wide, it grows well in humid as well as dry conditions. It is hardy from Zones 7 to 10.

Trunk-forming *Yucca rigida*, blue yucca, is slightly branched near its 12 ft. (3.7 m) top. Its powder-blue leaves are rigid, yellow at their margins, and tipped by a very sharp spine. Showy white flowers on 5–6 ft. (1.5–1.8 m) stalks bloom in summer. Supplement water in summer and plant in full sun or very light filtered shade. Blue yucca is hardy from Zones 6b or 7 to 10.

Beaked blue yucca, *Yucca rostrata*, is one of the most beautiful of all temperate types. It is a neat tree in every sense, with a tall, unbranched trunk, 6–12 ft. (1.8–3.7 m) tall, topped by a crown of narrow, pliant, powder-blue leaves that gives it the appearance of a picturesque miniature palm tree. Easily caught by the wind, leaves are always in motion. Beaked blue yucca is an elegant addition to the yucca repertoire, with many uses in the garden as a single or grouped accent or as an integral part of a larger mixed planting. It shows off especially well in a gravel bed against a stone wall, grouped with low-growing succulents. With age, the trunk, which may become branched, is embellished with flattened, dry foliage, a contrast to its head of fresh leaves. Its fruits resemble the beak of a bird, a characteristic preserved in the Latin epithet and common name. It grows well in a rocky, alkaline soil (which speeds its growth); in full sun or lightly filtered shade; and it is suitable for humid regions. Grown in lean, dry soil in full sun and without any protection, this yucca made it through several mild winters in *Horticulture* magazine editor Tom Fischer's Zone 6b garden in Boston, where its trunk doubled in size, from 1 to 2 ft. (0.3 to 0.6 m) over three warm years, until it was killed by normal winter temperatures of -10°F (-23°C). It might survive such frigid conditions if given added winter protection. It is hardy from Zones 7 to 10.

A tree form, *Yucca schottii*, mountain or Schott's yucca, produces an attractive dense rosette of broad, flat, rigid leaves to 3 ft. (1 m), strikingly steel-blue in color, on a single, unbranched trunk to 12 ft. (3.7 m) or more, and creamy white flowers on 2 ft. (0.6 m) spikes in early summer. Older specimens may produce more than one trunk. Originating in oak woodland and pine-oak forests, it is tolerant of heat and humidity but needs some protection from direct sun. It is hardy from Zones 6 or 7 to 10.

Native to rocky slopes in west Texas and into Mexico, *Yucca thompsoniana/ Y. rostrata* var. *thompsoniana*, Thompson's yucca, is a tree yucca with an arresting form for its head of narrow, radiating, powder-blue foliage; its thick, aging trunk, festooned with flattened, dried foliage; and its spring-blooming, white flowers on 4 ft. (1.2 m) or taller spikes. It grows well in humid areas and is hardy from Zones 5 or 6 to 10.

ZAUSCHNERIA
Common name: California fuchsia, hummingbird flower
Family: Onagraceae, evening primrose
Description: downy perennial
Origin: coastal areas, dry mountain slopes; western North America
Site and soil: sun; dry, well-drained
Height and width: 4–18 in. (10–46 cm) tall; 10 in.–3 ft. (25.5 cm–1 m) wide
Hardiness: Zones 5–10

Although a genus of only four species, *Zauschneria* is a taxonomic nightmare. According to some authorities, they are now listed under *Epilobium*. But since there is no consistency, we prefer to stay with *Zauschneria*, the name with which most growers are familiar. In any case, plants are highly variable. They range from less-hardy California coastal species to those that grow on dry mountainous slopes. Most are shrubby and upright, others sprawling and matlike, some with a decidedly woody base like a subshrub, while others are wholly herbaceous. Leaves from 0.75 to 1 in. (1.5 to 2.5 cm) long range from green to densely hairy and silver-gray. Flowers, generally bright scarlet and the plant's supreme attraction, are narrowly tubular to 2 in. (5 cm) long and invite hummingbirds from late summer to fall, when most types bloom. The genus was named after a German botanist, M. Zauschner. Zauschnerias need a hot, dry site by a sunny wall or walk, where other plants would wilt under the glare of the hot sun. They need especially hot weather to develop a strong root system, so favorable siting is vital in colder zones, where the growing season is relatively short. Soil should be kept on the lean side for best flowering. Although quite drought-tolerant once established, the first few years, where plants are marginally hardy, they should be watered when needed, especially during a dry winter period. Spreading by underground stems, some are potentially invasive. Keep them at bay and more attractive by pinching back tips of young plants to encourage bushy rather than rangy growth and deadhead as much as you can. In colder areas, plant in the spring or summer, never in the fall, and don't remove the season's spent growth until the following spring. Seeds may take from 30 to 60 days to germinate. Silver-leaved types look great, even when not in bloom, when they are trailing over walls, large rocks or boulders, or down a bank in a seminaturalized setting or rock garden. The best way to find out about zauschnerias is to visit specialty nurseries where you can see their different forms (upright and compact or more sprawling) and silvered foliage.

The most important and variable species is *Zauschneria californica*, whose range reaches from California to southern Oregon. It grows 8–18 in. (20.5–46.0 cm) tall and 30 in. (76 cm) wide; is woody-based with furry, gray-green foliage; and produces scarlet trumpets from midsummer to frost. It is hardy from Zones 7 to 10. Variants are confusedly classified as cultivars of this species, as subspecies, or as separate species altogether—something to keep in mind when looking for them. For a more compact and less sprawling form, look for *Z. californica*, Compact Form, 6 in. (15 cm) tall and 18 in. (46 cm) wide, offered by Siskiyou Rare Plant Nursery. *Z. californica* 'Etteri' is a superior plant with a low-spreading habit, 8 in. (20.5 cm) tall and 30 in. (76 cm) wide, with extra-large scarlet flowers. Once established in a favorable situation, its spread can reach 2.5 ft. (0.8 m). *Z. californica* 'Wayne's Silver' is everything a silver aficionado craves. It is a less vigorous spreader than usual, 12 in. (30.5 cm) tall and 3 ft. (1 m) wide, with good-sized scarlet flowers, and—most important—its narrow leaves on short, erect stems are heavily silvered. *Z. californica* subsp. *latifolia*/*Z. latifolia* is a hardier mountain species. It forms a substantial gray-green herbaceous clump, 10–16 in. (25.5–41.0 cm) tall and 10 in. (25.5 cm) wide, is covered with a solid red canopy of flowers, and is hardy to Zone 5. A good sort for tucking in small spaces, *Z. septentrionalis*, 8 in. (20.5 cm) tall and 18 in. (46 cm) wide, is valued for its gray-green foliage; dwarf, tufted, neat form; and noninvasive habit. It is hardy from Zones 7 to 10. Another noninvasive kind, *Z.* 'Mattole Select', has silvered leaves and the usual scarlet flowers, and it grows to 12 in. (30.5 cm) tall and 3 ft. (1 m) wide. It is rated hardy from Zones 7 to 10.

ZENOBIA PULVERULENTA
Common name: dusty zenobia
Family: Ericaceae, heath
Description: waxy shrub
Origin: coastal plain, bogs; North Carolina to Florida
Site and soil: sun or partial shade; moist, acid
Height and width: 4–6 ft. (1.2–1.8 m) tall and wide
Hardiness: Zones 5–9

The only species in the genus, dusty zenobia is a slow-growing, gracefully arching shrub that establishes spreading, somewhat suckering colonies along the coastal plain of the southeastern United States in bogs and among low thickets of evergreen shrubs. Its deciduous leaves, 1–3 in. (2.5–7.5 cm) long, are oval to oblong. These, as well as the stems, are lightly to heavily covered with waxy bloom that colors them gray-green to silver-blue. The phenomenon is recorded in its common name and in the Latin epithet *pulverulenta* (powdered). In the most silver-blue forms, the upper leaf surface is bluish and the lower surface is chalk-white. Bell-shaped flowers are like oversized blueberry blooms, but more wide open and fragrant, with a citrus or anise scent. They bloom on old wood in nodding clusters from late spring to early summer for two to three weeks. By fall, leaves tinged yellow with a touch of red hold on well into winter. Gardeners report that older leaves may turn green by summer. Look for blue-leaf forms or the cultivar 'Woodlander's Blue', introduced by Woodlanders nursery. Leaves retain their blue coloring in spring and summer, and yellowish fall leaves are tinged with reddish purple overtones. Although native to areas with moist, acidic soil with some shade, gardeners report that dusty zenobia does well in sun in most loamy soils. Michael Dirr has observed specimens at the Arnold Arboretum that were growing in full sun in sandy, rocky soil. It is tolerant of heat and some drought, but as Dirr suggests, plants should have even moisture in their early years while they are becoming established. Prune after flowering. Remember that seed-grown shrubs are variable and may not be silvery.

Our vote for the most valuable, underused native shrub goes to dusty zenobia, adaptable to gardens from New England to the U.S. Southeast. It is a great addition to any planting that features heaths and heathers or azaleas in a light woodland, or as a silver-blue accent in a green-dominated shrub border.

Beautiful Silvers for Tough Places

ACID SOIL

Calluna vulgaris
Chamaecyparis
Erica tetralix
Picea pungens
Zenobia pulverulenta

ALKALINE SOIL

Amorpha canescens
Artemisia californica
Atriplex
Cistus
Convolvulus
Elaeagnus
Helichrysum
Helictotrichon sempervirens
Hippophae rhamnoides
Leucophyllum
Shepherdia argentea
Verbascum

CLAY SOIL

Artemisia absinthium 'Lambrook Silver'
Artemisia californica
Artemisia canescens
Atriplex
Eryngium yuccifolium
Panicum virgatum
Salix purpurea 'Nana'

COASTAL CONDITIONS

(These vary from very to moderately salt resistant.)

Achillea
Amorpha
Anaphalis margaritacea
Antennaria dioica
Arctotis
Artemisia absinthium
Artemisia ×'Powis Castle'
Artemisia schmidtiana 'Silver Mound'
Artemisia stelleriana
Atriplex
Bismarckia nobilis
Buddleja
Calluna vulgaris
Caryopteris
Cedrus atlantica 'Glauca'
Cerastium tomentosum
Chamaecyparis
Cistus
Convolvulus cneorum
Cunninghamia lanceolata 'Glauca'
Cupressus arizonica
Dianthus
Dichondra argentea
Echinops ritro
Elaeagnus
Eryngium amethystinum

Eryngium giganteum
Eucalyptus cinerea
Festuca glauca
Gazania
Helianthemum
Helichrysum
Helictotrichon sempervirens
Hippophae rhamnoides
Juniperus
Lavandula
Leucophyta brownii
Miscanthus sinensis
Panicum
Perovskia atriplicifolia
Pyrus salicifolia
Salvia
Santolina chamaecyparissus
Sedum
Senecio cinerea
Serenoa repens
Stachys byzantina
Tanacetum ptarmicifolium
Thymus pseudolanuginosus
Verbascum
Veronica incana
Yucca

EROSION CONTROL

Acacia baileyana
Atriplex
Cistus
Elaeagnus
Hippophae rhamnoides
Juniperus
Panicum virgatum
Schizachyrium scoparium
Sorghastrum

EXTREME HEAT AND HUMIDITY

Achillea
Agave paryii
Artemisia abrotanum
Artemisia capillaris
Artemisia ludoviciana 'Silver King'
Artemisia ludoviciana 'Silver Queen'
Artemisia ×'Powis Castle'
Artemisia stelleriana
Asarum
Athyrium nipponicum
Bismarckia nobilis
Buddleja davidii
Caryopteris ×*clandonensis* 'Longwood Blue'
Cedrus atlantica 'Glauca'
Cistus
Cynara cardunculus
Dicliptera suberecta
Elaeagnus
Eucalpytus
Festuca glauca
Gazania
Juniper communis
Juniperus conifera
Juniperus inflexus 'Lovesick Blues'
Lamium
Lavandula ×*allardii*
Lavandula angustifolia 'Lady'
Lavandula dentata var. *candicans*
Leucophyllum
Mentha
Miscanthus sinensis
Panicum virgatum
Perovskia atriplicifolia
Salvia argentea
Salvia chamaedryoides
Salvia discolor
Salvia 'Neveh Ya'ar'

Salvia officinalis 'Purpurascens'
Salvia officinalis 'Tricolor'
Sedum bithynicum
Senecio cineraria
Serenoa repens
Teucrium
Tillandsia
Verbascum
Yucca glauca

EXTREME HEAT AND
PROLONGED DROUGHT

(These range from xeric—no watering needed after established—to deep soaking every one to two weeks in drought.)

Acantholimon
Achillea 'Moonshine'
Agave (many)
Amorpha canescens
Antennaria parviflora 'McClintock'
Artemisia abrotanum
Artemisia absinthium 'Lambrook Silver'
Artemisia cana
Artemisia ludoviciana 'Silver King'
Artemisia ludoviciana 'Valerie Finnis'
Artemisia ×'Powis Castle'
Artemisia schmidtiana 'Silver Mound'
Artemisia tridentata
Artemisia versicolor 'Sea Foam'
Atriplex canescens
Atriplex gardneri
Buddleja marrubifolia
Carex glauca
Caryopteris
Cedrus atlantica
Cupressus arizonica
Cynara cardunculus
Dichondra argentea
Echeveria

Echinops ritro
Eryngium bourgatii
Festuca glauca
Festuca idahoensis 'Siskiyou Blue'
Helichrysum
Helictotrichon sempervirens
Juniperus scopulorum
Juniperus virginiana
Lavandula 'Silver Frost'
Leucophyllum
Marrubium rotundifolium
Nepeta ×*faassenii* 'Six Hills Giant'
Penstemon palmeri
Penstemon pseudospectabilis
Perovskia atriplicifolia
Picea pungens
Ruta graveolens
Santolina chamaecyparissus 'Nana'
Salvia chamaedryoides
Salvia discolor
Salvia officinalis (dwarf forms)
Salvia pachyphylla
Sedum sieboldii
Shepherdia argentea
Stachys byzantina
Tanacetum densum subsp. *amani*
Tanacetum niveum
Teucrium aroanium
Teucrium polium
Thymus
Verbascum bombyciferum
Veronica
Yucca

INFERTILE SOIL

Amorpha canescens
Antennaria
Artemisia californica
Artemisia stelleriana

Atriplex
Ballota pseudodictamnus
Bismarckia
Cistus
Eryngium
Gazania
Hippophae rhamnoides
Panicum virgatum
Santolina chamaecyparissus
Senecio cineraria
Shepherdia argentea
Verbascum

MOIST SOIL

(These require steady moisture to wet conditions.)

Abies
Ajuga
Brunnera macrophylla
Carex albula
Chamaecyparis
Cunninghamia lanceolata 'Glauca'
Erica tetralix
Eucalyptus gunnii
Festuca cinerea
Juncus polyanthemos
Juncus reflexus 'The Blues'
Miscanthus sinensis
Plectranthus argentatus
Populus alba
Pulmonaria
Salix
Serenoa repens
Zenobia pulverulenta

SANDY SOIL

Amorpha canescens
Artemisia californica

Artemisia stelleriana
Atriplex
Bismarckia nobilis
Cistus
Eryngium amethystinum
Gazania
Hippophae rhamnoides
Panicum virgatum
Santolina chamaecyparissus
Senecio cineraria
Yucca

SHADE

Ajuga
Asarum
Athyrium nipponicum
Begonia
Brunnera macrophylla
Carex albula
Cyclamen
Heuchera
Lamium
Pulmonaria
Viola koreana

WINDY SITE/WINDBREAK

Acacia baileyana
Agave
Artemisia
Bismarckia nobilis
Carex
Cerastium tomentosum
Cupressus
Elaeagnus
Eryngium
Eucalpytus
Euphorbia
Euryops

Hippophae rhamnoides
Juniperus
Lavandula
Leucophyllum
Leucophyta brownii
Picea
Populus alba
Salvia
Santolina chamaecyparissus
Sedum
Thymus
Yucca
Zauschneria californica

DEER-RESISTANT

(Not their first choice, but deer may eat
them if they are hungry enough.)

Acacia baileyana
Achillea
Agave
Ajuga
Artemisia
Buddleja
Carex
Caryopteris
Cedrus
Centaurea cinerea

Cerastium tomentosum
Cistus
Cupressus
Echinops
Elaeagnus
Eryngium
Eucalyptus
Euphorbia
Euryops
Helichrysum
Lamium
Lychnis coronaria
Marrubium
Mentha
Origanum
Penstemon
Perovskia
Salvia
Santolina chamaecyparissus
Senecio cineraria
Stachys byzantina
Tanacetum
Teucrium
Thymus
Veronica
Viola koreana
Zauschneria californica

Where to See Silvers

In public gardens, look for silvers in conservatories, herb gardens, rock gardens, sensory gardens, Mediterranean gardens, native plant gardens, and xeriscape plantings that show off drought-tolerant plants. Check the *Garden Lover's Guides* book series (Princeton Architectural Press) for information about gardens in different regions and countries.

ARIZONA
Desert Botanical Garden
1201 North Galvin Parkway
Phoenix, AZ 85008
Tel 480-941-1225

CALIFORNIA
Huntington Botanical Gardens
1151 Oxford Road
San Marino, CA 91108
Tel 213-792-6141

Quarry Hill Botanic Garden
12825 Sonoma Highway
Glen Ellen, CA 95442
Tel 707-996-3166

Rancho Santa Ana Botanic Garden
1500 North College Avenue
Claremont, CA 91711
Tel 714-625-8767

University of California Botanic Garden,
   Berkeley
200 Centennial Drive
Berkeley, CA 94720
Tel 510-642-3343

CONNECTICUT
Twombly Nursery
163 Barn Hill Road
Monroe, CT 06468
Tel 203-261-2133

COLORADO
Denver Botanic Gardens
909 York Street
Denver, CO 80206-3799
Tel 303-331-4000

FLORIDA
Bok Tower Gardens
1151 Tower Boulevard
Lake Wales, FL 33853-3412
Tel 863-676-1408

Harry P. Leu Gardens
1920 North Forest Avenue
Orlando, FL 32803-1537
Tel 407-246-2620

Marie Selby Botanical Gardens
811 South Palm Avenue
Sarasota, FL 34236
Tel 941-954-1237

ILLINOIS
Chicago Botanic Garden
1000 Lake Cook Road
Glencoe, IL 60022
Tel 847-835-5440

MASSACHUSETTS
Berkshire Botanical Garden
Routes 102 and 183
P.O. Box 826
Stockbridge, MA 01261
Tel 413-298-3926

MINNESOTA
Minnesota Landscape Arboretum and
    Horticultural Research Center
University of Minnesota
3675 Arboretum Dr.
P.O. Box 39
Chanhassen, MN 55317
Tel 952-443-1400

NEW YORK
Central Park Conservatory Garden
14 E. 60th St.
New York, NY, 10022
Tel 212-310-6600
Entrance at 5th Avenue and 105th Street

The New York Botanical Garden
Bronx, NY 10458-5126
Tel 718-817-8705

Stonecrop Gardens
81 Stonecrop Lane
Cold Spring, NY 10516
Tel 845-265-2000

Wave Hill
675 West 252nd St. (249th and
    Independence Avenue)
Bronx, NY 10471
Tel 718-549-3200

OHIO
Western Reserve Herb Society
The Garden Center of Greater Cleveland
11030 East Boulevard
Cleveland, OH 44106
Tel 216-321-2583

PENNSYLVANIA
Longwood Gardens
P.O. Box 501
Kennett Square, PA 19348
Tel 610-388-1000

TEXAS
Barton Springs Nursery
3601 Bee Caves Road
Austin, TX 78746
Tel 512-328-6655

The Gardens at Festival Hill
International Festival-Institute
P.O. Box 89
Roundtop, TX 78954
Tel 979-249-5283

Peckerwood Garden Conservation
    Foundation
Rt. 3, Box 103
Hempstead, TX 77445
Tel 979-826-3232

VIRGINIA
Norfolk Botanical Garden
Azalea Garden Road
Norfolk, VA 23518
Tel 757-441-5830

BRITISH ISLES

Hestercombe
Cheddon Fitzpaine
Taunton
Somerset TA2 8LG
UK
Tel 01823 413923
Restored Jekyll Grey Border

Kiftsgate Court Garden
Chipping Campden
Gloucestershire
GL55 6LN
UK
Tel 01386 438777

Royal Botanical Garden Edinburgh
20 A Inverleith Road
Edinburgh EH3 5LR
UK
Tel 44 131 552 7171

Sissinghurst Castle
nr Cranbrook, Kent
TN17 2AB
UK
Tel 01580 710700

CANADA

Mediterranean Garden
Royal Botanical Gardens
680 Plains Road West
Hamilton/Burlington, ON L7T 4H4
Canada
Tel 905-527-1158

MAIL ORDER SOURCES

(* = display gardens)

Arrowhead Alpines ($2.00)
P.O. Box 857
Fowlerville, MI 48836
Tel 517-223-3581

Asiatica
P.O. Box 270
Lewisberry, PA 17339
Tel 717-938-8677
Asarums, woodland plants

Avant Gardens ($3.00)
710 High Hill Road
North Dartmouth, MA 02747
Tel 508-998-8819
Unusual, choice plants

Bluestone Perennials
7211 Middle Ridge Road
Madison, OH 44057
Tel 800-852-5243

Canyon Creek Nursery ($2.00)
3527 Dry Creek Road
Oroville, CA 95965
Tel 530-533-2166

Carroll Gardens ($3.00)
444 East Main Street
Westminster, MD 21157
Tel 410-848-5422

Digging Dog Nursery
P.O. Box 471
Albion, CA 95410
Tel 707-937-1130

Earthly Pursuits (in cooperation with Kurt
    Bluemel, Inc.) ($3.00)
2901 Kuntz Road
Windsor Mill, MD 21244
Tel 410-496-2523

Fairweather Gardens* ($4.00)
P.O. Box 330
Greenwich, NJ 08323
Tel 856-451-6261
Native trees and shrubs

Forestfarm ($5.00 in Canada)
990 Tetherow Road
Williams, OR 97544-9599
Tel 541-846-7269
Trees, shrubs, perennials

Goodwin Creek Gardens
    ($2.00 subscription)
P.O. Box 83
Williams, OR 97544
Tel 800-846-7359
Herbs, many lavenders, scented geraniums

Great Basin Natives
75 West 300 South
P.O. Box 114
Holden, UT 84636
Tel 435-795-2303

Heaths and Heathers
502 E. Haskell Hill Road
Shelton, WA 98584-8429
Tel 800-294-3284

Heronswood Nursery* ($5.00)
7530 NE 288th Street
Kingston, WA 98346-9502
Tel 360-297-4172
Wide range of distinctive plants

High Country Gardens
2902 Rufina Street
Santa Fe, NM 87507-2929
Tel 800-925-9387
*Drought-tolerant plants for the U.S. West
and elsewhere*

Kapoho Palms
P.O. Box 3
Pahoha, HI 96778
Tel 808-936-2580

LaPorte Avenue Nursery
1950 LaPorte Avenue
Ft. Collins, CO 80521
Tel 970-472-0017
Alpines

Las Pilitas
3232 Las Pilitas Road
Santa Margarita, CA 93453
Tel 805-438-5922
Native plants

Lauray of Salisbury ($2.00)
432 Undermountain Road
Rt. 41
Salisbury, CT 06068
Tel 860-435-2263
Tender succulents, begonias

Logee's Greenhouses* ($4.95)
141 North Street
Danielson, CT 06239-1939
Tel 888-330-8038
Begonias, scented geraniums, herbs

Mountain Valley Growers
38325 Pepperweed Road
Squaw Valley, CA 93675
Tel 559-338-2775
Certified organic herbs and perennials

Mt. Tahoma Nursery
28111 112th Avenue E.
Graham, WA 98338
Tel 253-847-9827
Alpines

Mulberry Creek Herb Farm* ($2.00)
3312 Bogart Road
Huron, OH 44839
Tel 419-433-6126

Plant Delights Nursery at Juniper Level
    Botanic Garden*
9241 Sauls Road
Raleigh, NC 27603
Tel 919-772-4794
Terrific selection of foliage and unusual plants

Plants of the Southwest ($3.50)
3095 Agua Fria Rd.
Santa Fe, NM 87507
Tel 800-788-7333
Drought-tolerant native plants

Prairie Nursery
P.O. Box 306
Westfield, WI 53964
Tel 800-476-9453

Rock Spray Nursery ($2.00)
P.O. Box 693
Truro, MA 02666-0693
Tel 508-349-6769
Heaths and heathers

Rocky Mountain Rare Plants
1706 Deerpath Road
Franktown, CO 80116-9462
Tel 303-660-6498
Alpines

Sandy Mush Herb Nursery
316 Surrett Cove Road
Leicester, NC 28748-5517

Seneca Hill Perennials
3712 Country Route 57
Oswego, NY 13126
Tel 315-342-5915
Hardy cyclamens

Shady Acres Herb Farm* ($3.00)
7815 Highway 212
Chaska, MN 55318
Tel 952-466-3391

Siskiyou Rare Plant Nursery ($3.00)
2825 Cummings Road
Medford, OR 97501
Tel 541-772-6846
Rock, alpine plants

Southwestern Native Seeds ($2.00)
P.O. Box 50503
Tuscon, AZ 85703

The Primrose Path ($2.00)
Charles and Martha Oliver
921 Scottdale-Dawson Road
Scottdale, PA 15683
Tel 724-887-6756
Heucheras, heucherellas, pulmonarias

Thompson and Morgan Seedsman
P.O. Box 1308
Jackson, NJ 08527-0308
Tel 800-274-7333

Well-Sweep Herb Farm*
205 Mt. Bethel Road
Port Murray, NJ 07865
Tel 908-852-5390

White Flower Farm*
P.O. Box 50
Litchfield, CT 06759-0050
Tel 800-503-9624
Tender and hardy perennials, trees, shrubs, vines

Woodlanders ($3.00)
1128 Colleton Avenue
Aiken, SC 29801
Tel 803-648-7522
Trees, shrubs, yuccas, grasses

Yucca Do Nursery*
P.O. Box 907
Hempstead, TX 77445
Tel 979-826-4580
Yuccas, agaves

CANADA

Fraser's Thimble Farms
175 Arbutus Road
Salt Spring Island, BC V8K 1A3
Canada
Tel 250-537-5788
Unusual plants

Gardens North* ($4.00)
5984 Third Line Road North
RR #3
North Grower, ON K0A 2T0
Canada
Tel 613-489-0065
Seeds of cold-tolerant plants

Richters Herbs*
Goodwood, ON L0C 1A0
Canada
Tel 905-640-6677

GLOSSARY

acidic soil: soil with a pH of less than 7 on the pH scale.

albi, albo, albus: white.

alkaline soil: soil with a pH of more than 7 on the pH scale.

alpine: a high mountain plant.

annual: a plant that completes its growth cycle in one season.

argentea, argenteus, argentus: silver, silvery.

biennial: a plant that usually completes its growth cycle in two seasons.

bloom: a thin protective layer of powder over a plant's normally green surfaces that affects its coloring but is easily rubbed off.

caesius: waxy or blue-gray.

candicans: white.

candidum: shining white.

canescens: becoming white or hoary.

canus: white-gray.

carpel: female unit in a flower, composed of ovary, style, and stigma.

cinereus, cinerascens: white-gray.

conifer: cone-bearing trees with needlelike leaves.

coppice: to cut down a tree or shrub to about 12 in. (30.5 cm) from the ground, usually in later winter, to encourage prolific sprouting.

farina, farinosa, farninosus: a thick concentration of powdery meal on a plant's leaves or stems.

frigidus: frosted.

glaucescens: somewhat glaucous.

glaucous: blue-green or blue-gray plant coloration, the result of a waxy or powdery coating of varying depth on plant surfaces that is easily rubbed off.

hirsutus: hairy.

hypertufa: absorbent, rocklike material made from a mixture of cement, sand, and peat to resemble tufa rock and used in making containers for growing alpines.

incanus: very gray and hoary.

lanatus, lanuginosus: woolly.

maculatus: spotted or stained.

marginatus: edged.

meal/farina: a dusty or powdery concentration of wax on a plant surface.

monocarpic: rosette-forming plants that die after flowering and may, like agaves, take a long time to flower.

moraine: a water-fed deep, rocky bed, natural or constructed, needed to grow certain alpine plants that need dry tops and water at their roots.

pallidus: pale.

pilous: covered with short hairs.

pinnate: arrangement of featherlike leaflets in two rows.

plumosus: feathery.

pollard: from the word *poll* (to cut short); a technique used to shorten trees by cutting off all the branches just above where they branch off from the main trunk.

prune: cut selectively.

pseudolanuginosus: rather woolly; from *pseudo* (rather) and *lanuginosus* (woolly).

pubescens: downy, hairy.

pulverulentus: a thick concentration of powdery meal on a plant's surface.

rhizome: a horizontal underground stem that forms roots continuously and produces new shoots.

RHS AGM: Royal Horticultural Society Award of Garden Merit.

scree: a natural or constructed slope of deep rock fragments that retains little moisture, for growing alpine plants.

scurf: minute scales on a plant's surface that give it a gray or silvery appearance.

sericeous: silky.

shear: to cut the whole plant back.

spinosus: spiny.

standard: a hard-stemmed plant, shrub, or tree trained or grafted to a single stem to produced a short to medium-tall treelike form, usually 3–6 ft. (1.0–1.8 m) tall with a bushy, weeping, or ball-like crown.

stomata: breathing pores usually on undersides of leaves or on conifer needles.

subshrub: a woody-based perennial with herbaceous top growth.

subtropical: plants usually from warm, frost-free regions; some may survive short spells of frost.

tender perennial: perennial that is killed by temperatures below 41°F (5°C).

tomentose: plants' surfaces are covered with dense, soft, and short hairs, causing it to have a woolly, cottony, or felted appearance.

topiary: pruning trees and shrubs into shapes, but usually applied to a plant trained to a standard form with its crown pruned into a ball shape.

tropical: plants from hot, steamy climates that do not survive below 65°F (18°C).

trough: generally any small stone or stonelike container used for growing alpines; real stone troughs were used to water barn animals.

tufa: very porous, weathered limestone rock desirable for growing alpines.

variegatus: variegated.

wax: a substance naturally produced by plants in response to a range of extreme conditions, whose purpose is to seal plant surfaces against evaporation. A thin layer is usually in the form of powdery bloom, and a thicker layer is called farina or meal. Depending on its concentration, plant color ranges from silver-blue and blue-gray to powder-blue.

woolly: hairy.

xeric: plants adapted to dry growing conditions.

xeriscape: a low to moderate water-use landscape based on water-conservation principles.

HARDINESS ZONES

Experienced gardeners know that USDA plant hardiness zones can be stretched a zone or two higher by careful siting, soil preparation, and winter protection. When in doubt about hardiness, we gave more than one hardiness zone number (Zone 5 or 6, for instance). In several cases, plants are so new their hardiness has not yet been determined. In any version of a hardiness zone map, the low zone number is based on collected data for average winter low temperatures, while the high number can be used to represent the limit of a plant's adaptability to heat.

USDA PLANT HARDINESS ZONES

ZONE	TEMP. °F	TEMP. °C
1	below -50	-46 & below
2a	-45 to -50	-43 to -45
2b	-40 to -45	-40 to -43
3a	-35 to -40	-37 to -40
3b	-30 to -35	-34 to -37
4a	-25 to -30	-32 to -34
4b	-20 to -25	-29 to -32
5a	-15 to -20	-26 to -29
5b	-10 to -15	-23 to -26
6a	-5 to -10	-21 to -23
6b	0 to -5	-18 to -21
7a	5 to 0	-15 to -18
7b	10 to 5	-12 to -15
8a	15 to 10	-9 to -12
8b	20 to 15	-7 to -9
9a	25 to 20	-4 to -7
9b	30 to 25	-1 to -4
10a	35 to 30	2 to -1
10b	40 to 35	4 to 2
11	40 & above	5 & above

BIBLIOGRAPHY

Adams, James. 1987. *Landscaping with Herbs*. Portland, Oregon: Timber Press.

Ardle, Jon. 2001. Structural harmony. *The Garden*. (June): 442–45.

Armitage, Allan. 1993. *Burpee Expert Gardener Series: Allan Armitage on Perennials*. New York: Prentice Hall.

Bennett, Masha. 2002. *Pulmonarias and the Borage Family*. Portland, Oregon. Timber Press.

Billington, Jill. 1994. *Using Foliage Plants in the Garden*. London: Ward Lock.

Bodnar, Tom. 2002. The Grandeur of Grasses. *People Places Plants*. (Autumn): 40–43.

Bradley, Fern Marshall, and Barbara W. Ellis. 1992. *Rodale's All New Encyclopedia of Organic Gardening*. Emmaus, Pennsylvania: Rodale Press.

Brenzel, Kathleen Norris, ed. 1995. *Western Garden Book*. Menlo Park, California: Sunset Books.

Brickell, Christopher, and Judith Zuk, eds. 1997. *American Horticultural Society A–Z Encyclopedia of Garden Plants*. New York: Dorling Kindersley.

Brown, Deni. 1997. *Encylopedia of Herbs and Their Uses*. New York: Dorling Kindersley.

Buchanan, Rita, ed. 1995. *Taylor's Guide to Herbs*. New York: Houghton Mifflin.

Buchanan, Rita, and Roger Holmes. 1994. *Taylor's Master Guide to Gardening*. Boston, New York: Houghton Mifflin.

Bussolini, Karen. A Study in Silver. *The American Gardener* (January/February): 32–37.

Cathey, Dr. H. Marc. 1999. *Heat-Zone Gardening: How to Choose Plants that Thrive in Your Region's Warmest Weather*. New York: Time-Life.

Charlesworth, Geoffrey B. 1994. *A Gardener Obsessed*. Boston: David R. Godine.

Chicago Botanic Garden, Holden Arboretum, Royal Botanical Gardens, Galen Gates, Chris Graham, Ethan Johnson. 1994. *Shrubs and Vines: The American Garden Guides*. New York: Pantheon Books.

Christopher, Tom, and Marty Asher. 1997. *The 20-Minute Gardener*. New York: Random House.

Clebsch, Betsy. 2003. *The New Book of Salvias: Sages for Every Garden.* Portland, Oregon: Timber Press.

Clifton, Joan. 1990. *Making a White Garden.* New York: Grove Weidenfeld.

Cole, Trevor. 1996. *Gardening with Trees and Shrubs.* Vancouver/Toronto: Whitecap Books.

Coombes, Allen J. 1994. *Dictionary of Plant Names.* Portland, Oregon: Timber Press.

Curtis, Benee Wise. 1995. Silver Leaf Sage. *The Herbarist:* 70–75.

Cutler, Karan Davis. 2003. *Pruning Trees, Shrubs and Vines: All Region Guides.* Brooklyn: Brooklyn Botanic Garden.

Damrosch, Barbara. 1982. *Theme Gardens.* New York: Workman Publishing.

Darke, Rick. 1999. *The Color Encyclopedia of Ornamental Grasses.* Portland, Oregon: Timber Press.

Deno, Norman C. 1993. *Seed Germination: Theory and Practice.* State College, Pennsylvania: Norman C. Deno.

Diboll, Neil. 2002. Rattlesnake Master. *American Gardener* (July/August): 51.

Dirr, Michael. 1997. *Dirr's Hardy Trees and Shrubs.* Portland, Oregon: Timber Press.

DiSabato-Aust, Tracy. 1998. *The Well-Tended Perennial Garden.* Portland, Oregon: Timber Press.

Druse, Ken. 2000. *Making More Plants.* New York: Clarkson Potter.

Ellefson, Connie, Tom Stephens, and Dough Welsh. 1992. *Xeriscape Gardening.* New York: Macmillan.

Fingerut, Joyce, and Rex Murfitt. 1999. *Creating and Planting Garden Troughs.* Wayne, Pennsylvania: B. B. Mackey Books.

Flook, Marnie. 1980. *Handbook of Rock Gardening.* Plants and Garden Series, vol. 36, no. 2. Brooklyn: Brooklyn Botanic Garden.

Foster, Gertrude B., and Rosemary Louden. 1980. *Park's Success with Herbs.* Greenwood, South Carolina: George W. Park Seed Co.

———. 1981. Sorting Gray Artemisias. *Herb Grower Magazine* (Summer): 28–33.

Foster, H. Lincoln. 1968. *Rock Gardening.* Boston: Houghton Mifflin.

Fox, Helen M. 1953. Herbs in Knots and Laces. *The Herbarist:* 9–12.

———. 1953. *The Years in My Herb Garden.* New York: Macmillan.

———. 1959. Color in the Herb Garden. *The Herbarist:* 35–38.

Francko, David A. 2003. *Palms Won't Grow Here and Other Myths.* Portland, Oregon: Timber Press.

Gardner, Jo Ann. 1997. *Living with Herbs.* Woodstock, Vermont: The Countryman Press.

———. 1998. *Herbs In Bloom.* Portland Oregon: Timber Press.

———. 1999. Precious Silver. *Canadian Gardening* (Spring): 54–72.

———. 2000. The Art of Artemisias. *Herb Companion* (April/May): 28–33.

———. 2001. *The Heirloom Flower Garden.* White River Junction, Vermont: Chelsea Green Publishing.

———. 2003. Silver Renaissance. *Herb Companion* (February/March): 20–23.

Gardner, Jo Ann and Jigs. 2002. *Gardens of Use & Delight: Uniting the Practical and Beautiful in an Integrated Landscape.* Golden, Colorado: Fulcrum Publishing.

Glattstein, Judith. 1991. *Garden Design with Foliage.* Pownal, Vermont: Storey Communications, Inc.

———. 2003. *Consider the Leaf: Foliage in Garden Design.* Portland, Oregon: Timber Press.

Greenlee, John.1992. *The Color Encyclopedia of Ornamental Grasses.* Emmaus, Pennsylvania: Rodale Press.

Griffiths, Mark, ed. 1994. *Index of Garden Plants: The New Royal Horticultural Society Dictionary.* Portland, Oregon: Timber Press.

Halpin, Anne, ed. 2001. *Northeastern Garden Book.* Menlo Park, California: Sunset Books.

Harper, Pamela, and Frederick McGourty. 1985. *Perennials: How to Select, Grow and Enjoy.* Los Angeles: HP Books.

Harris, Marjorie. 1993. *The Canadian Gardener's Guide to Foliage and Garden Design.* Toronto: Random House Canada.

Hawke, Richard G. 2001. *Plant Evaluation Notes: An Appraisal of Pulmonaria for the Garden.* Issue 17. Glenco, Illinois: Chicago Botanic Garden.

———. 2003. *Plant Evaluation Notes: Garden-Worthy Artemisias.* Issue 19. Glenco, Illinois: Chicago Botanic Garden.

Herwig, Rob, and Margot Schubert. 1974. *Treasury of Houseplants.* New York: Macmillan.

Hewitt, Jennifer. 1999. Well spotted. *The Garden* (February): 98–105.

Hill, Madalene, and Gwen Barclay. 1987. *Southern Herb Growing.* Fredricksburg, Texas: Shearer Publishing.

Hillier, Malcolm. 1991. *The Book of Container Gardening.* New York: Simon and Schuster.

Hinkley, Daniel. 2001. Collecting Silver. *Horticulture* (March): 49–51.

Hobhouse, Penelope. 1985. *Color in Your Garden.* Boston, Toronto: Little Brown & Company.

———. 1992. *Plants in Garden History.* London: Pavilion Books.

Hogan, Sean, ed. 2003. *Flora: A Gardener's Encyclopedia.* Portland, Oregon: Timber Press.

Holmes, Roger, and Rita Buchanan. 1999. *Home Landscaping: Midwest Region.* Upper Saddle River, New Jersey: Creative Homeowners Press.

Holmes, Roger, and Don Marshall. 2002. *Home Landscaping: Northwest Region*. Upper Saddle River, New Jersey: Creative Homeowners Press.

Hornig, Ellen. 2003. Hardy Cyclamen for Your Upstate Garden. *Upstate Gardeners' Journal* (Winter): 16–18.

Hudak, Joseph. 1993. *Gardening with Perennials Month by Month*. Portland, Oregon: Timber Press.

Hutchins, Alma R. 1991. *Indian Herbology of North America*. Boston: Shambala Publications.

Huxley, Anthony. 1982. *Huxley's Encyclopedia of Gardening*. New York: Universe Books.

Irish, Mary. 2003. Agaves. *Horticulture* (November/December): 32–37.

Isaacson, Richard T., ed. 2004. *Andersen Horticultural Library Source List of Plants & Seeds*, 6th Edition. Chanhassen, Minnesota: Andersen Horticultural Library.

Jacobson, Pamela D. 1997. Collecting and Nurturing Sea Herbs. *Herb Quarterly* (Fall): 30–37.

Jekyll, Gertrude. 1911. *Colour Schemes in the Flower Garden*. London: Country Life.

Jones, Millicent A. 1974. A Garden of Artemisias. *The Herbarist*: 14–16.

Kelaidis, Panayoti. 1993. A Celebration of Silver Leaves. *Fine Gardening* (May/June): 64–67.

———. 1994. More Garden Silver. *Fine Gardening* (May/June): 58–61.

Kelly, John. 1989. *Foliage in Your Garden*. New York: Penguin Books.

Klein, Carol. 2002. Touching Beauty. *Horticulture* (November/December): 40–43.

Kramer, Jack. 1969. *1000 Beautiful House Plants and How to Grow Them*. New York: William Morrow.

Lawton, Barbara Perry. 2002. *Mints: A Family of Herbs and Ornamentals*. Portland, Oregon: Timber Press.

Lee, Rand. 2002. Crazy for Catmints. *American Gardener* (May/June): 38–43.

Liberty Hyde Bailey Hortorium. 1976. *Hortus Third: A Concise Dictionary of Plants Cultivated in the United States and Canada*. New York: Macmillan.

Lloyd, Christopher. 1992. Silver and Gray. *Horticulture* (June/July): 54–57.

Lord, Tony. 1995. *Gardening at Sissinghurst*. New York: Simon and Schuster Macmillan.

Lord, Tony, ed. 2003. *Royal Horticultural Society Plant Finder 2003–2004*. London: Dorling Kindersley, Ltd.

Lovejoy, Ann. 1992. Seattle Symphony. *Horticulture* (August/September): 42–50.

Martin, Alex C., Herbert S. Zim, and Arnold L. Nelson. 1961. *American Wildlife and Plants: a Guide to Wildlife Food Habits*. New York: McGraw Hill, 1951. Reprint, New York: Dover Publications.

McDonald, Elvin. 2002. Winged Victory. *Traditional Home* (July): 73–78.

Meyer, Mary Hockenberry, and Courtney L. Tchida. 1996–97. *Miscanthus: Report on Viable Seeds.* Department of Horticultural Science, St. Paul, Minnesota: University of Minnesota.

Mineo, Baldassare. 1999. *Rock Garden Plants.* Portland, Oregon: Timber Press.

———. 2002. Create a Miniature Landscape. *Fine Gardening* (July/August): 66–67.

Mottau, Gary. 1989. Silver and Gold. *Horticulture* (December): 46–49.

Nabhan, Gary Paul. 1986. *Gathering the Desert.* Tuscon, Arizona: University of Arizona.

Nicolson, Philippa, ed. 1969. *Vita Sackville-West's Garden Book.* New York: Atheneum.

Ogden, Scott. 1992. *Gardening Success with Difficult Soils.* Dallas, Texas: Taylor Publishing.

Oliver, Martha. 2002. Praiseworthy Plants, ×*Heucherella* 'Quicksilver'. *Fine Gardening* (May/June): 26–28.

Olkowski, William, Sheila Daar, and Helga Oklowski. 1991. *Common-Sense Pest Control.* Newton, Connecticut: Taunton Press.

Ottesen, Carole. 1995. *The Native Plant Primer: Trees, Shrubs and Wildflowers for Natural Gardens.* New York: Harmony Books.

———. 2003. Heuchera Explosion. *American Gardener* (March/April): 42–47.

Peace, Tom. 2000. *Sunbelt Gardening.* Golden, Colorado: Fulcrum Press.

Phillips, Rodger, and Martyn Rix. 1991. *The Random House Book of Perennials.* New York: Random House.

Pleasant, Barbara. 2002. *Garden Stone: Creative Landscaping with Plants and Stone.* North Adams, Massachusetts: Storey Publishing.

Plowden, C. Chichely. 1968. *A Manual of Plant Names.* New York: Philosophical Library.

Powell, Eileen. 1995. *From Seed to Bloom.* Pownal, Vermont: Storey Communications.

Putievsky, Eli, and Arthur O. Tucker. 1991. It can take the heat. *Herb Companion* (October/November): 30–31.

Ritter, Chistopher. 2001. Glaucous Foliage. *The Gardener* (June/July): 28–31.

———. 2003. Blau Grass Fever. *The Gardener* (August/September): 11–13.

Roth, Susan A., and Dennis Schrader. 2000. *Hot Plants for Cool Climates.* Boston: Houghton Mifflin.

Salmon, David. Jeepers Creepers! *American Gardener* (November/December): 44–49.

Schenk, George. 1984. *The Complete Shade Gardener.* Portland, Oregon: Timber Press.

Scott-James, Anne. 1974. *Sissinghurst: The Making of a Garden*. London: Michael Joseph.

Sheldon, Elisabeth. 1989. *A Proper Garden*. Harrisburg, Pennsylvania: Stackpole Books.

Simmons, Adelma. ndg. *The Silver Garden*. Coventry, Connecticut: Caprilands Herb Farm.

———. 1974. *Herb Gardens of Delight*. New York: Hawthorn Books.

———. 1990. *Herb Gardening in Five Seasons*. New York: Plume, 1964. Reprint, Penguin USA.

Spencer, Roger. 1987. *Growing Silver, Grey and Blue Foliage Plants*. Kenthurst, Australia: Kangaroo Press.

Springer, Lauren. 1994. *The Undaunted Garden*. Golden, Colorado: Fulcrum Publishing.

———. 2002. From Drought to Deluge. *Horticulture* (July/August): 56–59.

Strabo, Walafrid. 1966. *Hortulus*. Pittsburgh, Pennsylvania: Hunt Botanical Library.

Tait, William A. Silver Plants in a Scottish Garden. *The Garden* (September): 568–570.

Taylor, Patricia. 2002. The Striking Blue of Foliage Shrubs. *The New York Times* (2 December 2002): CY14.

Taylor, Patrick. 1991. *Period Gardens*. New York: Atlantic Monthly Press.

———. 1998. *Garden Lover's Guide to Britain*. New York: Princeton Architectural Press.

Thomas, Graham Stuart. 1984. *The Art of Planting*. Boston: David R. Godine.

Thompson, Mildred and Edward. 1981. *Begonias: The Complete Reference Guide*. New York: Time Books.

Underwood, Mrs. Desmond. 1971. *Grey and Silver Plants*. St. James's Place, London: Collins.

Van Hevelingen, Andy. 2003. Rediscover a Fragrant Garden Friend. *Herb Companion* (February/March): 33–37.

Wasowski, Sally, with Andy Wasowski. 1991. *Native Texas Plants: Landscaping Region By Region*. Houston, Texas: Gulf Publishing.

Webber, William. 2001. *Colorado Flora Eastern Slope*. Boulder, Colorado: University of Colorado Press.

———. 2001. *Colorado Flora Western Slope*. Boulder, Colorado: University of Colorado Press.

Weinstein, Gayle. 1999. *Xeriscape Handbook: A How-To Guide to Natural, Resource-Wise Gardening*. Golden, Colorado: Fulcrum Publishing.

Welch, William. 1989. *Perennial Garden Color: Perennials, Cottage Gardens, Old Roses and Companion Plants*. Dallas, Texas: Taylor Publishing Company.

Whalley, Robin, and Anne Jennings.
1998. *Knot Gardens and Parterres.*
London: Barn Elms.

Wheeler, David. 2001. The Silver
Screen. *The English Garden* U.S. ed.
(October/November): 56–57.

Williamson, John. 1988. *Perennial
Gardens.* New York: Harper and
Row.

Wilson, Jim. 1994. *Landscaping with
Herbs.* New York: Houghton
Mifflin.

Woodward, Marcus, ed. 1985.
*Gerard's Herball: the Essence thereof dis-
tilled by Marcus Woodward from the
Edition of th. Johnson, 1636.* London:
Bracken Books.

Wright, R. C. M. 1973. *The Complete
Handbook of Plant Propagation.* New
York: Macmillan.

Wyman, Donald. 1969 [1949] *Shrubs
and Vines for American Gardens.*
Revised. New York: Macmillan.

———. 1990 [1951]. *Trees for American
Gardens*, 3rd ed. Revised. New
York: Macmillan.

Yang, Linda. 1999. *Topiaries and
Espaliers: Taylor's Weekend Gardening
Guides.* Boston: Houghton Mifflin.

WEB SITES

Desert-tropicals.
http://www.desert-tropicals.com

Floridata. *http://www.floridata.com*

The Heather Society.
http://www.heathersociety.org.uk

HortiPlex. *http://www.hortiplex.com*

International Plant Names Index.
http://www.ipni.org

Las Pilitas Nursery.
http://www.laspilitas.com

North American Rock Garden
Society. *http://www.nargs.org*

Paul, the Palm Doctor.
http://www.palmdoctor.com

Perry, Dr. Leonard. Perry's Perennial
Pages.
http://www.uvm.edu/~pass/perry

Royal Horticultural Society. RHS
Plant Finder.
http://www.rhs.org.uk/rhsplantfinder

United States Department of
Agriculture National Resource
Conservation Service. Plants
Database. *http://plants.usda.gov*

COMMON NAMES CROSS-REFERENCE

air plant, *Tillandsia*

alpine mouse ear, *Cerastium alpinum* subsp. *lanatum*

African daisy, *Arctotis*

    blue-eyed, *Arctotis venusta*

    cape, *Arctotis fastuosa*

artemisia

    beach wormwood, *Artemisia stelleriana*

    big sagebrush, *Artemisia tridentata/Seriphidium tridentatum*

    California sagebrush, *Artemisia californica*

    fringed wormwood, *Artemisia frigida*

    Japanese wormwood, *Artemisia capillaris*

    Powis Castle artemisia, *Artemisia* ×'Powis Castle'

    Rocky Mountain sagewort, *Artemisia scopulorum*

    Roman wormwood, *Artemisia pontica*

    sand sage, *Artemisia filifolia*

    sand sage, *Artemisia pycnocephala*

    silver sage, *Artemisia cana/Seriphidium canum*

    southernwood, *Artemisia abrotanum*

    tree wormwood, *Artemisia arborescens*

    western mugwort, *Artemisia ludoviciana*

    wormwood, *Artemisia absinthium*

artichoke thistle, *Cynara*

Australian silver bush, *Juncus polyanthemos*

ball moss, *Tillandsia recurvata*

basket-of-gold, *Aurinia saxatilis*

beardtongue, *Penstemon*

    desert, *Penstemon pseudospectabilis*

    parachute, *Penstemon debilis*

    rock, *Penstemon rupicola*

    wild snapdragon, *Penstemon palmeri*

Bismark palm, *Bismarckia nobilis*

blue atlas cedar, *Cedrus atlantica*

blue bunch grass, *Festuca idahoensis*

blue chalksticks, *Senecio serpens*

blue China fir, *Cunninghamia lanceolata* 'Glauca'

blue fescue, *Festuca glauca*

blue lyme grass, *Leymus arenarius*

blue mist, *Caryopteris* ×clandonensis

blue oat grass, *Helictotrichon sempervirens*

blue wheat grass, *Elymus magellanicus*

blushing bride, *Tillandsia ionantha*

buddleia

    butterfly bush, *Buddleja davidii*

    fountain buddleia, *Buddleja alternifolia*

bugle, *Ajuga reptans*

California fuchsia, hummingbird flower, *Zauschneria californica*

cardoon, *Cynara cardunculus*

catmint, *Nepeta*

  dwarf, Persian ivy, *Nepeta mussinii*

cenizo, *Leucophyllum*

century plant, *Agave*

  American, *Agave americana*

Colorado blue sprue, *Picea pungens* var. *glauca*

common rue, *Ruta graveolens*

common tansy, *Tanacetum vulgare*

  silver, *Tanacetum niveum*

  silver-lace, *Tanacetum ptarmicifolium* 'Silver Feather'

coral bells, *Heuchera*

cross-leaved heath, *Erica tetralix*

curry plant, *Helichrysum italicum*

cushion bush, *Leucophyta brownii*

dead nettle, *Lamium maculatum*

donkey tail, *Euphorbia myrsinites*

dusty miller, *Centaurea cineraria*

dusty miller, *Senecio cineraria*

dusty zenobia, *Zenobia pulverulenta*

eryngo, *Eryngium*

eucalyptus, gum

  alpine snow gum, *Eucalyptus pauciflora* subsp. *niphophila*

  cabbage gum, *Eucalyptus paucifolia*

  cider gum, *Eucalyptus gunnii*

  ghost gum, *Eucalyptus paucifolia*

  heart-leaved silver, *Eucalyptus cordata*

  mottlecah, *Eucalyptus macrocarpa*

  silver dollar gum, *Eucalyptus cinerea*

  silver-leaved mountain gum, *Eucalyptus pulverulenta*

  Tasmania blue gum, *Eucalyptus globulus*

  Tingiringi gum, *Eucalyptus glaucescens*

  weeping gum, *Eucalyptus paucifolia*

everlasting flower, *Helichrysum*

  silver everlasting, *Helichrysum thianschanicum*

false cypress, *Chamaecyparis*

  blue moss, *Chamaecyparis pisifera* 'Boulevard'

  Lawson, *Chamaecyparis lawsonia*

  Sarah Lawson, *Chamaecyparis lawsonia* 'Allumii'

  sawara, *Chamaecyparis pisifera*

false dittany, *Ballota pseudodictamnus*

fern

  Japanese painted, *Athyrium nipponicum* var. *pictum*

  southern lady, *Athyrium filix-femina*

fescue, *Festuca*

  blue fescue, *Festuca glauca*

feverfew, *Tanacetum parthenium*

fir, *Abies*

  blue noble, *Abies procera* 'Glauca'

  Korean, *Abies koreana*

  Spanish, *Abies pinsapo*

  Veitch's, *Abies veitchii*

  white, *Abies concolor*

foamy bells, ×*Heucherella*

fringed rue, *Ruta chalapensis*

frosty curls sedge, frosted curls sedge,
Carex albula

germander, *Teucrium*

felty, *Teucrium polium*

tree, *Teucrium fruticans*

globe artichoke, *Cynara scolymus*

globe thistle, *Echinops*

great, *Echinops sphaerocephalum*

small, *Echinops ritro*

golden daisy bush, *Euryops pectinatus*

golden mimosa, cootamundra wattle,
Acacia baileyana

gray rush, *Juncus patens*

hardy cyclamen, baby cyclamen,
Cyclamen hederifolium

heath, *Erica*

heather, *Calluna vulgaris*

hens and chicks, *Echeveria*

horehound, *Marrubium*

common, *Marrubium vulgare*

silver, *Marrubium incanum*

silver-edged, *Marrubium rotundiflorum*

hummingbird plant, king's crown,
Dicliptera suberecta

Indian grass, *Sorghastrum nutans*

blue, *Sorghastrum nutans* 'Sioux Blue'

Japanese silver grass, *Miscanthus sinensis*

juniper, *Juniperus*

common, mountain, *Juniperus communis*

creeping, *Juniperus horizontalis*

eastern red-cedar, *Juniperus virginiana*

Rocky Mountain, western red-cedar,
Juniperus scopulorum

shore, *Juniperus conferta*

silver red-cedar, *Juniperus virginiana*
'Glauca'

single-seed, *Juniperus squamata*

Korean violet, *Viola koreana*

lamb's ears, *Stachys byzantina*

lavender, *Lavandula*

English, common, hardy, true,
Lavandula angustifolia

fringed, *Lavandula dentata* var. *candicans*

giant, *Lavandula* ×*allardi*

lavandin, *Lavandula* ×*intermedia*

silver fern-leaf, *Lavandula buchii*

woolly, *Lavandula lanata*

lavender cotton, *Santolina*

gray santolina, *Santolina chamaecyparissus*

Neopolitan, *Santolina pinnata* subsp.
neopolitana

lead plant, *Amorpha canescens*

licorice plant, *Helichrysum petiolare*

little blue stem, *Schizachyrium scoparium*

lungwort, *Pulmonaria*

madwort, *Alyssum*

mescal, *Agave parryi*

Mexican snowball, *Echeveria elegans*

mint, *Mentha*

Miss Willmott's Ghost, *Eryngium giganteum*

monarch of the veldt, *Arctotis fastuosa*

mullein, *Verbascum*

    common, *Verbascum thapsus*

    Turkish, *Verbascum bombyciferum*

oleaster, *Elaeagnus*

    autumn olive, *Elaeagnus umbellata*

    Russian olive, *Elaeagnus angustifolia*

oregano, *Origanum*

painted lady echeveria, *Echeveria derenbergii*

partridge feather, *Tanacetum densum* subsp. *amani*

peacock echeveria, *Echeveria peacockii*

pearly everlasting, *Anaphalis*

pink, *Dianthus*

    cheddar, *Dianthus gratianopolitanus*

    clove, *Dianthus caryophyllus*

    cottage, *Dianthus plumarius*

prickly thrift, *Acantholimon*

pussytoes, *Antennaria*

rattlesnakemaster, *Eryngium yuccifolium*

ravenna grass, *Saccharum ravennae*

rock breaker, *Saxifraga*

rock jasmine, *Androsace*

rock rose, *Cistus*

rose campion, *Lychnis coronaria*

Russian sage, *Perovskia*

sage, *Salvia*

    Andean, *Salvia discolor*

    blue, Cleveland, *Salvia clevelandii*

    creeping, *Salvia somomensis* subsp. *cleve-*

    landii 'Gracias'

    germander, *Salvia chamaedyoides*

    rose sage, *Salvia pachyphylla*

    silver, *Salvia argentea*

    silver-leaf, *Salvia daghestanica*

saltbush, *Atriplex*

    four-wing, *Atriplex canescens*

    Gardner, *Atriplex gardneri*

    quail bush, *Atriplex lentiformis*

    sea orach, mountain spinach, *Atriplex halimus*

sand sage, *Artemisia pycnocephala*

saw palmetto *Serenoa repens*

sea buckthorn, *Hippophae rhamnoides*

sea holly, *Eryngium*

Siberian bugloss, *Brunnera macrophylla*

silver bluebeard, *Caryopteris incana*

silverberry, buffaloberry, *Sheperdia argentea*

silverbush, *Convovulus cneorum*

silver feather maiden grass, *Miscanthus sinensis* 'Silberfeder'

silver pear, *Pyrus salicifolia*

silver ponyfoot, *Dichondra argentea*

snow in summer, *Cerastium tomentosum*

soapweed, *Yucca*

Spanish moss, *Tillandsia usneoides*

speedwell, *Veronica*

    silver, *Veronica spicata* subsp. *incana*

spurge, *Euphorbia*

stonecrop, *Sedum*

sun rose, *Helianthemum*

switch grass, *Panicum virgatum*

Texas sage, *Leucophyllum frutescens*

Texas sage, Texas ranger, *Leucophyllum*

thistle, *Onopordum*

    Arabian, cotton, *Onopordum nervosum*

    giant, Scotch, silver, *Onopordum acanthium*

thyme, *Thymus*

    cooking, *Thymus vulgaris*

    silver, *Thymus vulgaris* 'Argenteus'

    silver posie, *Thymus vulgaris* 'Argenteus'

    woolly, *Thymus pseudolanuginosus*

treasure flower, *Gazania*

violet silverleaf, *Leucophyllum candidum*

western mugwort, *Artemisia ludoviciana*

white poplar, *Populus alba*

wild ginger, *Asarum*

willow, *Salix*

    coyote, *Salix exigua*

    creeping silver, *Salix repens* var. *nitida*

    dwarf arctic, *Salix purpurea* 'Nana'

    rosemary, *Salix elaeagnos*

    sage, *Salix tristis*

    woolly, *Salix lanata*

wormwood, *Artemisia*

    beach, *Artemisia stelleriana*

    Japanese, *Artemisia capillaris*

    Roman, *Artemisia pontica*

    tree, *Artemisia arborescens*

woundwort, *Stachys*

yarrow, *Achillea*

    Greek, *Achillea ageratifolia*

    silvery, *Achillea clavennae*

    woolly, *Achillea tomentosa*

yellow archangel, *Lamium galeobdolon*

yucca

    beaked blue, *Yucca rostrata*

    blue, *Yucca rigida*

    mountain, Schott's, *Yucca schottii*

    paleleaf, *Yucca pallida*

    Thompson's, *Yucca thompsoniana*

INDEX OF PLANT NAMES

Pages in **boldface** indicate a main text entry. Pages that include photographs appear in *italic*.